SELECTED ESSAYS

This page intentionally left blank

SELECTED ESSAYS

CLARK
BLAISE

EDITED BY

JOHN METCALF &
J.R. (TIM) STRUTHERS

BIBLIOASIS

FIRST EDITION

Library and Archives Canada Cataloguing in Publication

Blaise, Clark, 1940–
[Essays. Selections]
    Selected essays / Clark Blaise ; edited by John Metcalf and
J.R. (Tim) Struthers.

Includes bibliographical references.
ISBN 13: 978-1-897231-50-0
ISBN 10: 1-897231-50-4

    I. Metcalf, John, 1938- II. Struthers, J. R. Tim, 1950- III. Title.
PS8553.L34A6 2008   C814'.54   C2008-904364-2

Canada Council   Conseil des Arts
for the Arts   du Canada

Canadian   Patrimoine
Heritage   canadien

ONTARIO ARTS COUNCIL
CONSEIL DES ARTS DE L'ONTARIO

We gratefully acknowledge the support of the Canada Council for
the Arts, Canadian Heritage, and the Ontario Arts Council for our
publishing program.

PRINTED AND BOUND IN CANADA

To my granddaughters,

Quinn Xi Blaise and Priya Xue Blaise –

Imagine the stories they can tell!

This page intentionally left blank

CONTENTS

This page intentionally left blank

Autobiographical Essay: 1940–1984

THIS IS being written in Christmas week, 1984, in Iowa City, Iowa. I am forty-four, unemployed (I should be saying, bravely, self-employed as a writer), with a son in university, a son in high school, and a wife who has just started teaching in Montclair, New Jersey. The house I own has a literary history. It was in this house nearly a decade ago that John Irving wrote *Garp,* and the pillar-support of my garage bears the evidence – the autobiographical evidence, let us say – that writers turn life into metaphor, and mild misadventure into meaningful catastrophe.

Children and writers are both liars. The child's lie is uninteresting, a moral nullity, for it is based on denial – "I didn't hit her," "I didn't take it," "I didn't see it," "I didn't know," "You never told me." The writer's lie is all-inclusive, Faustian – "I was there, I suffered, I was the man." An inch of experience, a glimpse, a memory, a word, any special authenticating detail and the writer rushes in to claim a mile of responsibility. "I knew it," the writer says. "I saw it happening. It is my fault; I take the blame." Without the greed for guilt and punishment there is no art.

I have just finished writing an overt autobiography, a mixture of non-fictional essay and autobiographical-seeming fiction, entitled *Resident Alien.* It will appear (as of this writing) in about a year. I thought I was done with my Self, those dozens of fictional self-portraits I've executed through the years, and now I'm forced again to come clean, to claim more for my burdened memory than I can deliver. I'm tempted now to become a child and to say I don't know nearly a fraction of the things I've claimed to know, as a writer. I don't know the South, or Pittsburgh, or Canada, or India. I don't know languages, women, I was never a genius, I don't think the moves in my childhood made my life especially unhappy. I was never a Catholic or a Jew, I never lived as a Franco-American, I was never as poorly-off as the characters in my fiction, I never suffered their brutal derangements, I've not read as much as I've claimed, and I'm not the assured middle-aged, genial, avuncular, aesthete that I seem.

And yet, I am all those things, and more.

You see how dull real autobiography can be. I jazzed up my life for *Resident Alien,* while holding to the essential outlines my parents gave me. My first four books of fiction – the two story collections and the two novels – were scatsongs on a jangling but still intact pool of memories or linked possibilities from the life I had led. I held on to the flimsy memories of where I'd lived and what I'd seen; I let it serve as a garage-post to my own sense of loss and suffering. This time, I will scrape together all that I have not used before, and try to serve it in newly-designed bottles with different labels. It can't be helped if it comes out sounding like the same old fiction.

Most male writers I know, or have read about, had artistically-inclined mothers trapped in unhappy marriages to resolutely feckless husbands. My mother was from a stern prairie family in Wawanesa, Manitoba, where she was born, the eldest of ten, in 1903. Her father was the town doctor who later became the head of Canada's major insurance company, The Wawanesa Mutual. After he retired (early, because of encroaching Alzheimer's disease), the family moved to Winnipeg. My mother took a teaching degree at Wesley College, Winnipeg, in 1927, and spent three years teaching in Saskatchewan and Manitoba schools in Dauphin, Minnedosa, and Guernsey. Her students were generally the sons of Ukrainian farmers – or the farmers themselves – often older than she. The custom of the times was to give the village schoolteacher free room and board (she only earned a thousand dollars a year), and so, scrupulously, she saved. She was saving for nothing less than her deliverance.

She had a plan which her father had refused to finance. He was a patriarch, accustomed to pure devotion from his eight daughters. He gave them all his will – which they deployed, often in defiance. She wanted to be an artist, a designer, a calling of which he firmly disapproved. She had the talent from an early age – I've found her early sketches and had them framed – and it might have been the example of her will, more than her talent, that allowed her younger sister Ruth to get the California training she demanded. My mother wanted to go to Europe. She wanted to be, and this, I confess, is my conclusion, sophisticated. In 1930, she left for England (where else would a Canadian girl go?), and then to the continent. She sought, and discovered, the Bauhaus. And in the areas around that citadel of functional modernism, she found the Miessen ware, the Dresden porcelains, the ornamental culture that predated that cost-efficient, reduction geometry.

The poles of her taste define her character. Up-to-date and rational in nearly everything. Ferocious and self-denying in her independence. Punctual, responsible, scrupulous, ethical, excruciatingly fair-minded. Brave. A Bohemian and atheist of her time and place. For a literary analogy, I think of her in Huxleyan terms – scientific background, skeptical mind, bright and witty, with undertones of mysticism that pulled at her until she capitulated. Though she travelled the permissible world (Europe) in exciting times (the rise of Hitler), she retained the innocence of small-town Canada. She could not abide filth and Catholics, an effective barrier to wider travel. She was drawn to the occult – like many Englishy types – she had a talent for reading tea leaves. She could go into trances, and she quit it all when she felt herself getting "strange" and being perceived as just a little queer. All that atheism and rationality had to have an outlet. She'd rejected the organized religions of her day, but attended Theosophist lectures, read books on Buddhism, believed in reincarnation, and revered George Bernard Shaw. She had an enlightened Canadian's outlook on race and Empire: pro-India, pro-black, pro-American, anti-Imperial. (Canadian nationalists of her generation saw Britain, not

America, as the natural enemy; British institutions, not American policies, as the Yoke.) When she finally returned to Canada in 1937 to take over the head decorator's job at Eaton's Montreal store, she was thirty-four and unmarried. Her Montreal friends were all "bachelor-girl" professors at McGill. It was a world ready-made for her, and one she barely avoided.

From all that I know of the writing process, she was an ideal writer's-mother. A prototype. She'd had dazzling experiences in the world, the large world of Europe, and she could retell those stories for me, endlessly. She could illustrate them. I had an early drawing-talent – that was a link. If she was the ideal mother, I was probably the ideal son for her: appreciative, verbal, quiet. Through me, her ambitions would live. I don't mean to imply she was a stage-mother pushing me to performance, but the withdrawal of her approval filled me with awful terrors. I was raised, simply, to see my mother as an ally.

Being her ally meant equipping myself with the literary, artistic, and historical facts necessary to carry on a discourse. It meant appreciating certain facts and observing certain rituals; it meant always having something interesting to say. It also meant avoiding vast areas of coarseness, sexuality, and unwholesomeness.

Which brings me to my father.

I know very little about him. He was born Léo Roméo Blais, the son of Achille and Orienne (Boucher) Blais, in Lac-Mégantic, Québec, in 1905. He was the youngest of eighteen, until the birth of a final child, Rolland, five years later, after he'd already been sent to the monastery (a *donné*).The family bounced between New Hampshire and Québec for most of the first two decades of this century (part of a national pattern of migration), settling long enough in Manchester, New Hampshire, for his sisters Bella, Corinne, and Lena to marry. There was one brother, Oliva, who fought for the American Army in the First World War, then married a Frenchwoman and spent the rest of his life in France. My uncle, and the cousins I've met, and their children I've heard about, have probably balanced the ancient demographic books of emigration. The thirteen others never made it past childhood, including six who died in one week. At least, my father said so. My father combined the child's and the writer's art of lying; he lied to claim legitimacy, but he lied as well to avoid accounting.

The male writer's relationship to his father is often tension-filled, a case of bad receivers and bad transmitters, of static and silence. I wish I knew my father, for certainly a complicated man existed there, though he chose to show very little of it. He manufactured vast complexities, like a child, and like a child's lies they were uninteresting fabrications. He was ashamed of his origins (my mother had added the final "e" to our name, which he liked), so he never admitted to anything other than a Boston birth. He was ashamed of having no education, so he claimed nothing less than Harvard, sometimes Dartmouth. He was ashamed of the illiteracy of his family, and of his own difficult time with letters, so my mother handled all correspondence. He was ashamed, in short, of everything a son would find infectious and even exciting; all the occasions for pride were systematically obliterated. Thanks to my mother's storytelling abilities, and her pride in family accomplishments, I can reconstruct western Canadian life confidently. I enter my mother's world with ease and assurance; I know I will be received as a proper native. But my father never once spoke to me of his childhood and manhood, never spoke of his two earlier marriages (I learned of them only after my parents' divorce), and I witnessed the disintegration of his fourth and fifth marriages. He died on the last day of 1978 in Manchester, the victim of clots and vascular collapse, in pain and virtually alone, on his way to the medical facilities at Dartmouth.

And yet, *of course*, it is of my father that I write. He was the great mystery in my life, the great unknown teasingly at hand. My mother's life is the pedestal; his is the statue. His language, his origins, his life before my birth, his indifference to me, his rejection of all my ambitions. He was an athlete, a former boxer, a skier, a skater. He was a salesman, a violent, aggressive, manipu-

lative man specializing in the arts of spontaneous misrepresenta-
tion. And he was glamorous: short, dark, and handsome. As a
travelling salesman, he had women in every town; he drank to
excess every night, and hit the road at daybreak every morning.
After a critical accident, he took himself off the road and started a
second career as furniture-buyer for various department stores,
and in each of those small towns throughout the South and Mid-
west (we moved on the average of three times a year for my first
fifteen years), he found new women. Their sons and daughters
were invariably in my class at school; they became my ersatz
brothers and sisters and we kept a strange silence about our secrets. How I loved those girls! How I suffered from the bullying
of those boys! (I used some of those feelings in the first part of my
novel *Lunar Attractions*.) That strange silence, the strangled truths
we knew but couldn't communicate, is an essential part of the fiction I write and the fiction I most admire.

Anyone who has read my fiction knows how I have combed
those feelings, how the anguish of separation from my father's
world is an incurable ache. As I read over my stories from *A North
American Education* and *Tribal Justice*, and even from *Resident Alien*,
I see how I have extracted a certain revenge. The father in those
stories is often crippled by drink or an accident, often beaten. In
my novel *Lusts* he is dying of cancer; only in *Lunar Attractions* is he
arrayed in his glory. There are only isolated moments of unity: at
the close of the title story in my first collection, the offshore hurricane brings father and son together; in "The Bridge," the father
and his mistress save the boy from sunstroke. The violence of my
feelings sometimes frightens me; the consequences perhaps of a
strangled Oedipal fixation on my mother. I have never escaped the
family as the source of all my fiction and I doubt that I ever will.

Look, I want to say, fiction is really very simple to understand.
Northrop Frye has called it all part of a Great Code. Joseph Camp-
bell has related it all to a single hero and a single set of tests. Of
course, culture and language and experience all mitigate the single
story, but the great novels all say the same thing. They say: Once

upon a time there was unity. Once upon a time we floated in a basket under a benevolent sun on a serene ocean. Our lungs were pink as seashells, our arteries supple, our senses super-keen. And then a rupture occurred – call it a Fall, or consciousness, or some other Great Truth – and we are tipped from our basket into a monster-filled sea, under a scorching sky. There is no one to support us, and we struggle to find the shore. The great writers dramatize the struggle, they write from the consciousness of loss, from the knowledge that the natural world is an illusion of Eden, that social comforts have been purchased with the coin of forgetfulness. I think of the writers I most admire – Hemingway, Faulkner, Mann, Nabokov, Babel, Kafka, O'Connor, Malamud, Handke – and I realize that in each of them, a world is described, ironically, that has been severed from all that gives meaning, or dignity, to man or his discourse. I've called it "the Great Truth" that any writer must have in his head: for Hemingway it was the nihilism of the first war, for Faulkner it was slavery, for Mann the destruction of bourgeois society, for Nabokov it was expulsion from Russia, for contemporary Europeans, especially Germans, the awareness that their McDonaldized Europe is an infernal undergrowth fed by corpses.

I'd been born with a muscle condition, variously described as a dystrophy and *amyotonia congenita* (invariably fatal); I didn't walk till I was three and a half; I was, and am, pudgy and slow and lacking in good muscle tone despite dedicated efforts to control it. Naturally enough, the lack of physical grace, coordination (my only advantage over my father is that I outgrew him by six inches), and aggressiveness has made me, perversely, a lover of all sports. I am of that generation of small-town Americans for whom team-loyalty was a stepping-stone to some larger sense of purpose and steadfastness. However bad they were, those minor-leaguers were *ours*, they represented us, their losses were a test of our tolerance. I've never felt comfortable among winners in any competition; perhaps that's why I'm a writer and not a salesman.

Many of my friends from high school and college and on up find it an aberration in my otherwise respectable self. Something, they were sure, I'd outgrow – in fact, it would be a convenient benchmark of my maturing. Three hours a day in baseball season I am rooted to radio or television. Football weekends, basketball midweeks, hockey anytime. If anything, the off-season dreaming and the in-season attention have sharpened over the years. I remember moments in my Southern childhood of catching a touchdown pass. (Characteristically, the first pass I ever caught, when I was seven and playing with kids much older on a dusty street in Leesburg, Florida, was immediately after telling myself, "It's not hard to catch. They keep throwing to me and I keep dropping it because I think I can't do it. But throw it again and I'll catch it and no one is around me because they think I can't do it." George Stewart threw it again, and I caught it, and I remember his tattooed older brother Bunky, looking at me in wonder.) I remember one other time, in a schoolyard in Cincinnati, in the Avondale black ghetto. The quarterback lofted a pass to me and I caught it on the run, one of those perfect moments when the vectors of flight laid the ball on my fingertips with feather-lightness – I didn't know I'd caught it and neither did any of the incomparably faster defenders. I just ran and ran to the end zone, a legendary white boy for one afternoon.

Hey, man, way to go.

Years later, *Sport* magazine sent me on assignment out to both coasts to follow the Montreal Expos and report back on why they weren't winning. Dugout, locker-room, field, and press-box passes. Long talks with The Guys, the coaches, the opposition, the Hollywood types who follow them. Twelve hours a day of sheer, underbelly baseball; it still sustains me.

I am an autobiographical writer. Nearly all of my work is in the first person; there is a recognizable (even repetitive) "world" to my writing and to my characters. I've not veered too sharply from the path of "givens" in my life. That I am obsessed with the Canadian reality – the mysterious and unknown and the clear and confident, so close at hand. That I am the manchild of such disparate forces, that French and English, America and Canada, Pittsburgh, Montreal, Toronto, Winnipeg, and the deep rural South all mingle in me. That India, through marriage, should have become a vital test, an escape from all my subjectivity.

More than most authors, I am dependent on autobiography. Raymond Carver, in his *Paris Review* interview, cited my work as "purely autobiographical," which is not exactly true – only the outline and the first-person mode of telling are autobiographical. The content is imagined. Until now I've avoided quoting from *Resident Alien*, but since I've said this all before, and said it better when I thought I was saying it for the last time, I'll quote it one more time:

> Where does the impulse come from, and why, after fifty stories and two novels, does the voice and the shape and the subject-matter remain fundamentally the same? Why am I wedded like a reborn Wordsworth to the epic of my own becoming? I've hounded my life like a tied-up dog, digging it up, soiling it, as though where I've been and what I've seen is somehow prototypical, epic, and exemplary rather than sheltered, eccentric, and utterly accidental.
>
> The cataclysm in my life was my parents' divorce. Absurd, I know; it was the most predictable of occurrences and it happened late enough in my life – nineteen – when all parental obligations had been met. But no matter how calmly I took it, I realize that I never accepted it, never forgave it, never really survived it as the person I was. Their divorce formed a knot in my character; my life collapsed around it like a compacted star.
>
> I am dependent on a world made explicable by my mismatched parents in their improbable, even heroic, marriage. So long as they are together, all things are possible. Their incongruity calls up, and somehow justifies, the harshest and most beautiful images of my experience and imagination.

Most of my stories are told from an undisclosed adult perspective, in the first person, and most take place in childhood and adolescence, at a time when the parents are together, when the potential for divorce, the logic for divorce, the imperative for divorce, were being ignored. Life without their unspoken, unacted, erotic violence is literally unimaginable to me, just as life *after* their divorce seems lacking in moral authority. I need the shelter of their marriage; their complications and polarities are still the food-source of what Edwin Honig has called their "aging embryo." They function for me as God served Nietzsche – keeping a few things impossible, while justifying everything else. They are the heavens and the landscape of my imagination – the indispensable maps leading north and south, into French and English, to Europe and beyond.

I will never surpass my parents in their passion, their guts, their improbable adventures. While I am clearly the inheritor of my mother's genes – for art, for contemplation, for thick legs and deep-set eyes and, I fear, a certain gene for Alzheimer's disease (she lies now in a Winnipeg nursing home, eighty-one and utterly, utterly lost) – I've also taken over my father's wanderlust, his self-made vanities, his inability to settle on a single role in a single place. I am steady in my profession of writing and there it ends.

My father could not hold jobs. He was unstable, he got drunk or abusive, or impatient. His desperate climb from the deepest pit of rural Québec obliged him to accept any job, anyplace, that offered more money than the job he had. Being a salesman, he of course was gullible. If he heard of a horse to bet on, he'd bet. Of an innovation in appliances, cars, or medicines, he'd buy. Of a better job, he'd jump. Aesthetics, inconvenience, hours, played no part. I share his impulses; I honour the concept of rootedness, yet I've behaved abominably. In another context I've called myself a Bluebeard of the Interstates.

I was born in Fargo, North Dakota, where my father was a furniture-buyer for Sears. It was his first American job. In 1940, many
Canadians feared that the war was already lost. England would
fall; Canada would be occupied. If not, Canada would fight on,
alone. Newfoundland, a British colony, would be occupied like
the Channel Islands. Québec would refuse to fight an "English"
war (in this, my father as well as Pierre Trudeau were in perfect
agreement), and the brownshirt fascists of Adrien Arcand were
poised for a *putsch*. America was viewed as secretly fascist. I
own a book, written by a Canadian diplomat, called *Canada:
America's Enemy*, published in 1940, in which he urges an
invasion by the U.S. to preempt the coming collapse of the Commonwealth. The move to North Dakota, then, was seen as a way
of protecting their precious cargo. America would never go to
War.

We moved a few months later, still with Sears, to Cincinnati.
A year later to Pittsburgh. In 1945, to Atlanta where my father
launched his first business. It failed, and he was forced to go on
the road. We moved to northern Florida, the towns of Leesburg
and Tavares in the lake-rich, citrus-laden hills. In 1947 he suffered
his near-fatal accident, and we slid into desperate poverty. I went
to one-room schools with teenage morons. It was three years before we saw electricity and indoor plumbing again. And those
were the years that gave me my first writing-world. I was a
Southerner, I breathed that air and suffered those parasites, and
was awed by all I saw. When my father recovered his health, he
went back to furniture-buying, in West Palm Beach, Fort Lauder-
dale, and Jacksonville.

Had we stayed in any of those towns and cities, we'd be
millionaires by now. The people we knew, our old neighbours
who'd come down south just after the war, they've made it, just as
my father had always dreamed. They have gates in front of their
houses, Continentals in the drive, yachts in their backyards. By the
early sixties, when I backpedalled south one last time at the
beginning of my writing life, my father was living in a Pittsburgh

rooming house with five paroled drunks in a kind of halfway house for the deranged and unemployed.

In 1950, pursued by accumulated demons, we fled one night to Canada. Back to Winnipeg, to live in my grandmother's house, under the shelter of their fame and money. My background till that time was as self-made as any child out of any book. I drew pictures, I memorized lists and texts and bird-guides and fish-books, I listened to baseball games from places that could thrill me, names like Shibe and Briggs and Fenway. My schooling had been haphazard, amounting to three dislocations a year, in shanty-cars and unpainted one-room shacks, in the deep, segregated South. These are the years of the deepest sense-impressions I've ever received, of colours and smells and tastes that are as clear to me today as they were then.

When I came to Canada, it was the beginning of reason. For the first time, there were people I respected – my aunts and uncles and gifted teachers – to put my life in a context. I was a freak, with my Southern accent and my self-taught ways. Yet I was also of The Family, a famous family, and perhaps my skills at drawing and my feats of memorization (I knew all the capitals of all the political divisions in the world; I knew the county seats of every county in America; I knew all the kings of England and Germany and France; I knew the call letters of the major radio stations) were more than mere *idiot-savanterie*; maybe there was a guiding intelligence, despite the fact that I, at ten, had never worked a math problem or written an assignment. The teacher was faced with a dilemma, either to install me three or four years back, or keep me in grade five and force-feed me like a goose, with penmanship, math tables, British history, and formulae.

Less than a year later, we were back on the road to Springfield, Missouri, Cincinnati – city of my immaculate reception – and finally Pittsburgh. From grade eight till graduation and slightly beyond, I was a Pittsburgher. It is a city of natural confluences, ethnic and establishment, sports and intellect, working-class and upper-management. I loved Pittsburgh, and I hope I have done justice to it in *Lusts* and *Lunar Attractions* and several stories. My father, after getting fired from the first job that brought him there, and taking us to Montreal where for a crazy couple of weeks he thought of resettling (he'd done something very bad, that day of his firing), decided to return to Pittsburgh and start a furniture store of his own. My mother to sell and to decorate; he to sell and order. They were, by then, fifty years old. And for six years, and through two stores, until I began college at Denison University, they prospered.

There too, had another woman not interposed herself, they might be millionaires today. They had their shot. In 1962, I saw everything being auctioned off, our only house sold, my parents dispersed to rooming houses. My mother returned to Canada and to teaching; my father remarried and went to Mexico. He'd bagged a great deal of money in the liquidation (my mother got twelve thousand dollars from it, thanks to his smart accountants and her ethical refusal to contest a thing). The new wife took it, brained him, and deserted him in Mexico. He made his way back to Pittsburgh, to the halfway house, then worked his way back down to Florida, to a nephew he'd never met. The nephew introduced him to his last wife, a widow from New Hampshire, and the rest belongs to a different story.

Now, at last, I can speak of the writing. I went to Denison University in Ohio, hoping to be a scientist. For two years I was a Geology major, then I discovered writing. Eventually, thanks to Paul Bennett, a great teacher who has headed Denison's writing program for nearly forty years, I learned that there was an outlet for all the suppressed quirkiness in my life. I *wasn't* just another lovesick suburban mooncalf from Pittsburgh dozing through endless science labs, looking for Friday night dates. I had known worlds before their passing; I had seen extinct animals – Florida cougars, ivory-billed woodpeckers, Key deer; I had witnessed the Klan in power, floggings, segregation; I had parents with different nationalities, different languages were spoken in my house; I had lived without conveniences and in different countries: my life, if viewed from just a degree or two off-centre, was in fact a riot of colour and drama and story.

If, that is, I learned to lie like a writer and not like a child. I dropped out of school, overwhelmed by what I'd learned, battered by my parents' divorce. I went to Florida to work, started reading a novel a day, and declared myself an English major. I took out loans to see me through a senior year, I wrote, and when I graduated in 1961, I was editing the campus literary magazine and I had won the writing prizes. My stories were Southern in the extreme, so swampy they should have been drained, then sprayed. I thought I was Southern; the inauthenticity of my accent, the brevity of my exposure to that world wouldn't bother me for another few years.

What about the stories, I wonder now. The stories are all linked by water. My first story, "Broward Dowdy" (it's in *Tribal Justice*, but was written first at Denison, then eventually published by *Shenandoah*), is about a moss-picking family I'd known, deep in the swamps by the shores of Lake Harris. My second, as yet uncollected, was published in a short-lived magazine called *Chrysalis* and was called, rhapsodically I felt, "Giant Turtles, Gliding in the Dark." It was a remembered response to the glass-bottomed boat rides I'd taken as a child through Silver Springs. The third, "Relief" (also in *Tribal Justice* and first published in *Shenandoah*), concerns the same shanty-settlement on the shores of Lake Harris, this time during the confusion of a hurricane's passing. (Is this the time to acknowledge the bravery of editors who take a chance on beginners? James Boatwright has published five of my stories; I owe him a lot and have met him, very briefly, only once.) In all of those stories, there is no hint of Canada, of our temporary residence, our highborn Yankee origins. A fourth story, "Growing Pains," first written in Bernard Malamud's seminar at Harvard, was published in *The Carolina Quarterly* (in an issue with two young writers later to become friends, Leon Rooke and Raymond Carver), and concerned Erskine Caldwellian manipulations of rape, incest, and retardation among those memorable moss-pickers. I picked up the tone, slightly, using a more literate narrator, in another *Shenandoah* (and *Tribal Justice*) story, "Notes Beyond a History." All very murky and gothic, but nevertheless, deeply felt at the time. There were other stories, some from Denison, some from Harvard, "A Fish Like a Buzzard" and "Saranac, in October," that have not, to date, been collected and reside now with the hundreds of other drafts and letters and attempts at novels, at the University of Calgary.

Before the South passes entirely out of view, however, I'd like to resurrect one sentence from one of those stories. It's a line I'm proud to have written, and I think it continues to live for me after twenty years because it's really about writing, more than the scene it describes. It's from "Relief," discussing the meteorological phenomenon of a "seiche." When air pressure suddenly lessons over a large, enclosed body of water – as when, for example, the eye of a hurricane passes over an enormous lake – the water withdraws to its centre, forming a dome. (A tornado over open water gives a waterspout.) That dome of water then relaxes when the eye retreats, and a kind of bore-tide can come crashing out of nowhere into the recently uncovered shoreline. This scene describes the retreat of the water:

> We looked out again, beyond the inlet which now was guarded by logs that had been submerged. On the open lake the wind blew whitecaps off the tops of swells. There were ripples now on the inlet. The stench of mud, as it dried, made even the migrants back off. The inlet – now shrunk to the outline of its deepest depressions – roughened, and the congregations of fish frothed to the surface, drinking in air with little gasps. We stood at the end of the dock and looked into the water. There were boats, far below, long sunk, housing bass and larger turtles. We hadn't known that the inlet was so deep.

It's that little aside – "now shrunk to the outline of its deepest depressions" that still has some residual power over me, for I think now it strikes close to the heart of my Southern experience. I was not a Southerner and could never be, but the memorable qualities of Southern poverty rubbed me against the deepest depressions in the available (white) American culture of that time. It has always been water – the water, for example, at the end of "A North American Education,"

> There was another Sunday in Florida. A hurricane was a hundred miles offshore and due to strike Fort Lauderdale within the next six hours. We drove from our house down Las Olas to the beach (Fort Lauderdale was still an inland city then), and parked half a mile away, safe from the paint-blasting sand. We could hear the breakers under the shriek of the wind, shaking the wooden bridge we walked on. Then we watched them crash, brown with weeds and suspended sand. And we could see them miles offshore, rolling in forty feet high and flashing their foam like icebergs. A few men in swimming suits and woollen sweaters were standing in the crater pools, pulling out the deep-sea fish that had been stunned by the trip and waves. Other fish littered the beach, their bellies blasted by the change in pressure. My mother's face was raw and her glasses webbed with salt. She went back to the car on her own. My father and I sat on the bench for another hour and I could see behind his crusty sunglasses. His eyes were moist and dancing, his hair stiff and matted. We sat on the bench until we were soaked and the municipal guards rounded us up. Then they barricaded the boulevards and we went back to the car, the best day of fishing we'd ever had, and we walked hand in hand for the last time, talking excitedly, dodging coconuts, power lines, and shattered glass, feeling brave and united in the face of the storm. My father and me. What a day it was, what a once-in-a-lifetime day it was.

Water has always summoned up the binding images of terror and of love. It did so with the giant turtles grinding their beaks under my Florida pillow, it did so with the ghastly images of alligator garfish, of alligators themselves, of water moccasins, of mudfish, and later in my Canadian stories, of the leeches covering my character's body ("At the Lake" in *Tribal Justice*).

The novella "Snow People" begins with a broken jaw – a baseball off the bat of the same George Stewart who once threw me a touchdown pass – and a quick memory of being saved by George from drowning the summer before (true, as a matter of fact, on both counts); the opening scene of *Lunar Attractions* has the boy and his father fishing on a Florida lake in a pastel sunset, when an alligator shatters the stillness and breaks forever the bond that had formed. I ended the novella "Continent of Strangers," set mainly in Sweden, with the spurned American lover standing in the Baltic breakers as a Finnish girl comes to join him, and I had begun with his fantasy, arriving in Europe on his first, romanticized trip, of crashing and being joined in the life raft by his Icelandic stewardess and washing up on the shores of Greenland. Well, all stories *are* the same, banal in their retelling, redeemed by their details. They contain the memory of a unity shattered, and the painful crawl back to shelter. We participate in myth as we write, by whatever disparate paths we take to get there. For me, water – for some unknown reason – has always held the secret of every revelation.

I am one of those writers who would have had a career, thin and obsessive no doubt, if he'd fallen in a manhole at the age of twenty and never come out. Of my Self up to twenty, I am in complete sympathy. I seemed, unconsciously, to have absorbed the movies, the songs, the sports, the politics, the landscape of the American forties and fifties. What I didn't absorb I can convincingly distort, or fabricate.

In 1961 I graduated from Denison and headed for Harvard. I'd read Malamud at Denison – one of two people to do so – and he was for me the personification of all I admired, all I wanted to be.

Real writers were rare on American campuses in those years – I'd never seen one. When I met Malamud for the first time, handing him my "Broward Dowdy" story from the Denison literary magazine, I was shaking, my mouth was dry. When he accepted me to the class of ten (the others were all Harvard students, or nearby locals), I felt the first validation of my life. I was at Harvard; I was with Malamud. Now my education could begin.

In every sense, it did. Bennett had given me confidence to trust my story (to "lie" in that special sense of telling the truth); Malamud began the rigorous process of getting me to think about my material. He stressed the dramatic element – every part of the story had to dramatize, had to characterize. Nothing that failed that test could remain, however pulsatingly "beautiful" it might be. (I had a lot of pulsatingly beautiful images in those days; I was the Cambridge Faulkner.) I began to see the intellectual dimensions in my life; I wasn't just Southern, I was Southern from a Yankee perspective, and I was Yankee from a Canadian perspective, and I was Canadian from a French and English perspective, and on it went. Two years later, when I was writing for an M.F.A. degree in Iowa, I began seeing those successive layers and learning how to frame them. I put a frame of "the War" around the core of "Broward Dowdy" and Shenandoah took it. I wrote "The Fabulous Eddie Brewster," the first of my stories to use my parents, recognizably, and Florida, and Canada, and my barely recalled French uncle who'd visited us just after the War. I wrote "Grids and Doglegs," a Pittsburgh story that borrowed from the family I had lived with when my parents were starting their store, the love I'd felt for all those ersatz sisters, the movingly intellectual qualities of Pittsburgh – the Carnegie Library, the Museum and Planetarium – and its proletarian excesses – its devotion to the losing Steelers and Pirates and Pitt Panthers – and my anguished attempt to find a place for myself between them.

There are two more things to talk about: marriage and Canada. After Malamud's course I wrote more stories in Boston and worked in a bookstore, but I knew that I was one of those writers cut out for teaching. I wanted out of my eight-hour-a-day, $37-a-week job. Malamud had given me the only "A" in his course and that grade – I've learned – was a kind of promissory note always to help me. I had heard of Iowa, and though Malamud had come up the hard way and was fundamentally opposed to artificial writing communities, he believed in supporting talent wherever it led. I entered Iowa in February 1962, with a scholarship from Omaha Power and Light.

My teacher was Philip Roth. His interest in me was confined to the Malamud connection (odd that I, still the unreconstructed Southerner in my writing, should know Malamud, and he, later to be linked through dozens of pseudo-scholarly articles and *The Ghost Writer*, knew him not at all). I wrote more Southern stories, took his literary seminar devoted to books he'd been told to read but never had (*Young Törless, The Good Soldier, Confessions of Zeno*, and many others), kept reading a book a day (as I've been doing for the past three years), and prowled the stacks of the library, reading every story in every English-language quarterly in the world. (I was becoming a goddamned expert. Those are names, however obscurely they began, that dominate the scene today.) Roth left and I started learning from R.V. Cassill, and Cassill – a difficult and demanding man – had much to teach, as well as to preach. Where else in America in 1963 would a self-conscious young writer be asked to analyze, exhaustively, the fictional techniques of Jean Stafford in *The Mountain Lion*? Yet the qualities that made him difficult also made him brilliant; he could analyze a work, making every part fit, bringing out every nuance, with the special insight of a paranoid overhearing imagined conversations.

I was learning literature from masters, but I was learning critical responses from my peers, my friends. The Writers' Workshop in the early sixties remains for me a touchstone of dedication; even a partial listing of our classes contains the saplings if not the forests of contemporary American writing. Ray Carver, Joy Williams,

Bette Howland, John Yount, Mark Strand, Jim Tate, Charles Wright, Marvin Bell, Andre Dubus, Phil O'Connor, Mark Costello, Ted Weesner, Bill Harrison, Jim Whitehead, Paul Friedman, John Stewart, David Benedictus, Jerry Bumpus, with bigger names (novelists, not story-writers) – John Irving, Tom McHale, Asa Babar, Nicholas Meyer – massing in the wings.

I have written of this, exhaustively. Read *Lusts*, read *Resident Alien*, read Steve Wilbers' history of the Writers' Workshop. I believe in communities of writers, artificial or not. I tolerate their excesses and pretensions all in the name of energy and performance. In the twenty years since I've left the Workshop, I've founded a similar program in Montreal, served in one in Toronto, and have settled in Iowa City, after a year of teaching. If I am to teach for a living, which seems inevitable, it must be writing courses and it must be where serious, ambitious students gather. Anything else raises the inflation and pretension level too high.

I have left the hardest part for last. Surviving childhood and becoming a writer is the painless part of living. Marriage, fatherhood, citizenship, meeting the expectations of manhood – those are the crushers.

I met my wife, Bharati Mukherjee, on my first night in Iowa City, in February 1962, at the home of Paul Engle. She'd entered the Workshop from Calcutta that September, and was staying in the dorms. Whenever people were to be impressed, Paul would bring her out. Impressive she is; the most beautiful woman I had, or have, ever seen. The most improbable move of my lifetime of moves was the move I put on her. The early sixties, in its widest divergence from the mid-eighties, was still a time of marriage. Everyone was married; no one had divorced. We all lived in cramped apartments with playpens and diaper-hampers, and those of us who arrived without wives or children felt the ache of incompletion. (Roth caught the mood perfectly in *Letting Go*. You were not "mature," not complete, until you married. You were an existential neuter, pontificating on experiences you'd only read about.) I, too, was married before I left graduate school; I, too, had a son before graduating.

A man like myself, so aware of the failings of his father, enters marriage and fatherhood with a clear set of priorities. The child shall be loved; the wife shall be, first of all, one's closest friend. I had taken on not just a wife with special talents and very special charms – I had taken on an alien culture, the widest possible world available to me. Indian men often married American women; the opposite only rarely occurred. Bharati received death-threats from men – spurned suitors – in the Indian community. Her reputation, impeccably upright until my proposal, plunged overnight into lewdness. (How else would a good Indian girl meet an American boy? Every Indian knew – knew existentially – Americans were only interested in fornication and imbibing strong spirits.)

The child slowly became a man in marriage. We graduated and took jobs in Milwaukee for a year, Bharati at Marquette, I at the city campus of the state university. For the first time I saw myself eclipsed; it was she who (naturally) garnered the attention, whose contract would have been extended. I, with my *Shenandoah* acceptances, my refusal to go for the Ph.D., was terminated. We returned to Iowa a year later so that she could finish her Ph.D. requirements – one of those hellish years for a young mother and a still-incomplete husband – and I could plot our next move.

It was now 1966. I had been involved in the teach-ins in Milwaukee, my mother had returned to Winnipeg, and my Southern stories were losing their steam. I wrote a novella, "Thibidault et Fils," set in Franco-American New England, and it was taken by *Prism*, in Vancouver. I was learning to lie, claiming knowledge of French and Catholic life that I had brushed against for less than a week in my life. I wrote "The Fabulous Eddie Brewster," finding the inventions, the resonances, absolutely natural, and it was taken by Canada's leading quarterly, *The Tamarack Review*. I had found a voice, which means, finally, I had found something I commanded.

The conclusion was simple – my mother had triumphed; I was a Canadian after all. All that was unforced in my life came from

Canada. The stutterings in my life were all American – the moves, the squalor, the terrors, the poverty. McGill offered Bharati a lectureship, and me a nighttime job teaching English. We immigrated in the summer of 1966, skirting Toronto for which I had a Montrealer's scorn. It would be bilingualism-or-bust; I would be the crowned prince of a coming renaissance. Single-handedly, if necessary, I would forge a cultural identity that was continental in scope and national in expression . . . all I had to do was follow the simple outline of my life.

I make it sound arrogant only from residual regret and instinctive irony. I was a young writer seeking his voice, and that is one of nature's irresistible forces. Speaking entirely for myself, the decision was correct, and my work in Canada and on behalf of Canada is, on the whole, honourable. I recreated as best I could an Iowa in Montreal at Sir George Williams University (now Concordia); I wrote stories, read them in high schools and colleges, edited books, taught a generation of younger writers in Montreal, Toronto, Saskatchewan, and British Columbia, wrote for radio and television, and knew, for a few years, a kind of national prominence that is possible only in a smaller culture. And all that while, Bharati – Canadian before me, a published novelist (*The Tiger's Daughter*, 1972; *Wife*, 1975) before me – did not receive a single invitation to read, did not receive a fraction of the reviews given even to chapbooks by our students.

Simply, I was the prodigal son, the American who'd returned to Canada, who knew some of the stories and some of the keys to turn. Bharati was the exotic whose material was Indian (bad enough) or American (far worse). We had achieved comfort in Montreal with dual tenured professorships, with foreign travel as a matter of course, a house in Westmount, children (a second son) in private schools, but we'd achieved it in a failing society.

René Lévesque's independence-minded Parti Québécois was elected in 1977. Overnight, the English-speaking community of Montreal withdrew to Ontario or the West. The literary community that we drew from, that our writing program had practically created, vanished overnight. York University in Toronto offered me a position at a time when Montreal teachers were accepting watchman's jobs in Ontario. Mine was a vast promotion. Bharati won a Guggenheim grant. It looked, as a sportswriter once said, like it would last forever.

That's when, thanks to a Federal government initiative against "non-traditional" immigration, Canada emptied its spleen against its "visible minorities." Paki-bashing was alive and well on the streets of Toronto and Vancouver. We'd been protected from it in Québec, as happily French-speaking Anglos; in Toronto my reputation kept growing, while Bharati found shopping impossible, even in our tiny neighbourhood. We stayed the minimum two years and then we applied for immigration, fourteen years after that happy day entering Canada at Windsor in 1966. We were now Canadians with two kids, forty years old, with seven books between us, and a job to split at Skidmore College in upstate New York.

That takes me back to the beginning paragraph. I'm starting my third life now, in my early forties. The old American life of Pittsburgh and the South is irretrievable. Canada is still alive, as *Resident Alien* will show, but a new America has taken hold. I wrote *Lusts* during my National Endowment year; I wrote *Resident Alien* under a Guggenheim, the same year I quit Skidmore and moved to Iowa. Our children demanded Iowa – it was the first school system they truly loved. This year I've written my third novel, *Embassy*, my first book without Canada, without adolescence, without identity crises forming the core. Bharati has found her voice, not as an Indian in exile but as an Indian immigrant, and her first book of stories, *Darkness*, will be published in the summer of 1985. She lives thirty minutes by bus from the Port Authority, in an apartment in Upper Montclair. I live here, surviving on a second mortgage, readings, and hope. In six months I will join her.

Despite my best efforts, this is still Irving's old place, still the *Garp* house. I'll point out the garage-post when I sell it, for surely in this town I'll be selling it to someone who knows modern books. I am aware, reading this over, how long forty-four years really is. What a privilege it's been, witnessing things that are gone for good. That's the kind of writer I am – a memorialist. Writing this piece today, December 20, 1984, in one long burst, I see old areas I've never exhausted. The love of those ersatz sisters, the odd relationship between the children of a man and his mistress – there's a story there. When *Embassy's* done, I'll write it.

Mentors

I BEGAN TO WRITE from a desire to impress my experiences on the obvious blank understanding of my fellow undergraduates at Denison University. I had known a time and place in America – the Deep South in the late 1940s – that was already history. I had been let out of school to watch Klan floggings, cross-burnings, and lynchings. I had attended segregated schools, and I had seen alligators, manatees, mountain lions, chain gangs, gar fish, mudfish, sharecroppers, and I had attended schools with morons and half-wits, been doused with delousing powders, had my feet swabbed with carbolic acid for hookworms and my hair shaved for ringworm. I'd run away from encampments of Seminole Indians who were not out to sell blankets or wrestle gators, and I'd seen my father, beaten to a pulp by three town marshals under the direction of a court order, as our little factory was stolen from us.

In the beginning, then, I thought of myself purely as a Southern writer on the basis of five potent years in my life – ages six through ten – spent in the swamplands and hamlets of north-central Florida. Faulkner was my guide; his language, his evocation of doom, of age, of the implacable determinants of race, class, and history. My small world fit perfectly in the Yoknapatawpha legend; I had seen all the same types, gone to schools with them, seen the towns with their statues to the Confederate dead, been dismissed from school for Confederate Memorial Day and Jefferson Davis's Birthday, and listened to my teachers' rapturous litanies on the sins, lineage, and unspeakable practices of the arch-villain, Abraham Lincoln. We'd been given little Confederate flags at school so we could line the streets of Leesburg at night, cheering the unmasked parade of the Klan, and the motorcade they led, as it proceeded to Venetian Gardens, a doubleheader, and the crowning of the Watermelon Queen. Where are you now, Dolly Beard, Watermelon Queen of 1948, Senior at Leesburg High?

And like a child out of Faulkner, or Marjorie Kinnan Rawlings, or Willie Morris, I had roamed woods, fished, played, and slumbered in the midst of a tropical torpor that was also a tropical maelstrom. I remember years, it seems now, of retiring to a screened-in porch with nothing but a Coke and the radio playing *The Game of the Day* from somewhere up North, but I also recall the furies of Florida: hurricanes, the scream of a mountain lion, the thrashing of a gator just under a rotten pier, the braiding of water moccasins in my path. I remember trailing an enormous woodpecker so deep into cypress swamps that I was knee-deep in warm water with no path out, and the bird – maybe a classifiably extinct Ivory-Billed, or maybe only a Pilated – was tapping above me while gators whistled nearby and deer could be heard plunging into deeper water that seemed to surround me.

I understood those favourite words of Faulkner, and I used them myself: *deeper, beyond, further.* It was Faulkner, to his glory, Faulkner the divine and sometimes tangled rhetorician, who had the extraordinary faith to title a story simply and forever, "Was."

Those were a few of the realities I wanted to convey to my suburban-bred mid-western classmates at Denison University. That I might look like them, sound like them, behave imperfectly like them, but that I shared nothing of their experience, outlook, values, or ambitions. For the first three or four years that I wrote, I considered myself nothing more than a Southerner, and if the truth dare be told, nothing less than Faulkner's heir.

"Write what you know," the instructors teach, but the better instructors know that the process is far more devious than that. If we *know* it, chances are it's too boring to write. Grace Paley has amended the truism somewhat: "Write what you don't know about what you know," and that comes closer, for it takes us back into Faulkner's dark caverns of *beyond, deeper,* and *ago.* If we wrote only what we knew, and showed and never told, our writing would be crippled of authority (emphasis on the first two sylla-bles). What I *knew*, at the age of twenty, was suburban life in Pittsburgh in the mid-fifties; I knew it cold. I knew the retail trade in furniture, paper routes, baseball, the charms and terrors of women, astronomy, archaeology, and gobs of facts about geogra-phy. (It would take five years before I composed those elements in a story, "Grids and Doglegs"; if I had tried it as an undergraduate – and probably I did – it would have come out like warm, flat soda water.)

We are talking of alchemy. Taking the facts, the common lan-guage, the world and characters we know, and transforming them into something never before seen, hitherto unknown, and forever fresh. (Do you know what's wrong with that sentence, the Faulk-nerian in me asks? It's that last word, "fresh." Not wrong because of meaning, but wrong because of rhythm. "Never before seen" is a synonym for "fresh" to balance the scales of "forever." But I also like the alliteration. "Fragrant?" Or a good Faulknerian "fecund"?) Forever fertile.

Denison has a professor of English, a poet, and a great teacher of poets and fiction writers by the name of Paul Bennett. He gave me a "B" in my senior year advanced fiction class, so he's no push-over. He also gave me an "A-" in my first writing course in my sophomore year, when I was a struggling Geology major, other-wise doing poorly. He has in common with all great handlers of young talent (I'm thinking specifically of certain baseball coaches, movie directors, and finally, any teacher, any parent) the qualities of faith and patience. Yes, he taught us to write what we knew about, and to write clearly and to show, not tell, but he also empha-sized trusting ourselves, trusting our story, pushing beyond what we knew into the realms of discovery. His patience rewarded me with a career: I wrote bad poems, bad character sketches (pure *Readers' Digest* stuff), bad stories about men in life rafts, and West-ern shootouts, and then one last story at the end of the course, a story called "Broward Dowdy" which excited him. It was the rea-son he taught: to see the emergence of talent, to be there when it started to happen. But I was still a Geology student, and I thought I was going to transfer to Pitt – my parents had just started their divorce, and the money for an expensive school like Denison had dried up. But the divorce dragged on and my father was solvent for one more year and I returned to Denison for a third year, bottoming out at the end of the first semester, dropping out for a semester and returning for a senior year, after a summer in Chicago, as an English major and as a writing student. In the two years remaining to me at Denison, I vowed to read a book every day and did so; I started a book-reviewing column for the weekly paper, co-edited the two literary magazines on campus, and published my stories and poems in them. Three years later, when I was married and living as a graduate student in Iowa, "Broward Dowdy" became my first story accepted by a national magazine, and I put it at the head of my second book of stories, fifteen years after writing it.

When I graduated in 1961, after winning the various campus writing prizes – which I also judged (this was in a politically innocent era) – with stories so swampy they should have been sprayed, I went on to the summer writing class of Bernard Malamud, at Harvard. I needed validation – Denison was fine and Paul Bennett is a great man – *so far as they went*. The question was, how far did they go? There was only one way to find out, perilous as that way might be. There were hundreds of Denisons out there, and thousands of campus hotshots; but there was only one Malamud, one Harvard, and only ten places in his class.

The luckiest move in my writing life was the acceptance to Malamud's class. I've had some good breaks since, though I like to think my credentials at least softened the odds, but this first one was pure luck. Malamud was coming to Harvard from Oregon; the ten slots in his class were already chosen by readers in the Harvard English Department. Who knows what criteria – but Harvard and Harvard Square is never lacking for dozens of young Updikes and hundreds of young Thomas Wolfes, talents and egos abounding.

Fortunately, I hadn't known the course was closed weeks before I'd even sent in my deposit, and my story. Fortunately, it was Bernard Malamud teaching and not some other (at the time) reasonably obscure immortal looking for a well-paid summer vacation in the heart of genteel academia. I went to the English office in Warren House, after hitchhiking in from Pittsburgh. "Oh, that course was closed weeks ago," the secretary told me. "Is there a waiting list?" I asked. "I sent in my manuscript as soon as I heard Malamud was teaching –" I must have thought that even having heard of Malamud, let alone having read him from the heart of Baptist America, was evidence of sufficient grace to insure admission. To the two of us at Denison who had read Malamud and engaged in a frantic search to uncover the elusive first novel after having devoured *The Assistant* and *The Magic Barrel*, he was the greatest writer in America. I had never seen, let alone met, a "real" writer.

"You can go up and ask him," she suggested.

He's there? I can ask him? It was, I should stress, a different era. Those of us from the provinces had never seen an author we truly admired. I was terrified and I walked around Warren House so many times I was afraid he'd sneak out before I could rehearse my presentation. Finally I confronted myself: You borrowed a hundred dollars for the course. You hitched here. You have a friend in Belmont Hill who's putting you up. You've told yourself you're going to be a writer. Face him, you idiot. Your life is over, here and now, if you can't take his course.

This is your moment of truth, Blaise.

He was seated at the end of a long room. The bookcases were empty but for shoeboxes and stacks of manuscripts, thick bundles bitten by rubber bands. (*That's* a nice little phrase.) There were more stacks on his desk. He was not particularly smiling or welcoming. He said, "I asked them to send me the manuscripts in Oregon, but instead they made the selections. That's not fair to the people who submitted in good faith. Find yours up there and give it to me."

"It's just this story," I said – I'd brought a second copy, razored from our Denison campus magazine. The catalogue hadn't mentioned thousand-page novels as a minimum consideration. "Come to the first class tomorrow, Blaise. I can't promise you're in, only that I'll read it."

I wrote two more very Southern stories for that class. All that Malamud had seen of my work, in fact, were stories with such heavy Southern dialogue that I felt absurd reading them aloud in class. There was something of an impostor about me – feeling myself Canadian more than American (the divorce had opened up the floodgates of an urgent nostalgia; I was hitchhiking on all long weekends up to Quebec City from Belmont Hill), and obviously sounding like any other college-bred Easterner. I was writing scenes that Erskine Caldwell would shun. And the class was as expected: bright, ambitious, and accomplished (at least four others that I'm aware of have gone on to establish writing careers). I was a little embarrassed by my material in that Ivy League, half high-WASP, half Jewish setting, and I felt the disapproval of my classmates, if not of the teacher. It's so easy to appear the buffoon when you follow your illiterate young characters down a swamp on a gar-hunt, or when idiot brother rapes nympho sister while out gigging frogs. My classmates were writing *European*-set stories, love affair stories, abortion stories, even Africa stories, and they were submitting *chapters*, not stories. Or they were turning out high-powered intellectual farces and fantasies that echoed Barth and pre-figured Pynchon, Heller, and Vonnegut. The big book of those in the know was Gaddis's *The Recognitions*. Harvard was the big time, all right; the overflow of the next-ten rejectees from Malamud's course was being taught by John Hawkes, just down the hall. At Malamud's prompting, I read *The Lime Twig*, and everything earlier. So: it was possible to keep the rhythms of Faulkner, the rhetoric and incantations of voice, and get rid of that inauthentic Southern material. I rejoiced.

That was the terror I faced. I wanted to write, and life itself had given me a boost by smearing me in the paste of a memorable

Southern childhood. But it was an accident. Those memories were a shopping list, and I was quickly exhausting the menu of available experience. Then what? Be a Pittsburgh suburbanite? And so I wrote one very strange story for Malamud that summer; a typically over-ambitious piece of incomprehensible (also Faulknerian) monologue of a senile Canadian doctor, remembering and living (in his hospital bed) his heroic service during the influenza epidemic of 1919, while (in searing irony!) he is really an eighty-five-year-old whimpering husk soiling his sheets in a Winnipeg hospital. My grandfather, obviously. At the very least, it was a change of material, though of course (as Malamud pointed out), I had scrambled a good story and a strong character for the dubious pleasures of sophomoric experimentation. Of all the things to lift from Faulkner, I had to choose the Benjy monologue.

Malamud's instructions are as simple as the universal reader demands and as complicated as the most ambitious author expects: focus on character, make every act, every detail, dramatic. Fiction, he said, is "the dramatization of the multifarious adventures of the human heart" – advice that we young Barthists (we'd all read *The Sot-Weed Factor* and *The End of the Road*) and Gaddisites probably associated with the death of literature. That was Dickensian! We wanted the clean lines and sharp edges of Modernism, we'd been raised on irony, juxtaposition, and every conceivable complication of structure. On days when we didn't provide stories of our own, Malamud introduced us to Isaac Babel, Flannery O'Connor, Hemingway, James, Moravia. He read us stories – well-received ones by nameless contemporaries – and asked us to think twice before admiring such clever tricks, such facile manipulations. If a title was mentioned in class, by teacher or student, that I hadn't read – a simple enough event in those days, despite the two years of book-a-day reading – I'd have it read twice before the next class.

The mentors that last in our lives are those who do not press a case, do not try to shape, or inflate; do not lust for miniatures of themselves, or even try to leave much of an impression at all. They are anything but charismatic (I have known many inspirational writing-teachers in my day); they teach by their tolerance and their conviction. They are calm, even serene, in that reconciliation of tolerance and authority, and, I think, they have one other great quality. Malamud, as a reader, as a teacher, and as a writer, takes *delight*; there is no other way of putting it. It was possible to *delight* this man, to see his eyes, mouth, brow suddenly dance over a sentence, a word, an idea. Oh, it is possible to enrage a teacher, to infuriate or embitter him or her, and many teachers make their point by great shows of anger and fury, or of scathing wit and sustained comedy; only the rarest, I think, instruct by an almost private show of delight.

When the summer school ended and Malamud went on to begin his career at Bennington (odd to think he was forty-seven that summer, so old and powerful and socketed in eternity to me at the time, and how quickly I'm closing on that age now), I stayed back in Boston, getting a job in a bookstore and taking an apartment with one of the wilder members of the summer class. I stayed with the job all winter, thinking I could remain out of university and somehow in the flow of that thing called "life" (we were in the American butt end of existentialism, after all), working just enough hours to finance my writing. As for living, I'd leave that to my apartment-mate. I hitched up to Bennington to visit Malamud one weekend; he came down to Harvard one afternoon while I was working, found the stack of his recently-issued novel, A New Life, signed them, and as the manager came running over, he pointed to the books and said, "A deposit on Blaise's freedom for the afternoon. Let's beat it." And there I was, on a cool day in Harvard Square, walking with the writer I most admired (and still do), answering as best I could *his* questions about me: What did I intend to do with my life? Was I working? Was I happy? What could he do to help?

I do remember, one evening after work in the bookstore, slipping into the Lamont Library, taking out a new notebook and writing a story, "How I Became a Jew," that was literally a transi-tional story between South and North, as well as a tribute to Malamud. In one sitting; shades of Thomas Wolfe! I had started a novel, "The French and Jewish War," about my parents and I sup-pose about myself and twisted loyalties, and most of it was set in Canada. I would be writing it a year later, in Iowa, after the most momentous year in my life. I vomited the night on Dubuque Street in Iowa City when I read through those two hundred yellow pages with the big inked number at the top of every page (my God, *me*, at one hundred! at two hundred!!) and then unclipped the pages from the binder I had bought on the first day of Malamud's class at the Harvard Co-op, marched outside in the cold, lifted the lid of my garbage can, and ripped the pages into shreds.

This page intentionally left blank

The Border as Fiction

"How do you get eighteen French Canadians into
a Volkswagen?"
"Tell them you're going to Plattsburgh."
—old joke

IN THE LAST DAYS of 1987, during our latest move, while unpacking boxes of books that had lain in storage for over two years, I uncovered a slim, discoloured volume entitled *The Borderland and Other Poems*, by a certain Roger Quin, poet and Bohemian (born 1850). The book is updated (but is circa 1910), and is published by A. Walker & Son of Galashiels. That, I take it, is in Scotland. The discolouring comes from smoke, a reminder of our house fire in Montreal in 1973. Books purchased before that fire, and preserved through two dozen moves since, are signs of a certain naive commitment. I had probably purchased Quin's book at a church rummage sale in rural Québec in the mid-sixties.

Anything to do with borders speaks to me personally. I am animated by the very thought of borders; crossing the border is like ripping the continent, tearing its invisible casing. I look upon borders as zones of grace, fifty miles wide on either side, where dualities of spirit are commonplace.

The Scots, of course, first cultivated border consciousness to a bardic art. That invisible, near-mythical Scottish border is a primeval literary marker, and the prototype for the border that obsesses me, the Canadian-American. I'm not Scottish, and have never set foot in Scotland, but at one time in my life the thought of such a border appealed to me, as it would to many Canadians. Now, as though to prove that no written word is ever lost, I put Roger Quin ("the tramp poet") at the head of an essay, a piper to his lost, disparate clan.

In the introduction to a book of nineteenth-century Scottish short stories, the editor, Douglas Gifford, writes of the conflicts in the characteristic Scottish story: "Disorder, romance, imagination and feeling" are set against "rational Order." Sir Walter Scott's novels are "seen as extended metaphors for the dissociation in Scotland of thought and feeling, materialism and imagination, repression and sensitivity." Later Gifford notes that "two major forces shape the major fiction" – namely, "protestantism and profit."

These divisions have their echoes in Canada, certainly in my own family and in my sense of what Canada and the United States represent, and of the purpose of the border that lies between them. In an autobiographical essay, the late Québec (actually Franco-Manitoban) novelist, Gabrielle Roy, speaking of her own family, wrote, "with which side should I identify myself especially? With the Roys, troubled people, strict, Jansenists according to what I had been told, but also idealists and dreamers? Or with the Landrys, vivacious, impulsive, gracious and smiling? Where should I turn to to learn from where I came?" The borders in Québec do not require a checkpoint.

This dissociation, or at least conflict, between Protestantism and profit, secularism and the Church, seems to me a useful point of departure for discussing Canadian visions of the United States. Surely the United States has embodied to Canadians a promise of wealth and self-assertion, and a threat to stability, while the border – increasingly mythical, one might add, as free trade and modern communications erode its ancient protections – affords only a tattered shelter. Canada's initial mission on this continent was the extension of parliamentary civilization – anti-republican, and anti-individualist – and there are substantial segments of Canadian society, and deep responses in the collective Canadian cortex, that resist the anarchic, litigious sprawl of American life, even when attracted, or pulled, to the American marketplace. This tension is the transparent casing that supports the border; it is central to the reading of the Canadian character and, not incidentally, to its literature.

Wouldn't most Canadian thinkers, and writers, agree with the proposition, drawn from the Scottish example, that adherence to Canada (an ideal of Canada that is every bit as operative as the stars-and-stripes ideal of America) implies a certain material sacrifice? One clings to Canada out of inertia, yes, but faintly from virtue as well. One gives up Canada – the conclusion is inevitable – for the same reasons a Glaswegian treks to London: guilt and greed.

Look again at the self-awareness in that little joke (a québécois joke, actually, told in French) that heads this essay. See the disparity between a Quebecker's image of Plattsburgh, and an American's sense of the same dreary air-base town. In the United States, Plattsburgh is seen as the last outpost; from Canada, it is the shopping mall of milk and honey.

Our move this year is deeper into Manhattan; last year was Queens. In the past eight years we have lived in Iowa City, British Columbia, Atlanta, Saratoga Springs, Toronto, and Montreal. From a lifetime of crossing borders, I have developed a border consciousness. Borders mean metamorphosis, personal transformation. They offer the opportunity to be and not be simultaneously, or to be two opposing things without deception. I suspect I am not alone in sensing the pull of alien gravities, yet I've often felt lonely, wondering if anyone else out there on our continent of rootless adventurers ever felt as I did.

For me, growing up in a map-strewn apartment in central Florida, countries were like bodies, and borders were their skin. I attributed personalities to shapes, and learned to recognize and respond to outlines of states, countries, and even counties the way salesmen do to faces. I projected personalities on barren outlines.

I fantasized the embrace of Vermont and New Hampshire; they share their diagonal slice of a rocky rectangle like lovers. I approved the tentacular, border-state handshake of West Virginia and Maryland, snaking over Virginia and sliding under Pennsylvania. I detected disloyalty, however, in West Virginia's dagger thrust into the latitudes of Ohio and Pennsylvania. (The suspicion was borne out years later, in the late fifties, when I used to drive between my Pittsburgh home and my Ohio college, crossing that West Virginia panhandle at Wheeling. Between two abolitionist states stood the stark "coloured-white" motel signs.) I thought of Tennessee and North Carolina as a sliced earthworm – two separate bodies from a single diagonal cut. I inferred hostility between Mississippi and Alabama as they turn their backs on each other, just like Arizona and New Mexico. I saw Arkansas as a chipped flowerpot, Louisiana as an overstuffed armchair, Minnesota as an enveloping protoplasm about to ingest Wisconsin. I liked broad, smiling Iowa, with its bulging cheek. I wondered about the twinning of inanimate objects – why Missouri and Georgia took on similar shapes, even to tiny nipples at their lower right. Alberta and British Columbia were bloated and blunted versions of Nevada and California. The Yukon mimicked Idaho, and Montana played the American version of the Northwest Territories. Canada leaned its Western provinces vertically, while the Western states were boxes, cut square for stacking.

Later, watching television weather forecasts, I wondered how the Americans could cut off their borders at North Dakota and complain of "Canadian cold" emanating from sheer blankness to the north. Books as well seemed to end at the border. I loved Faulkner's sense of Canada, the use of Shreve McCannon, Quentin Compson's Harvard roommate, as the implied audience to the greatest of all American novels, *Absalom, Absalom!* It's Shreve who asks the major question of the book and in Faulkner's writing – "Why do you hate the South?" – and it's to Shreve, a Canadian, that Quentin cries his response: "*I don't.*" (At one time, I made something of that formulation: the Southerner and the Canadian, back-to-back brothers with the belt of individualist, ahistorical Yankeeland in between.) The only other American author with a consistently continental sense of origins was Ross Macdonald, and he, of course, was an old Canadian.

There is, I think, a border mentality, just as there is a small-country mentality (as recently expounded by Milan Kundera), or an exile mentality, a ghetto mentality, an imperialist mentality, an island mentality. The border mentality is alert to differences to calculating loss and advantage. It watches for tinctures of change as one demographic landscape blends into another.

And there is a border mentality that can take liberty with borders as they are drawn, and that seeks to arrange things more coherently. I've written in the past of my own helpless fascination with the observed facts of the atlas, my attempts to memorize everything on the face of the globe, until finally those facts were not enough and I embarked on a childhood reinvention of the world, of countries, cities, continents, on a movement from history and from memoir into fiction. I was inspired to read, in a *Paris Review* interview, of Carlos Fuentes's literary reinvention of the world. There is, for Fuentes, a Caribbean literature, subversive of history and language, a multilingual literature of history's castaways: "There is a culture of the Caribbean . . . that includes Faulkner, Carpentier, García Márquez, Derek Walcott, and Aimé Césaire, a trilingual culture in and around the whirlpool of the baroque which is the Caribbean, the Gulf of Mexico." The point is, there are many more borders in the world than those we traditionally honour. In the process of growing up, we writers reinvent borders in the same way politicians and businessmen rediscover constituencies and markets.

The two borders of the United States offer interesting contrasts. The Rio Grande appears as a giant bug zapper, a lure behind a grid. The attraction is greater than the risk, and risk is a physical calculation compounded of jail time, humiliation, and possible death. Presumably few of the millions of Mexicans and Latin Americans who attempt to breach the Mexican-American border annually are much concerned with possible loss of culture and identity, or with the new political and psychological landscape they'll be asked to inhabit. The same cannot be said of those who cross the forty-ninth parallel and its New England equivalent. Because the Canadian identity is consciously maintained, the border is as much a psychological as a physical one. Each Canadian emigrant must come to America prepared to die a subtle, psychic death.

Some borders are cages; others are mirrors. Some purely political borders rasp on our consciousnesses – the various Koreas, Germanies, Irelands, Lebanons, "Bantustans," and West Banks. They seem to defy the common meaning of *border*, which is to define differences – these are borders that separate likenesses. Traditional borders, such as those in Europe, are natural reminders of where ancient armies ran out of steam, where languages and religions died, where empires faltered. European countries, so far as European consciousnesses are concerned, are separate but equal. (It would be hard to imagine a Danish joke using the nearest German city, Flensburg, in the same way the Quebecker uses Plattsburgh.) A few borders are aesthetic or cultural, such as that of Scotland, or the Mason-Dixon Line, or hundreds of others with poetic and psychological potency – the various *Gaeltaecht* regions of Ireland, the Breton, Welsh, Basque, Kurdish borders that don't really exist except as maintained fictions. There are borders made of the thinnest membrane, such as that between Canada and the United States, which is undefended because the two sides have reached a mental stasis. (To call the border "undefended" is an absurdity; Canadian defensiveness is a standing army of twenty-five million. We stand on guard for thee.) And there are the new, economic supraborders: the post-colonials, and those dividing east and west, north and south, industrialized and developing countries, and free and communist ones. Increasingly, they are the borders with which our children will be dealing – my obsession with minute shapes and whimsical curlicues will be seen as a harmless hobby akin to stalking stamps with a magnifying glass.

I trust, however, there will always be ambiguous borders like the Canadian-American – not exactly a fiction, yet clearly special. As a child, I thought of borders, or at least the ones that I knew well, as force fields. I was powerless to move. I could see across them into a pure Canada or America, but those places were not for me. Borders threw back a likeness that partook of parody and distortion. The images were like us, but just a little strange. The border seemed to move with me, hanging overhead like a cloud.

I would say now that borders are fictions. Within a given territory's boundaries, and determined by the nature of those boundaries, exists a collective character: the European confidence, the Japanese insularity, the American naive openness, the African touchiness, the Canadian desire for identity. Africa suffers a surplus of borders, none of which speak to the consciousness of the people. Africans live, simultaneously, within three or four sets of borders (tribal, religious, racial, linguistic). Canada has only one external border, which is a protection against assimilation (like Scotland's), and a host of regional and linguistic barriers that are internal variants of the same thing. To be Canadian is to state a preference, and to maintain that preference every day in a series of symbolic acts. By their borders ye shall know them.

My Canadian parents, fleeing the war, dipped into North Dakota in 1940 to have me. And so I carry a mythical birthplace around for life – Fargo – a place we left within the year. And then we hit the road, my French-speaking father and my aristocratic mother: Cincinnati, Pittsburgh, Atlanta, a dozen stops in Florida, New York, Cleveland, Chicago, Winnipeg, Springfield (Missouri), Cincinnati, Montreal, and Pittsburgh again. All of this before I was twelve. In stories and novels I've treated my suitcase-and-Greyhound life as an uncommon existence and I'm sure it is, but it's not unknown. Many children of feckless parents travelled as much or more – but not all developed a border consciousness. I was overdetermined, but I'm not sure where it came from. If I had to guess, I would say that my parents were so profoundly different from one another, that I grew up loving and fearing a border consciousness every day of my life.

A border means that certain things are more likely to occur on this side, *here*, than *there*. Certain other things are probably impossible. There is comfort in knowing that in Canada chances are you won't be gunned down by a random psychopath. You probably are safe from serial murderers. You will not be beggared by medical bills and education costs. The part of the country from which you come will determine your outlook; you will be regionally determined. (A Canadian friend, now married to an American novelist, remarked to me this winter, "I've been here two years and only now am I learning not to ask 'Where do you come from?' as a first question.") It means, if you're a writer in Canada, writing about high school, you're more likely to sympathize with the teacher over the student (with Laurence's *A Jest of God* and Metcalf's *Going Down Slow* over Knowles's *A Separate Peace* and Salinger's *The Catcher in the Rye*). If you're writing about small towns, you are necessarily advocating the use of an incendiary device to obliterate them. Members of Parliament, policemen, or clergymen will not be seen, necessarily, as fools, thugs, or hypocrites.

I was a passionately Southern boy in the segregated Deep South of the late forties, and I was a fervent Canadian singing "O Canada" and "God Save the King," and I was a child of the Ozarks, and a member of the Reds' Knothole Club in old Crosley Field, and I passed out of my boyhood in Pittsburgh's post-Kiner, Clemente era. Pittsburgh, my home for seven years, the American city I know best.

I suffered for all the rebukes that clung to grim, sooty Pittsburgh and so I memorized – it always helps to have a hungry memory – lists of Pittsburgh's accomplishments. (Why, I wonder now? Native-born Pittsburghers could be merciless about the city's patent ghastliness. I never had the confidence to ridicule. The city was me. Every place I've ever been has been me; I've expanded myself right out to everyone's borders.) Pittsburgh's great fortunes were my benefactors; its institutions were mine for the taking. Loving Pittsburgh wasn't easy – except as a lover of losing efforts, a true Scotsman, or perhaps Southerner, Canadian, or one of Fuentes's Caribbeans – back when the Pirates, Steelers, and Pitt Panthers were all at the bottom of their respective leagues. We had Duquesne basketball to cheer, and the rest was civic endowment: the Carnegie Library and Museum, Buhl Planetarium, the Civic Light Opera, the Pittsburgh Symphony, the Art Students League, and the astronomy clubs and archaeology clubs that worked out of the basements of those grey-granite institutions. I belonged to all of them, they developed my talents, they gave me friends who were nerdy, just like me. They carried me through high school, as proud of my city as any New Yorker or Parisian is of his.

Which is, of course, the point. By the age of fourteen I had manufactured myself half a dozen times into a native of a place. Border crossing could have made me feel alien, and deep down it probably did; overtly, however, I responded only with a puppylike loyalty. Seeking always to blend in, I did so by memorizing the box scores and the trolley grid, and tracing out the city maps at night and poring over the regional maps so I could picture each outlying town and suburb as it surfaced in the news. Oh, the satisfaction gained from those Friday night high-school football scores, and knowing, after a few months, where each of those schools were located! Thirty years later, as I drive the continent at night and KDKA (Pittsburgh's fifty thousand watts) weaves the airwaves, I realize I *still* remember. But I'm not a native of anywhere, and I still fear the inevitable question: "Where are you from?" Fargo, North Dakota?

Or Montreal, the city where my parents had met and married, and from which they'd emigrated, and which is still the place I feel most attached to, and have lived in longest? Or the Deep South, which I remember with a special ferocity, a place whose smells and visions still assault me? Or Manitoba, the only repository of my family, where my maternal grandparents and cousins and aunts and uncles lived, and the family had its farm, and I was sent most every summer? My mother is buried in Winnipeg, in the family plot, with her parents and sisters. (My father is buried in Manchester, New Hampshire, next to his last wife's first husband.)

Or perhaps, in the hungriest leap of all, Europe, where my mother spent the most exciting years of her life, studying art and design in Germany from 1929 until the closing of her school in 1933? Crossing the border into Denmark in 1935, she told me, and seeing a smiling porter sweeping the platforms, had made her cry with gratitude. She hadn't realized, until leaving Germany, the strain that she and everyone else had been under inside those Nazi borders. Her stories had made a vanished Europe, or a pre-World War I Saskatchewan winter, more real to me that anything in my experience.

I wanted to be anything but what I was, and to come from anyplace but where I had. The real me was always somewhere else, but I never found it. Which is the other side of saying, with Roger Quin (poet and Bohemian), that "my errant Muse" lives only here, "in the ruins of Lincluden, Torthorwald, Caerlaverock" (or Montreal, Pittsburgh, Europe, Winnipeg, and the Deep South, with stopovers in India, due to my exotic marriage).

Until my recently married Canadian friend mentioned it, I hadn't thought of intense regionalism as a national trait of Canadians – it was always so much an urgent aspect of my personality – but of course she's right. Canadians ask where you're from, because where you're from reveals relatively more about you if you're a Canadian than it does if you're an American. Being from Saskatchewan or Nova Scotia, at a Toronto cocktail party, probably accounts for sharper self-definition than being from Kansas or Maryland does in New York.

That is, I *think* it does. One feature of a psychologically maintained border, a subjectively felt border, is its porosity, the fact that it blends differences but does not eliminate them. Border mystique exists in Scotland, where differences must be internalized and perpetuated, formed into symbols, and rehearsed as works of art. But some people, alas, are not good actors. *Historical* borders – solid, traditional, European-style borders where fifty metres on the other side of a striped kiosk people speak a different language and practise a different religion, share a different history, and even look a little different – do not require symbols or rehearsals. Those borders served only to define territory and protect against invasion. *Maintained* borders, such as Canada's with the United States, protect against assimilation. Presumably, a group of young Italians would not identify a group of German tourists on a camping trip as anything but German (nor would it occur to them to question the Germans' identity), but in Margaret Atwood's *Surfacing*, the narrator discovers – with a shock and with depression – that some typically loud and vulgar American campers and fishermen, despoilers of a pristine Canadian nature, turn out to be Canadian (that is, they may be *from* Canada, but that fact is not contiguous, in the self-conscious Canadian psyche, with *being* Canadian). If Canadians do not suffer continuing identity crises, then they are contaminated with the American virus of total, blank, unselfconsciousness.

There are, conversely, many Americans who hold classically Canadian opinions of the United States and think of themselves as "belonging" to a different culture (Canada being an alternate of choice). Such people, I feel, act from sentiment. They feel Canada embodies an innocence or purity lacking in America, that its border is somehow an ecological and social time tunnel. A clean, progressive place to fish and ski and swim. "Toronto's like New York was thirty years ago," say wonderstruck friends, reflecting New Yorkers' contemporary anxiety over dirt and violence. For most Canadians and Europeans, to visit New York City is also to engage in time travel; the city poses many of the shocking confrontations of a pre-industrial age.

Psychological borders are, by their nature, unequally felt. The English don't feel oppressed by the Scottish border. If they think about what it means to cross the border at all, their thoughts are probably folkloric, full of stags at eve and Highland flings. Such a border crossing involves rugged, ecological time travel. Americans don't feel cramped by the Canadian helmet tight on their heads. The fugitive virtues of Plattsburgh are differently weighted in the two cultures. For Canadians, however (especially for those who would strenuously deny it) the American border is a central, imaginative fact of life. Proportionally, I suspect there are many more Canadians who feel themselves to be "basically American," and do not weigh the cultural and psychological costs of free trade (for example) with the same scales as they do the economic costs. My father, who gave up the French language and Catholicism, was such a person. For all of his American life he lied about his background, his names, and his origins. He claimed, like me, to be a native of anyplace he lived. My mother, who went along with all the moves, never claimed to be anything but a Canadian, from "the West," Wawanesa born and North Battleford and Winnipeg educated – these places were truly the frontier West when she was a child.

Borders are a supreme fiction. For the once colonial, newly liberated, borders are a deformity. They do not define, they do not protect, they do not express a collective will. Borders, in fact, exacerbate instability. Borders are madness, they separate natural brothers, they enclose natural enemies.

It took a psychic insurrection for V.S. Naipaul to realize he was not defined by the accidental quadrant of his birth, the island of Trinidad, but that paradoxically, his accidental, colonially determined birth as an uprooted Hindu in a Caribbean barracoon made him a citizen of the colonial master, Britain, as well as the rest of the postcolonial world. So, too, the India-born residents of the United States, Vikram Seth and Bharati Mukherjee. Guyana-born Wilson Harris sails the world in his imagination, as does the nominally Pakistani, Brazil-anointed American resident Zulfikar Ghose. Small wonder that in the works of all these writers madness lurks at the edges. They have seen too much, twisted themselves into too many shapes. They are extensions of Fuentes's super-Caribbean – new border crossers, new mapmakers, citizens of a new world literary order.

For Europeans, borders are definitions, especially perhaps for the British and Scandinavians, who fortify their ancient identities with island-like isolation (that's why the few of them who travel do so in such an entertaining manner). Authors such as Bruce Chatwin and Jonathan Raban are not travelling to discover new selves – they know what they are. They travel without the edge of danger, the risk of character loss; travel, if anything, enhances their confidence.

For Canadians, borders are a protection against assault, which always happens elsewhere. When they travel, it is to try on possible new identities; what they often encounter is a mirror of themselves they can't accept. In Alice Munro's story "Miles City, Montana," the narrator and her young husband and two daughters drive from British Columbia to Ontario. To reduce the story rather brutally to a portion of its plot, something happens when they enter the United States. In their car game of "Who Am I?" (yes, of course, one thinks), the older daughter identifies herself as "somebody dead, and an American, and a girl." (She turns out to be a shot doe, seen slung on a pickup truck that morning.) They want to swim in a pool, but it is closed between noon and two-o'clock. The young lifeguard, however, is accommodating, if somewhat distracted by her boyfriend; she lets the girls use the pool. The parents stay in the car. The mother eventually gets out to stretch her legs, then has a sudden jolt of recognition – "Where are the children?" Of course, she intervenes just before the younger girl drowns. The lifeguard was inattentive; her boyfriend smiles and turns down the radio. The family drives off, and eventually rejoins the Trans-Canada north of North Dakota.

In Munro's story, death and recognition are averted, but not forever. The grace of good fortune *this time* becomes a moral wariness, a realization of vulnerability. The mother sees an equivalence between the heedless young Americans and herself and her husband, as they seek approval from his Ontario parents, wanting to prove themselves as grown-up and responsible.

In Atwood's *Bodily Harm* and *The Handmaid's Tale*, the assault is not avoided. Canada is an incubator of innocence for the protagonist of *Bodily Harm*, whose sanitized Toronto trendiness offers no protection from, and no warning of, the impending violence on a tiny Caribbean island. In *The Handmaid's Tale*, Canada exists as an unaffected bystander to American fundamentalist violence, a place to which fugitive women, the runaway slaves of the late-twentieth century, may escape. In the work of another poet and novelist, Michael Ondaatje, violence is also animating, embraced as consciousness's dark companion. In Ondaatje's *Coming Through Slaughter* and *The Collected Works of Billy the Kid*, violence as an art form arises south of the border.

The worst that can be said of Canadians is that they are frequently silly, tasteless, indecisive, or vulgar – for confirmation, see the collected satires of John Metcalf or Mordecai Richler. The best that can be said is that they are rational, sober, decent, humble – see the *New Age* cycle of novelist Hugh Hood. Or – because of their peculiarly passive position on this continent, torn between the American beast and the European ideal, acted upon but essentially powerless – Canada and the Canadian psyche becomes the proper testing ground for the anima/animus formulations of Robertson Davies.

Space has run out, but the border lingers in my mind. I want to speak of borders and margins, borders and frontiers, borders and mimicry, borders and subversion. I want to say my childhood perceptions were entirely backwards: I was not imposing character on the maps I studied and tried to memorize – the map I was born with had imposed its character on me.

Kerouac in Black and White

TWO IMAGES HAUNT ME.

Vanished French-speaking empires, multiracial and multilingual, the only two *truly* multicultural societies ever created north of the Rio Grande. One was Indian – the Métis (Cree-Ojibwa-French) nation of Manitoba, exterminated by the Anglo-Canadians, its leader, Louis Riel, hanged in 1885 – and the other is Cajun, black and white, a little Indian and a little Spanish, colourful but threatened, of bayou Louisiana. The same dream haunted Faulkner (in *Absalom, Absalom!* and in the character of the Indian Chief "Doom" whose name derived from "Du Homme"), and haunts Carlos Fuentes (a vision of a lost multilingual Afro-Franco-Hispano-Dutch-Anglo, Voodoo-Catholic-Animist empire of the Caribbean), but it still drums in the hearts of most present-day Québécois (their fate – extinction, or the recipe-book – if they don't protect themselves) and of a few Franco-Americans, for whom, as they well know, it is already too late. Franco-Americans clung to the edge of the life raft, the dream of *survivance*, much longer than most immigrant groups, but now they're gone. They're ghosts. That nightmare, and that dream, existed in the imagination of Jack Kerouac, French-America's most famous son, after Rudy Vallée and Leo Durocher.

An impotent, alcoholic, ruined, middle-aged, mill-town Franco-American living in Lowell, and finally in St. Petersburg with his jealously protective, corrosively ignorant and loudly bigoted mother, or with a wife he alternately loved and hated while trying to divorce, is not a candidate for progressive opinions on race, class, or sexual politics. Forget Kerouac in his youth, the beautiful boy with his breathless tales of breaking away from *canadien* Catholicism nightmared in *Doctor Sax* or tapestried in *Visions of Gerard*; forget the trips he took us on, like swatted rubber balls on their widest orbit in *On the Road* and *The Dharma Bums* and *Mexico City Blues* before they crashed back to the paddle that propelled them. That was then; this is later, much later.

We're looking at two pictures and one is not pretty: the *"Don't you know me? I'm Jack Kerouac!"* vulture dining on his own corpse in his paunchy, woozy, premature middle age. The *don't-you-know-me* conventional Catholic, virgin/whore sexual moralist. The *you-can't-be-Jack Kerouac* who exposed himself at parties, ranted in interviews, who wouldn't go to parties if Negroes were invited, "Jack Kerouac" the anti-semite, "Jack Kerouac" the would-be basher of Vietnam protesters. "Jack Kerouac" the cat-petting Buckleyite. Not *ti-Jean*, the Horace Mann and Columbia freshman football player; not *Jack* (for he still has single-name recognition), that recurrent American literary icon, the darkly handsome mute genius from improbable origins, and our national need to celebrate romantic excess even as we condemn it, not that tortured brew of innocence and superstition and omnivorous sexual, literary, and geographical hunger. We're talking instead of the ruined hulk, the alcoholic, the exposure-artist, the anti anti-Vietnam patriot, the hoarder of resentment, the racist, the bigot and what, if anything, they tell us of his people and their relationship to race.

Dreiser, Saroyan, Pound, or Brando, or Presley, and of course Kerouac, were concoctions of Americana, those pure products who named a landscape (Wabash, Fresno, Tupelo) and were doomed to madness. Hard lives, all of them, making for unpleasant men. Auden was right: "Those to whom evil is done/ Do evil in return." Or, they keep on doing evil to themselves, in punishment and atonement. I don't think they'd agree with one of the final statements by Martin Luther King Jr., speaking of black history in America, that "unearned suffering is redemptive," unless they sought that redemption through their compulsive self-expression.

Do the despised become despicable? Or ennobled? That's one difference between history and literature. In literature, we try to make it happen.

By extension, through Jack, we're talking of a particular time and place in the United States – New England in the first half of this century – and of the four or five million first- and second-generations of French-Canadian immigrants to the mill towns of New England, like my father – Leo's – Manchester, New Hampshire, like Kerouac's father – Leo's – Lowell, Massachusetts, or his mother's Nashua ("nash-way"), New Hampshire. Geographically, or at least demographically, it doesn't hurt to note at the outset that the four states that received the vast majority of turn-of-the-century Quebeckers – Maine, New Hampshire, Rhode Island, Massachusetts – probably had, collectively, more black bears than black people. In other words, he was a high-school football star on, presumably, an all-white team. Then he went to New York.

Race in the normal American black/white sense was never a reality for Kerouac, never part of his early personal history – only a metaphor for freedom, or temptation. He carried his blinkered childhood within him like a malignant unborn twin, and a white, Catholic, lost, pure French empire was part of that childhood. But for the likelihood of Indian blood, which he (like most French Canadians) embraced, Kerouac was *pure laine*, a proud, full-blooded, full-culture French Canadian. ("Go back," he wanted to call to his Breton fishermen ancestors, "*ils vous jouent un tour.*" That is, America's going to play a trick on you.) Against the backdrop of the Church, and his own monochromatic background, "Negroes" offered only occasions for sex, drugs, and music. And since those are also occasions for merging identities, they specifically challenge the corrosive dream of racial and religious purity. Gerald Nicosia, in *Memory Babe*, mentions that Jack would have married Mardou Fox, the heroine of *The Subterreaneans*, if she'd been white. A strange inhibition for a Beat. "Purity" rose up early, and later consumed him, his vulture-twin pouncing on a helpless host.

The French Canadians *were* the African-Americans of that melanin-challenged time and place, just as Saroyan's Armenians were the "gypsies" of central-valley California. Like Kerouac, Saroyan famously embraced life whole, offered in his hundreds of stories a palate of amused social and ethnic tolerance. Yet, his marriage collapsed over anti-semitism. Saroyan, whose career and personality parallel Kerouac's in many ways, was Jack's earliest major literary influence.*

The nature of Kerouac's gift was for suggestiveness, a quickness of apprehension, a helpless reproduction of association and atmosphere. Capote, famously, demoted it to "typing." Some of the attitudes Kerouac ingested and never spat out, like Pound's "suburban prejudice" of anti-semitism, were (as a "putter-inner" on the Wolfe-Céline-Saroyan-Pound and Faulkner model) the ancestral voices and ongoing bigotries of his life. Childhood attitudes and suppositions can be (must be) separated from adult discourse, of course, but Kerouac would not be Jack if he'd been cursed with self-consciousness. His father, eventually, hated Roosevelt, Jews, Democrats, and (other) minorities. So did Jack, eventually.

Outwardly in his final Lowell and Florida years with his mother he was indistinguishable from many other fat drunken pugnacious Canucks, the very image of his rabidly prejudiced, right-wing father. All those other great putter-inners also struggled against the conventions of their growing up, struck rebellious early attitudes, but settled finally on an essentially racist, right-wing (or in the case of Céline and Pound, perhaps Wolfe, perhaps Lawrence, fascist) politics.

---

* In Saroyan's childhood, attempts were made in the Central Valley to ban the entry of Armenians as "Asians." The same prejudice continued into the 1940s when deportation and seizure of their hard-won landholdings were a popular cause. For similar treatment of French Canadians see my *I Had a Father*, particularly the editorials of *The New York Times* a century ago.

I think of Kerouac as belonging to the great, eternal "B-list" of American writing, Farrell and O'Hara, Steinbeck and Dos Passos, Cozzens and Marquand, Saroyan and di Donato – the uncanonized voices of second-generation ethnicity, shanty Irish bitterness, or near-WASP snobbishness. Many came from the newspaper world – Saroyan was the fastest teletype operator on the West Coast, and Kerouac typed off shelving-paper rolls. They typed a lot, they knew life and trusted their experience, they were cynical, they were bitter, and most of them drank a lot.

But Kerouac at his best – no, that's too academic – Kerouac at his most Jack-like – had a generous heart and all-embracing energy that is, in the American context, *ethnic*: non-WASP, giving, awkward, curious, unembarrassedly affectionate. At his worst, admittedly, he was a monster. But thirty-five years after first reading *The Subterraneans*, as a self-styled undergraduate rebel-writer, I recently read it again, wincing at my underlined enthusiasms, but not willing, finally, to change a thing. The great gift of Kerouac's ersatz Buddhism (which he strenuously denied later on) became the credo of an age not-yet born (this was 1959, after all), but it is planted in the mind of every young writer: *The bad news is, everything's connected, but the good news is, nothing matters.* What freedom! What licence! We see now how he arrived at his truths, against a deep, contrary, Gothic Catholicism. (*Everything matters, everything's connected and you're to blame for all of it, especially the death of your saintly older brother, and your mother is here to tell you that you'll never be pardoned.*)

Consider this (that is, go with it), part of a two-page sentence, a riff, gratuitous, about Mardou Fox's (Jack's half-black lover's) Indian father:

– Concern for her father, because I'd been out there and sat down on the ground and seen the rail the steel of America covering the ground filled with the bones of old Indians and Original Americans. – In the cold gray fall in Colorado and Wyoming I'd worked on the land and watched Indian hoboes come suddenly out of brush by the track and move slowly, hawk lipped, rill-jawed and wrinkled, into the great shadow of the light bearing burdenbags and junk talking quietly to one another and so distant from the absorptions of the field hands, even the Negroes of Cheyenne and Denver streets, the Japs, the general minority Armenians and Mexicans of the whole West that to look at a three-or-foursome of Indians crossing a field and a railroad track is to the senses like something unbelievable as a dream – you think, "They must be Indians – ain't a soul looking at 'em – they're goin' that way – nobody notices – doesn't matter much which way they go – reservation? What have they got in those brown paper bags?" and only with a great amount of effort you realize "But they were the inhabitors of this land and under these huge skies they were the worriers and keeners and protectors of wives in whole nations gathered around tents – now the rail that runs over their forefathers' bones leads them onward pointing into infinity, wraiths of humanity treading lightly the surface of the ground so deeply suppurated with the stock of their suffering you only have to dig a foot down to find a baby's hand. – The hotshot passenger train with gnashing diesel balls by, browm, browm, the Indians just look up – I see them vanishing like spots – " and sitting in the redbulb room in San Franciso now with sweet Mardou I think, "And this is your father I saw in the gray waste, swallowed by night – from his juices came your lips, your eyes full of suffering and sorrow, and we're not to know his name or name his destiny?"

Kerouac was a Presley-figure, one of the dark, transitional drug-taking, groupie-gathering (and groupie-escaping), mother-besotted, all-absorptive, grotesquely-gifted princelings, one of those famed "pure products of America," going-or-gone mad. The "putter-inners" ingested everything, filled every cavity (*you must know, do, everything*), and when the habit of absorption outlived the raw nervous edginess, they got fat, sluggish, fetid. They are the legion of America's open-mouthed, wonderstruck, gullible, affirming, uncritical, experimental but finally brittle self-taught shapers. Their tragedy is, they cannot learn, or grow; they reject editing, rewriting, and criticism. They are not Jamesian, or Iowa-bred, they can't handle fame or a public. Their talent is to spend, not invest. Needless to say, their defects are the measure of their virtue. (Joyce, in English, is the only one who succeeded, and would he have made it had he been American?) They don't live long, or happily. They have seen too much, they can't close their eyes, they can't edit life, they repeat themselves, they're abusive, and they reject all help. Like Kerouac, their ambition finally is not art; it is religion. They want to be saints, or, like Faulkner, God.

I always believed, as Saroyan and still more, Céline, and of course Joyce did, that the secret of fiction is the ability to design a structure and a language that is apparently all-inclusive, that is plot-blind, time-free, and psychologically-unbound. But the implications of that belief are close to the symptoms of madness, and can be found, abandoned, on scraps of paper in the back of a million drawers. The mad inability to disconnect the voices in the head from dialogue with the outer world. The world is their map, Kerouac's map, on a fatal scale of 1:1.

The person named Jack Kerouac came to hate niggers and Jews, though, like many a French Canadian, he loved Indians. In that, he recognized probable forebears (there were no French women in those original stockades) and to accept the corollary that French-Canadian life on this continent is obviously tribal. French Canadians are a Latin-American people with a history less obviously interracial than the Mexican, but utterly similar in all outer and many inner characteristics. Think of upper New England at the turn of the century as a kind of south Texas today. They are also like the Boers of South Africa, a founding people locked inside a homeland, obsessed with survival, surrounded and outnumbered by would-be attackers, but deeply challenged by inner temptation.

As I said at the outset, survival as a linguistically and culturally-intact people is limited now to the province of Québec. "French Canadians" exist only outside of Québec, in other parts of Canada. Inside Québec one finds only Québécois. Francophone Montrealers are not taking well to immigrant Haitian and French-Africans; turbaned Sikhs in the Mounted Police set Quebeckers' teeth on edge. They draw little satisfaction from contemplating a fully multicultural city, or province – Québec is not bilingual – nor do they share enthusiasm over the 20th century adventure of recasting a continent's gene pool. Survivalists, in other words, are not necessarily the most welcoming, the most accommodating of people.

Occasionally, French Canadians think with their blood, see themselves as a founding race equal only to the Indians, unbeholden to newcomers, and, as hardpressed resisters of conquest, free of guilt. (Some blacks in America assert that by definition they cannot be termed prejudiced, and one hears similar arguments in Québec.) There was some of that in Jack Kerouac: he was here first, and he resented "aliens" determining his standing, and his income.

Outside the walls of a protective Québec, or the self-imposed walls composed of guilt and nostalgia among her sons and grandsons in the various diaspora communities, French-Canadian culture is slowly sinking into Americanness, an irritating minority Canadianness, or a Blue Bayou anachronistic quaintness. Some would say, "It's time, let it go." Others, like Faulkner over Yoknapatawpha, Kerouac in *Vanity of Duluoz*, would choose to grieve.

The Smuggler's Son Grows Older

R OBERT FROST had a lot to say about borders, though he called them walls, and the people who maintain them and those who question their value. Even if his scale is tidy, and the location is bucolic Vermont, certain implications apply to us, global mariners that we are.

"Something there is that doesn't love a wall," he wrote, and ended up giving ironic voice, though not endorsement, to the oft-quoted rejoinder, "'Good fences make good neighbors.'" To the poet, walls are *literally* unnatural. Nature knocks them down every winter. Hunters rip them up, flushing rabbits. In "Mending Wall" there are no cows to protect, or pen; the wall separates pine trees from an apple orchard. In short, Frost's wall serves no practical purpose. The poet wants to plant a notion in his neighbor's head. He contemplates saying "Before I built a wall I'd ask to know / What I was walling in or walling out, / And to whom I was like to give offense" even as the neighbor carries more stones for mending, "like an old-stone savage armed." Yet, as they talk, they keep the wall between them and the doggedly dull neighbor cannot go beyond repeating his father's bromide: "'Good fences make good neighbors.'"

Well, there you have it, or part of it. Frost is describing a border in need of redefinition. Mature borders, we might say, like those in Western Europe since the EU, or Canada-U.S., and, at times and in certain places, Mexico and the United States. What do we think of fences, or borders? Or for that matter, what do we think of those rabbits disturbed by hunters, since Frost's rabbits are really the subjects of this talk? Do we need borders, do they serve any purpose when they are protecting nothing within, or guarding against nothing from without? Do good fences build good neighbors, or do they give offense? I confess I am as conflicted as the poet is in reaching an answer.

(To the obvious objection that global terrorism has once again tipped the scales in favour of more stones, more barbed wire, more sniffer-dogs and armed guards, I would say, hold on, friend, do you know what you are walling in, or walling out? Do new threats demand old responses? Since we can never be sure of anything, must we exclude everything? I'd hate to think that terrorists are subtler and more at ease in the global village than we are.)

This talk is my plea on the behalf of rabbits everywhere. Clever creatures, those rabbits in "Mending Wall," hiding safely inside the very bowels of borderhood until the hunters dislodge and scatter the stones. Or to put a different name on the same phenomenon, see this as a modest assertion of smugglers' rights. What is a smuggler, after all, but someone with unquestioned access to both sides of a border, in possession of something more valuable *on the other side* than back here, someone who can calculate in a moment the relative worth of anything, in two currencies? In an unbound world of unprecedented leaps and dramatic transformations, where millions of shape-changers are on the move every year and continents are in upheaval, I want to pause a moment to celebrate the smallest gesture, the tiniest and least heroic of steps, the rabbit's hop, the smuggler's spontaneous deceptions.

What is a border? Is it a frontier, as its French equivalent implies, a marker that defines the farthest defendable extent of one's national, cultural, or linguistic property? Or is it a moat, meant to keep others outside? The classic borders of the European nation-states seem like scars, long-healed welts that mark the melancholy fate of stalled armies, of silenced religious battles or tribal loyalties. Those borders now exist as memories, their guard posts unmanned, their customs houses unvisited, quaint as cathedrals. Ideologies, or their breakdowns, however, continue into our day to create new kinds of borders – rasping cages, like East Germany's or central and eastern Europe's were, or North Korea's or the Israel-Palestinian divide, keeping people separated from their cultural kin, or like Cuba's, penning one's own people against perceived contamination.

Today I'm talking about something almost ethereal. It's not a classic border, but it is more than a quaint memory: it's the *consciousness* of a border. Since the border between Canada and the United States is as much psychological as physical (but more physical than a contemporary European's wave of the hand), it's a little pretentious – especially in south Florida, with so many Canadians in the audience, including some of my own relatives – to talk of border-crossing as a kind of life-defining moment. It's hardly in the league with my wife's coming from India, or our new Chinese granddaughter setting up life in New York City.

For the most part, well-adjusted Canadians, meaning people that know who they are and what they want, do not have to change their identities in order to pass, and presumably live happily, in the United States. Well-adjusted Canadians don't even consider it much of a border at all, just an inconvenience; they want to burrow south or west, away from winter. For the Canadians I lived among, the United States was a kind of permanent spring thaw with better shopping. From Winnipeg, we thought of weekends in Minneapolis as the poor man's Florida, a chance to leave our boots behind. If they wish, Canadians can pass undetected, like a Dutchman entering Belgium, with just the slightest of giveaways, those famous Peter Jennings "aboots." As for well-adjusted Americans, the Canadian border seems more temporal than geographical, leading to exclamations like "Oh, I love Toronto! It reminds me of New York forty years ago." Furthermore, the U.S.-Canada border is really two sub-national borders: one English, stretching from the eastern tip of the Great Lakes all the way west to the Pacific, and the other French, separating Québec and New Brunswick from ethnic kin in upper New England.

For the ill-adjusted, however, the border seems designed as a personal torment. Because of my parentage – an Anglo mother from Winnipeg and a French father from rural Québec – and even the year of my birth, 1940, when my parents sought to save me and themselves from a rumoured fascist coup in Québec by having me born in reliably isolationist North Dakota, I have crossed all the borders and lived atop all the fault lines the northern half of this peaceable continent has made available. I share a birth-state with William Gass and Roger Maris, Louise Erdrich and Larry Woiwode. But probably the emblematic North Dakotan in my life should be "Jay Gatsby" *né* Gatz, the invention of that urbane Minnesotan, Scott Fitzgerald, who must have found North Dakota as deep a source of mystery as I do.

For someone like me, who is not particularly well-adjusted, borders bring no comfort. A border means: Who are you? What are you? Why have you come? How long will you stay? Those are the terrifying questions I cannot answer. The border says: *You cannot be both.* But that is, profoundly, what I am. I am what you say I cannot be. I am a rabbit with unicorn ambition.

From a lifetime of crossing borders and living inside their fretwork, I have developed a border consciousness, off everyone's radar. I carry news from one side to the other, publishing my life's work in Canada but living here in the U.S., publishing my first six books in the U.S. when I was living in Canada. I tell Americans the news of Canada; I assure Canadians that Americans are as uncertain, as identity-challenged as they are. It is not a profitable smuggling operation. Borders stand for decisions and definition, but border-crossers are identity-smugglers, shadowy, anonymity-seekers, keeping a bland face, denying their purchases, waiting fifty miles to unpack their goods.

My mother was not one of the well-adjusted Canadians. She was not a shape-changer. Wherever we lived in the United States, in northern Florida, in Pittsburgh or Cincinnati, she was an outpost of Canada. She never changed her Canadian ways: the food she cooked – steamed, crunchy vegetables drenched in lemon juice, organ meats – and the magazines she read, her socialist politics, her prairie accent, her unforgiving views of certain American icons. (I think especially of Bob Hope, John Wayne, and, most irrationally, Tom Harmon, the football-hero-turned-sports-broadcaster.) My father, who was overtly more "foreign" in the American context, a man with an identifiable accent, with a checkered past, changed his life-story in every new town, with every new job, and no one, except his wives and doctors, ever questioned him. My father was a French-Canadian Jay Gatz.

An attraction to maps is the first sign, to the pre-literate child, that the seamless world is riven by difference. Maybe it's the first sign that the kid is headed for trouble. Maps are colouring books of the real world; stay within the lines and you're assured good grades and a comfortable future. I was one of those map-conscious boys who knew the outlines of states and countries and their capitals and rivers and mountains even before I could properly read. Borders did not settle disputes – they seemed to speak of splits, of arguments and uprootings. Maps were narratives, shapes were characters; I could read the stories as plainly as with any comic book. The stacked, indifferent blocks of western states, the Wyomings and Colorados, who would want to live there? The carved intricacies of New England, the odd thrust of West Virginia into the belly of Ohio, the bizarre embrace of West Virginia and Maryland, over the head of baffled Virginia, under the Mason-Dixon complacency of Pennsylvania; they spoke of betrayals and a bloody history. One stout Canadian province, Ontario, did the work of eight lazy American states, keeping a lid on the Great Lakes. If I could learn enough about maps, I could understand the subtler mysteries that surrounded me.

Firm, secure borders, "good fences," are for the law-abiding. Border-anxiety, "Something there is that doesn't love a wall," is a mild form of paranoia. The world is bristling with borders, sadly, with more borders every year as new Turkmenistans and Slovakias assert their identity. The fence-builders are winning, even as other barriers are coming down. But with apologies to the world's aspiring Chechnyas and Acehs and Kosovos, they're not very interesting. They are a return to the past, they are posted properties. Their borders don't even bother to ask, "Who are you?" They say only, "No trespassing."

And yet I must admit that the world can suffer unspeakably for the lack of borders.

Travelling west from Belgrade in a rented BMW in the early 1970s, my wife and I crossed an invisible border and came upon a mosque and minaret in a picturesque mountain village. I'd known there were European Muslims, of course, but I never thought I'd see them. The integration of a desert faith into the lake-and-river-rich Balkans seemed miraculous. The name of the nearest town was Tuzla. Sitting at a roadside tea stall was a group of large, loud Slavic truck drivers in skullcaps roasting a lamb. I saw only what I wanted to see in that innocent decade – a celebration of sorts: two Canadians, a dozen Yugoslavs, a Hindu, some Muslims, some Croats, sharing lamb and tea and a vile red wine owing more to radishes than grapes, over an historic fault line, speaking German. A transcendent moment, I thought. The only border that seemed important at that time was the political east-west, between NATO and the relative freedom of a breakaway Soviet alley. It was, innocently and ignorantly, a vision of possibility. They were big, strong, bold men, but they were rabbits. In other picturesque villages, the hunters were gathering, the map-makers were biding their time.

History shows the first celebration of borders to be the area lying between England and Scotland, a bardic invention maintained by minstrels and mythology. There's even a secondary invisible sub-national border, like Canada's French and English, between Highland and Lowland Scots. Like Scotland, Canada is a border-hugging country; 90% of its population lives within fifty miles of the American border. (Think what the U.S. would be like if a quarter of a billion people lived along a thin line strung between Seattle and Bangor.) No wonder Canadians know America so well, just as the Scots know England. No wonder Americans know so little, and care even less. We're the smugglers, the rabbits, hiding in the fence.

Those invisible Scottish borders are prototypes of the border that looms attractively and forbiddingly in my imagination. The closest thing I know to that ancient Scottish border is something like today's northern Maine, or, as others have written, the Rio Grande Valley of Texas, where cultures are contiguous and the population on each side of the border knows the other intimately. Twenty miles north of the Québec or New Brunswick-Maine or New Hampshire border, English is rarely spoken. Twenty miles south, French disappears, and with it, delicate suspensions of identity. When I was a child, those buffers were wider; when my father was a child, he travelled hundreds of miles into the United States, speaking only French. That sense of indeterminacy once had a name: "The Republic of Indian Stream," located in a pocket of Québec's Eastern Townships and adjacent northern New Hampshire. It lasted for four years, with its own constitution.

I was the map-conscious, border-clinging child who noticed names on mailboxes or the proprietor's name above the door of gas stations. I saw signposts and shouted them out. I knew when "our" names, meaning French names, started to appear in upper New England, and then predominate, like mosques and minarets. My father noticed it too. Somewhere in upstate New York he'd pull into an Esso station and order the gas in French, *twa' pyastr'*, three bucks' worth, *à craquer*. He trusted me to make the smuggler-calculations. The Canadian dollar in those days was worth more than the American. The Canadian gallon was larger than the American. The American price was lower. So where was the advantage, really?

True borders, those that are psychologically maintained, are zones of grace where dualities of loyalty are tolerated and commonplace. When we bought gasoline from someone with a French name, my father would joke with the gas jockey, trying to reduce the price a penny or two. They'd haul an old man out of the back of the station, and there would follow a series of questions: Where were you born? What village are your people from? What parish? (The first time my father entered the United States was in 1912, and he crossed the border from Lac-Mégantic, Québec to Long-Lac, Maine on skis. Half of his family is buried in Long-Lac, which was part of the same Ste.-Anne's parish.) And then, to my mother's distress, would come the tracing of relatives, since all French Canadians are cousins to one degree or another. And at those stations – if you knew how to ask – you'd be taken to a back room and they'd uncover a one-armed bandit and give you a couple of pulls on the handle. Or there'd be a game of cards going on with a modest pot, and again the language of the game would be ours. I understood very early that the language of my father's people was not quite legal, and what they considered legal was not approved by my mother, and my father's people were not, in fact, quite acceptable. It was the language of scruffy old men, hidden in the back. I understood this and learned to keep it quiet, just as my father did. It gave me a sense of myself that has sustained me for many years.

My father was a settled furniture salesman in the early 1950s. But thirty years before that, eighty years ago, he'd had a different job. He'd been a boxer in Montreal, an aspiring young thug. In the 1920s, he was recruited by Canada's greatest export industry, distilling, to distribute bribes to local sheriffs and to ride shotgun on the nightly convoys of liquor that made their way from Montreal through Adirondack back trails down to Albany. I've tossed these names around with the great Albany novelist, William Kennedy; I've read the accounts in Mordecai Richler. The Jews of Montreal brewed the liquor, the French Canadians smuggled it in, the Irish Mafia picked it up and transferred it to the Italian Mafia in New York City. It was a glorious joke on American Protestantism, on Prohibition and rectitude. Everyone made money on their blind hypocrisy. It was a smuggler's dream.

My father paid a price of course. He shot a man, maybe several would-be hijackers, and spent time in American jails. He was deported back to Canada. He married twice in the States and deserted both women, met my mother in Montreal and lived with her nearly twenty years, married twice more and died, still a Canadian, and is buried in the old French-Canadian ghetto of Manchester, New Hampshire in a graveyard called *"le petit coin du Canada,"* although it is the last place he would have acknowledged as home, and the place that most abused him as a child. And so, I am the smuggler's son. I know about exploiting a border for all it's worth, understanding what I'm looking for and never finding it, trading everything away, holding on to nothing. My kind of border-crosser lives on either side in equal degrees of alienation. In fact, that's how he survives.

I even remember when it ended, when for me, at least, that perfect balance snapped. Forty years ago, I was a student in Boston, trying to maintain a life in Cambridge as well as Quebec City. Usually I hitched a ride every weekend, but one night I took the Greyhound bus. The driver's name was Leo Legare, on the Boston-Quebec City overnight route. A group of old French-Canadian women had come down on a shopping trip and were all headed back with their bags and overnight cases, and, seeing his name on the placard above his seat, started asking him questions. He threw up his hands and said, in English, "They don't pay me to speak French. They pay the Portuguese drivers extra, but they don't pay me nothin' extra to speak French." I shared that moment a kind of shame as he told the old ladies to board and keep their questions to themselves. He was right, in the American way, but wrong in the Québec sense.

Border-crossing, be it from Manitoba to North Dakota, or Québec to Maine, is an intimate act, a performance act. You might not be carrying anything of value or have anything to declare, yet you always feel you do, that you've left something out of the calculation. Your whole life is a declaration. You have yourself to declare.

Just as Willie Sutton visited banks because that's where the money was, so does a smuggler look for borders. And when the smuggler grows up to be a writer, he continues to look for borders, or imperfect transitions. He sees them everywhere, in an accent, a name, tea with milk, that old tingle when our names start appearing, when motels display two flags and licence plates passing are more likely than not Canadian. In the old days, Manitoba cars all sported block-heater cords and vinyl frost-guards on the driver's window. Seeing them was a comfort. But down the road there's the border: five miles, two miles, five hundred feet, and a looming confrontation. *Who are you?* This time, they'll catch me. They'll say, you've used up all your visits. You must decide once and for all. They'll say, you can't come back. Or they'll say, welcome home.

A month ago in Montreal I was having dinner with an old friend, Ray Smith. I was describing the pleasures of Southampton, where I now live, comparing it with San Francisco, where I also live, and Ray said to one of his sons, "There he goes again." I'd said something about Southampton not being quite New York, nor quite New England, not quite urban or suburban, something about the accents perhaps, and the Irish and Italian Catholicism of my undergraduate students, but he heard something else: "With Clark, it's all about establishing borders."

I was amazed when he said it, but he's absolutely right. It's all about borders and the people who live just outside them, the tribes of the "not quite." I find authenticity in their compromises, and security in a word I often use but can't define: I find residence in my "unhousement."

Ideas Suggested by Nerves

L IKE MANY of you here, I am troubled by my responses to the
work of V.S. Naipaul.* For many years I have wanted some
kind of magic formula that would permit me to reconcile certain
violent objections with many absolute pleasures. How much of it is
my own outraged liberal, Western, Commonwealth, Indophilic,
Anglophobic background speaking out (and crying, "No, NO!"),
and how much of it is *his* calculated outrageousness, his own
updating of Trollope, Froude, and Macaulay, I cannot say. One
recalls, however, from the brief essay "The Little More," Naipaul's
almost wistful reflection, delivered early in his career as a journal-
ist, ". . . I wonder whether anyone anywhere will ever be able
again to write with that mid-Victorian certainty: that unapologetic
display of outrageous prejudices . . . ."

Roughly speaking, Naipaul's expertise breaks in three areas:
the Caribbean, the extended "Third World," and England. To date,
1981, the masterworks are probably *A House for Mister Biswas* and
The Mimic Men; his most successful non-fiction book I find to be
The Loss of El Dorado, followed by *The Middle Passage*. If the Caribbean, not unsurprisingly, feeds his most sustained and finished
works, this should not distract any reader from the achievements
of *In a Free State* and *A Bend in the River*, or from the solid but ulti-
mately too tidy pleasures to be gained from *Mr. Stone and the
Knights Companion*. I am withholding comment on his latest book,

---

* The title of this essay echoes a phrase in Naipaul's *Among the Believers: An
Islamic Journey*. In context, a reference to spotting African workers on the
Karachi docks, a vision so perfect and so preposterous that the author
initially remembered it as delirium.

Among the Believers, until I develop a wider context for what I want to say.

Our diffuse field of World Writing in English embraces three distinct literary worlds, which we might do well to keep distinct. The first offers little problem – it's the literature of the various "developed" nations of the Commonwealth – all the little Englands on their way to becoming little Americas – from Ireland (still the model of success) through Canada, Australia, and the other Southern Hemisphere outposts of empire. Many interesting things can be said about distinct and consanguinary traits in these literatures, and they all evoke parochial passions, but that is not my concern here. It seems to me they differ from American and British literature mainly in matters of scale (just as American departs from classic English in the same way): less history, fewer texts, less of a canon, less of a bibliography, less of a body of commentary. But all contain their recognized masterworks – the Gallants, Laurences, Atwoods, Gordimers, Lessings, Whites, Keneallys follow in the tradition of the first great exiled islander, James Joyce, who remains for me the justification for this often-cramped specialization – and none need stand ashamed in today's literary market place.

The second literature is vastly more complicated to discuss. In some ways, though it has interesting works to offer us and sophisticated authors who write them, their very existence poses a problem for us, and for the cultures they come from. I am referring to the literatures of the subcontinent, and of Africa – those vast, partially-subjugated, imperfectly-transformed super-colonies. They were, and are, vast areas with complex histories, embracing mythologies, ethnicities, societies, religions, and languages, of which English is but a late and minor manifestation. In these societies, raging disputes still surround the very use of English, along with the assumed alienation of the English-speaking elites, and the forms of English that best describe, say, the Indian or the Nigerian experience. We are all aware of the Tutuola debate in Nigeria, or the Narayan controversy in India, questions arising from the degree of distortion, delirium, simplicity, poetry, "folkishness" or international standard that is somehow "proper" for an English-language author from countries the English had tampered with but barely transformed. One cannot help concluding that English might even be a transitional step in the evolution of an eventual national literature in some mutually-agreed-upon national language, awaiting only the requisite literacy, and cultural funding.

(In making such a statement, I am aware that a single work of genius might render the entire speculation somehow purely academic. In reading Salman Rushdie's *Midnight's Children* for a review last year, I realized that the whole tortured question of a "proper English" for the rendering of an Indian experience can never be closed. Also, that it need never be raised.)

The third literature, of course, is that of the synthetic societies, the impoverished, utterly created (and forsaken) absurdities of the Caribbean or the South Indian Ocean: total colonial constructs, slave-societies, imperial enterprises undertaken purely for short-range economic gain without the slightest regard for pre-existent African or Indian cultures, preferences, or survival. These brutal half-baked barracoons (in Naipaul's phrase) lacking any coherent *raison d'être* or any reliable inner gauge to their own worth or identity, are the most ill-served of all the British legatees. Colonial authority alone granted them a language, a religion, a décor, law, dress, games, a literature – everything was imposed and rewards were disbursed for excellence in mimicry. The overtly military violence is largely missing. Instead, the imperialism is internalized; they are islands of conquered psyches.

In this description you see the outlines of Naipaul's thought. People of course remain people and they will struggle for identity on Trinidad as they will in New York or Paris – only the odds against them, without a history, without a place in the world's consciousness, without a guide apart from cricket stars and reggae, without an economy apart from filling imported tubes with imported toothpaste, are simply too great. They go mad. They behave erratically, self-destructively, superstitiously, incoherently, hypocritically, and worst of all (to appropriate the title of Austin Clarke's Barbadian autobiography, *Growing Up Stupid Under the Union Jack*), stupidly. Joyce as usual saw it first, understood its origins, and its vicious circularity. After writing his *Dubliners*, the only way out is an act of self-creation.

Naipaul also grew up with it, watched its deadly work up close, and made his famous vow to leave, and has transcended it with his own form of silence, exile, and cunning. For him, however, the sickness has metastasized; it seems a generalized condition of the unhoused, impotent, deluded, ahistorical, post-colonial man. It seems to be the condition of the entire world except for the areas of conspicuous material and intellectual achievement (and they are in decline). It's Naipaul's beat, a vast area of darkness beyond the competence of most British and American critics to evaluate for themselves – Naipaul is their immediate authority. The possibilities of misreading are enormous; I remember the frustrations of a Bahamian critic announcing in a packed hall in a Commonwealth Literature conference in New Delhi some four years ago, "You have not travelled to the West Indies. You have travelled to Naipaul!" Under their genial surfaces of steel bands (which he despises) and tourist hotels, he seems to be saying, lurk the viciousness and shallowness of racial and religious pride, narrowness of thought, and a blight of utter conformity. This is the legacy of the original conquistadors, we learn from *El Dorado*: savage, ignorant men who would kill for a material dream. Murderous dreamers have left their legacy through Latin America and the Caribbean; the sins of the ancestors are alive today. As he remarks in *Guerrillas*, apropos of what seems to be a placid, green, Caribbean pastoral, "When you get to know them, every country is that kind of country." Meaning, of course, an abattoir.

In his latest book, *Among the Believers: An Islamic Journey*, an imposingly large and often grand tale of travel through four militantly Muslim states, Naipaul extends his thesis even further. The

Spanish conquistadors learned *their* trade from the Muslim invaders of Spain; the typical Latin-American village encountered from Yucatan to the Pampas is itself a copy of the Iranian desert village. In other words, new links in the chain of accountability have been forged; Spain is now a New-World vector of an older disease, not the source. The source of intolerance is not Inquisitional Spanish Catholicism – it's rather the original dreamer-killer, redeemer-plunderer from Arabia. He made the caudillo as well as the Ayatollah. Naipaul calls the Arabs "the most successful imperialists of all time, since to be conquered by them (and then to be like them) is still, in the minds of the faithful, to be saved."

He does not reflect on a related irony: Islam is no more successful than European imperialism. Naipaul's loudest critics see *him* as a colonial apologist. Naipaul's dispute is not with the phenomenon of imperials; it is rather with variant notions of salvation.

What has been missing is a study linking Naipaul's fiction to his reportage, seeing it all as an *oeuvre*, as we have learned to see Mailer's, Orwell's, or D.H. Lawrence's. Clearly, Naipaul never rests, that is, he takes no mental vacations as the Edwardian novelists were expected to do. (The maintenance of a unified voice and high aesthetic seriousness, an acute self-consciousness of one's essentially priestly-role, is what separates the Moderns from the rounder Victorian era.) The same themes and the same matchless prose style permeate all his work, and one certainly gains the same impression of the fatigued, irritated, disappointed, impatient author behind it.

From the entirety of his output, which by now contains more raw encounters than in any English writer outside of Dickens, we have a consistent portrait of the author. The minutely-cultivated public and political persona, coupled with the perfect exclusion of a psychosexual selfhood, is for me the most striking quality of Naipaul's writing. The *whole* self is lived in history and in issue and in public event. He is certainly the least "internal" of any major contemporary. That refusal to animate an inner self separates him from us, I believe, in many of the ways a Trinidad is inevitably foreign to us, despite the shared use of a language.

The opus is thus heavy on judgement and interpretation; social to the exclusion of psychological. Familiar motivations, the normal contexts for opinion, have been banished from his work. The resulting clarity is sometimes striking; so too is the brutality of some of his judgements.

What we *do* know of his values we know very well, and we have seen them tested in more settings than any authors of our time. We know that his commitments are impeccably liberal, even when they seem calculated to outrage Third-World sympathizers. We know he supports progress, creativity, science, personal ambition, social prosperity, and all the normal freedoms. We know that he is uncompromising with enemies of those values – even when they may possess considerable charm or counter-value of their own. Like steel bands, which seem at first an irrational hatred. (But they function, of course, as substitutes, in the Trinidad mind, for great art. The steel drums are the debris of colonial exploitation; they stop their practitioners at a relatively low level of conventional mimicry; they reward a pimpish desire to turn a tourist trick.) Religion – that is, empty observation of religion, like the West Indian Hinduism, or fanatic devotion like the contemporary Muslims – may be the sorts of things that outsiders politely ignore, or would be reluctant to ridicule: not Naipaul. Racialism, ignorance, tyranny, materialism, poverty, aimlessness – these are the enemies.

Early in this new book, in discussing a recent Iranian novel, Nahid Rachlin's *Foreigner*, he terms the heroine's choice of remaining in Iran for her spiritual fulfillment a "death pact" when she renounces a return to her American husband and her life of scientific research in the West. Naipaul will not engage the dialectic of that particular novel; it's as though he knows first-hand the terrors of tropical torpor, racial-exclusiveness, mindless ritual, and the humiliating rigmarole of being a good colonial, and has lifted himself up from it all single-handedly and has impatience border-

ing on contempt for anyone who refuses to make the same sacri-
fices. He abhors colonial "stupidity" in all its forms (including
Black Power, and the politics of separation or vindication), and
makes no excuses for its victims.

In another example from *Among the Believers*, he confronts his
young Iranian driver and translator with a few simple facts of life
that are liberally-intended and even justifiable, but which lend
themselves to a reactionary interpretation, even to an apology for
the Shah. I mention this in some detail because it is applicable to a
vast range of difficult encounters in his other books as well – many
of which cause great discomfort to his well-intentioned admirers.
The driver, a twenty-six-year-old graduate student in science, an
adept English-speaker, an articulate (or perhaps merely vociferous) Communist, a skier, a driver, with an educated, employed
Communist girlfriend, is also the son of a mountain shepherd.
Naipaul points out that all of his advantages derive entirely from
the Shah's regime – Khomeini would have surely kept him ignorant in the mountains, tending sheep. Yet the driver, like most of
us, is a violent opponent of the Shah and all he stood for. On balance, Naipaul is saying, the Shah for all his repressiveness, and for
all his personal loathsomeness, was a far greater force for liberal-
ization, even radicalization, than the Ayatollah or the band of
romantic Marxists who deplaned with him. The Shah, whatever
his faults (and Naipaul is never one to dwell on them), came from a
world that would eventually lift the centuries of delusion off the
people's backs; the Ayatollah, whatever his overwhelming demo-
cratic support, is out to enslave his people once again. Which of us
would have defended the Shah in the name of liberalism in those
frantic months before the taking of the hostages?

I've taken only a few steps towards resolving my Naipaul problem; some are in this paper and some are still to be formulated. I
think his Caribbean work is his strongest, not only because it is
closest to his experience of growing up, but also to his style of free
movement, externalization, his cartoonist's art of vital caricature.

Perhaps he doubts the value of psychology because he views the West Indies as pre-psychological. But when he appropriates the vision and experience of an Indian, or an Ismaili Muslim, he needs more reach, more complexity, and he doesn't have it. He becomes all too obviously a fictionalized V.S. Naipaul, surrounded by a rich outer world. The work tends towards reductiveness; minor characters no longer existing in their own humanity but rather in order to fill a predictable role; each scene determined to make a conclusive point. In works that are calculated to be harrowing – the novella "In a Free State" or the story "Tell Me Who to Kill" in the same volume – the claustrophobic plotting works. In an expansive novel like *Guerrillas*, it's loud and over-demonstrated. The tone of *A Bend in the River* is, I feel, unbalanced: intense fiction erupting from ruminative autobiography.

I stated at the outset that Naipaul is partially the victim of his very great success. He achieved his masterpiece of island fiction so early in his career that ambition drove him on to new material, and to appropriation of new visions. Feeling perhaps as he does about the West Indies, he had no desire to deepen the portrait of *Biswas*, except for the brilliant island set-pieces in *The Mimic Men*. By then, he had rejected the idea of being a "West Indian Writer" – understandable enough in any writer, Canadian as well – but for some reason he also rejected both race and sex as appropriate subjects. He felt he did not know Americans or British well enough to write from inside their experience (although he had been living among the British for over a decade, he felt no such timidity with characters from other "free states"). He rejected, too, on grounds of simple boredom (although there may be more to it than that), the immigrant novel: all that tedious manipulating – as he stressed in an interview by Ian Hamilton – of the foreign character inside English society. (All that special pleading for patience and understanding, all that implied sympathy for the victims of ignorance or prejudice, one is tempted to add.) No; Naipaul's fictional concerns are of the highest order: nothing less than the clash of the world's two consciousnesses (I think he sees only two); the half-made world struggling to be born, or tempted to retreat completely. And to do it all in the lucid glare of public event, without the particularizing base of psychology, and in the miniaturizing beam of irony.

An issue that remains to be taken up is that of the uses of psychology in the novels of the Third World; the simple fact that history and politics and group consciousness may render psychology and individual consciousness limiting and irrelevant factors in the delineation of character. (For "group consciousness" read "race" as in the novels of George Lamming and Wilson Harris, the other prominent Caribbean-based novelists who have constructed major fictions without recourse to psychology as we know it. The perception of the multitudes within one, as in *Natives of My Person* or *In the Castle of My Skin*, may very well be the starting point for a new kind of inquiry into the richness, and the limitations, of Naipaul.) If the richness of an "authenticating" experience has been denied one – as Naipaul has argued through his middle and now later career – then what, precisely, is the use of so much intellectual refinement? (Strangely enough, only Bobby in "In a Free State" seems to have been endowed with a conventional clinical past, and that past does very little to explain his pathological character.)

I find myself still at odds with Naipaul when he carries over the inquest into a Trinidad to its parental Indian culture, without a compensating change of voice (merely a drastically narrowed scope and cast of characters). Or when, in an interview by Bharati Mukherjee and Robert Boyers, he dismisses Africa – an Africa we know from reading Achebe, Armah, Laye, and Kane – as little more than the dreaded "bush." Or when the heads of Indian women are declared to be "empty" (and that comment is dutifully displayed on the front page of *The New York Times Book Review*). It's when I have had the opportunity – admittedly rare – of comparing direct experience with Naipaul, India for India, Africa for Africa, that I begin suspecting along with that Bahamian critic that I have been "travelling to Naipaul" and that Naipaul has not left Trinidad either, and the straitened, tragic world that created him.

This page intentionally left blank

The International Novel

O F COURSE it's impossible to talk about international writing. It doesn't exist, except as a tabulated summation of about three hundred separate national and subnational literatures. It would take an intellect far greater than mine to make sense of such variety, or to find patterns in the midst of such randomness. It would be like reading a thousand of the world's leading newspapers, concentrating only on the headlines, and determining the trends and major events in world affairs.

Fortunately, as Director of the world's largest international authors residency, I come to the topic with certain advantages. All I have to do for three months every year is to sit back and read, and listen to, the thirty-three writers in the International Writing Program. Those writers, and the thousand who have preceded them in the past thirty years, generate more work, in more languages, than any single person in the world can read, but if you are the kind of person who listens closely, if you write and travel yourself – that is, if you're the kind of person who breathes the air of Iowa City, or who's part of The Loft – approaches to the question of international writing, if not answers, begin to suggest themselves.

With your indulgence, let me start with the autobiographical approach. How big, and how elusive, is the subject? So big, that I want to start with my own personal origins, just to maintain perspective.

Growing up in Canada, or in various parts of the United States, under my mother's strong Canadian influence and my father's even stronger silent contempt for anything that couldn't be sold, drunk, or eaten, I learned there were four distinct measures of size, importance, and greatness. I'm not talking of metric vs. imperial measures, or French vs. English words; I mean a whole system of counting that an inquisitive, ambitious, adolescent boy from the (literal) provinces could internalize. These were the terms of measurement that permitted a chauvinist from an underpopulated and underachieving country like Canada to compete on this continent with a certain pride and dignity. The standards were: Canadian, American, North American, and Commonwealth. Hovering above them all was the granddaddy of all standards: world. Never in my memory did we use the word "international," which was just another threatening word for American.

There's even a fifth category, invented by Mordecai Richler: "world famous in Canada."

Here's how it worked, forever encapsulated in one of the most moving moments in my athletic memory. It's 1954, and I'm fourteen. It's the track announcer's placid account of Roger Bannister's sub-four minute mile. "Ladies and Gentlemen, here is the result of event 9, the one-mile: 1st, No. 41, R.G. Bannister, Amateur Athletic Association and formerly of Exeter and Merton College, Oxford, with a time which is a new meeting and track record (okay, okay), and which – subject to ratification – will be a new English Native (sure, sure), British National (get on with it), All-Comers, European, British Empire, and World Record. The time was 3 . . . (roaring crowd noise muffles the completion)." And *then* I knew. World history had been made, but we had to pass through at least five screens before believing it.

A Canadian record was a nice thing to win, of course, but like inclusion in *Canadian Who's Who*, we still needed to know how it stacked up, and unless it related to ice hockey, chances were great that a Canadian record would be wiped out at the next international competition. A Commonwealth record was a little more of the same, meaning, in essence, "better than anything in England or Australia." In Montreal I taught in the "largest academic building in the Commonwealth." That immediately tells a Canadian two things. First, nothing in Jamaica, Nigeria, Australia, or even the grand old U.K. matched us. But the grim truth was that something in the United States, or Russia, or Mexico, obviously did. The fifty or so nations of the Commonwealth, embracing all continents and races, were a *smaller* concept than North America, a two-country affair for a Canadian of my generation. For all we knew, something right next door in Buffalo or Detroit or dare I say Minneapolis was larger than my fourteen-floor, city-block, downtown Montreal building. Maybe there were a thousand such buildings, stretching from Albania to Zaire. Our boast turned hollow and tinny; we were humiliating ourselves even by mentioning it. It's a curious form of humiliation, to boast of victory over something as intangible as the Commonwealth, while avoiding the proximate and obvious opponent next door.

That particular quality of shame, more deeply and violently felt, is something known in all parts of the world. The writers reflect it, Salman Rushdie has even written a novel with *Shame* as its title. It's an elusive feeling, one that Americans, in my experience, have trouble grasping. And why shouldn't they? Shamelessness is an even more difficult concept to dramatize.

And so, boasting as an art form was something best left to Americans, not because they are more boastful or chauvinistic than anyone else – Canadians *yearn* to be boastful, as I've tried to indicate – but because they never had to consider other scales of achievement or competition. There always seemed to be calculation to a Canadian boast, a sweaty, almost legalistic hedging that diminished its effect even as it met all possible challenges. Americans weren't trained to look over their shoulders, or over a border, or to make adjustments in mid-sentence before declaring their supremacy. "Wait," they never had to say, "I think they're putting up something taller in Kuala Lumpur that will wipe this Sears Tower off the map." American boasting was, by contrast, so pure and innocent.

Even the *desire* to build something taller than the World Trade Towers, or the Sears Tower, is a curious kind of compliment. It doesn't rid the country of shame; it only rubs it in deeper. When

Malaysia built their trade centre towers they were described as "taller than the Sears Tower" (which they are) because such a comparison would be immediately challenged and the answer, right down to the centimetre, had to be ready. "So this is your taller-than-Sears office building. Very nice," an American might say, much as he might of Toronto's CN Tower, "So this is your world's tallest free-standing uninhabited structure. Very impressive."

Such are the satisfactions of supremacy; even when bested, the world plays on your terms. The terms are set here, because the publicity is here, the markets are here, the money is here, the innocence is here, the confidence is here.

Holding the North American record for anything says quite a bit, at least to a Canadian. "North American" – as a measurement – is a Canadian invention. Whenever I hear "North American" as in "North America's oldest," or "North America's largest," I don't have to wait for the accent that follows; I know a Canadian has spoken or that a Canadian achievement, like the CN Tower, or Montreal's Comedy Festival, is about to be mentioned. To an American, the *idea* of North America doesn't really exist – that is, as an imaginative space – with anything like the force that it does for a Canadian. "North America" in fact *diminishes* the notion of "America," the larger geographical unit is somehow a smaller imaginative concept.

All of these Canadian memories are inspired by the topic I've been asked to speak on today: international literature. If you've been following my laboured analogies, I think you're beginning to get a notion of international, vs. national, writing. It's indescribably vast. It's amorphous. And because it's so monstrous, living at such depth, we can fly right over it. All too often, I suspect, the adjective "international" is employed more dismissively than expansively. (Has Miss Universe or Miss World begun to outshine Miss America? Maybe by now, with a world television market, it has. Congratulations: Miss Universe is the Malaysian Trade Tower of beauty pageants, but we know what inspired it, what it's copying.) Americans don't think too much about "international" as a category, any more than they think of "North American." It might be mentioned out of politeness, as in the term "international best-seller," or the way in which Lata Mangeshkar holds the international record for sales by a female vocalist, or Jackie Chan is an international star, but the serious business, the real action, is here. Quite literally, in thinking of international *anything*, as opposed to multinational, there's no 'there there'. Multinational means Tokyo or Frankfurt, London or Zurich; it means EC or perhaps NAFTA or GATT. International means Kuala Lumpur or Djakarta – everything that isn't American or directly competitive.

The word "international" in American usage means something smaller or lesser than "national," something to be handled on the side columns of newspapers or in quasi-comic, half-horrified bytes like "The World in a Minute" on local news. The moment we learn that an author is internationally acclaimed, it means, subliminally, they are culturally homeless. Acclaimed everywhere, at home nowhere, international becomes a kind of concession prize. *Only* international? we might ask, like some Swedish group that sings in English? Or a Czech Bluegrass band, or some Macedonian pop group that just won the European song festival?

Broadly international events are difficult to judge. In this country, the Booker Prize, Britain's highest literary honour, is respected because it is perceived as British (the entire Commonwealth is eligible), and British standards are trusted. The Pegasus Prize for world literature, on the other hand, despite the size of its award, the breadth of the competition, the prestige of its international panel of judges, is largely unknown. The Nobel Prize, the Rose Bowl of literary competitions, is of course prestigious and international as all hell, but its reliability, by now, is presumed to be compromised by political correctness or some kind of proportional voting. In other words, it has internationalized itself to death.

The fact is, there's little evidence that America moves to the same literary rhythms as the rest of the world. Our readers reflect the

American confidence that anything out there that's any good will be found, translated, published, advertised, reviewed, and made available in precisely the same way as any other book – in other words if it's any good, it will come to me on my terms, in familiar packaging, at Prairie Lights or The Hungry Mind. The unstated contract is that it won't pose political or historical headaches; that the familiar will outweigh the confusing and the remainder is pleasant exotica. A trusted reviewer will tell me why I should care. After all, they did it for Rushdie, they did it for Márquez, and they did it for Solzhenitsyn.

The United States still admits fewer foreign works to its commercial lists, we have fewer foreign books on our bestseller lists, and fewer in our trade catalogues, than any country I know. Finding good translators is hit-or-miss, and is certainly *not* a commercial priority. The foreign-language writer attempting to crack the American market faces not only the barriers familiar to all of us, but the fact that no agents, no editors in New York read foreign languages, and must commit several thousand dollars for translation even before beginning to consider the work. By contrast, my wife, for example, knows that every editor she has, in the various languages where she's published, has read her in the original language.

The commercial American houses make – it seems to me – relatively little effort to seek out interesting foreign writers and to publicize them for an American audience. Victor Pelevin, who is with us here, is an extraordinary exception, and for good reason. In my position at Iowa, it's part of my responsibility to find agents for our visiting novelists or short story writers, and I can tell you, it's a rare agent or editor who sees my inquiries on the behalf of foreign authors as a favour. Even for writers who work in English, and who pose no immediate language barrier, the unfamiliarity can be off-putting. The book must connect with American problems and project an American sensibility. The only exception I can think of, the writer who swept away all such objections, is Gabriel García Márquez, a foreign author who transformed our sensibility. I think he's the only contemporary translated author that Americans can comfortably claim as an influence on our writing.

The danger is that in the absence of the full literary landscape, one dominant voice from a region is likely to crowd out all others. If we translate only the Grand Canyons, only the Mount Everests, we deprive ourselves of the continuity, the context, the foothills of a literature. When we are unexposed to the variety of voices from a language or a region we become like literary tourists, Sears Tower readers in Kuala Lumpur. "Ah, very impressive," we say of a Latin-American writer, "but where's the flying virgin?" Magic Realism is one genius's way of apprehending his special society; it is unforgettable in its presentation, but it colludes with many of the evils, like the savagery, the corruption, the military cruelty and sexism, that it seems to condemn.

Many years ago, I attended a Commonwealth Literature conference in New Delhi, where the focus was on work from the Caribbean. After about ten straight papers on the work of the Trinidad-born, India-descended V.S. Naipaul, one of the Africa-descended critics from Barbados stood up and exclaimed, "You people haven't gone to the Caribbean. You've gone to Naipaul!"

The same can be said of central Europeans who no longer share, or who never shared, the outlook and experiences of Milan Kundera, of Germans who find Günter Grass a blank monument, Russians who long ago rejected or who never accepted socialist realism as a method, and who see the template of suffering and resistence celebrated by Solzhenitsyn, for example, as just another variant upon it. And what of the children of Salman Rushdie in the country of his birth, postmodernists, risk-takers, sophisticates, envelope-pushers, who will nevertheless be held to a vision, or judged by the style, that is Rushdie's alone, but only one out of many?

Just last week back in Iowa, I was reading a work by a Spanish writer in which the woman on the beach says to her boyfriend, in effect, "Not right now, Carlos. I want to start the new John Irving novel." This is the kind of casual acceptance that a writer waits a lifetime for, one that is more common in the outer world in regard to American writers than it is even here in the United States. In fact, I can't think of an equivalent statement from a character in our literature, in reference to a foreign work, except in an early Woody Allen movie. Writers in the Iowa program every year astound me with their encyclopedic knowledge of American writing; an Argentine asked me only yesterday if I could arrange a meeting with Lee K. Abbott, whom he considers the heir to John Cheever. How many people here know Lee's work? How many could trace the influences of Borges, or Cortazar, say, on the work of young Argentines? No one here knows that young Argentine's work, or the Spanish writer's work, despite their dozen books and a handful of prizes. It would be a rare American who can name even one living Spanish or Argentine author, despite José Cela's recent Nobel Prize.

My point is not to browbeat readers in this country and certainly not in this room; far from it, for you and the independent bookstores where you browse are the lifeblood of literature. I do want to draw a picture, however, of innocent confidence slowly yielding to false confidence, America's reigning centrality, at least in literary terms, becoming marginal for the lack of curiosity, the lack of exposure, and the huge disparity between our influence on the world and the amount of the world that we allow to influence us. Sooner or later, we will lose the advantage we're not even aware that we have.

Finally, I want to discuss just a few trends that I've observed in just a few selected works that I think could stand for hundreds more that I'll never see. There is an international literature beyond the neutral fact of "work by foreign authors." Part of it, as it has always been, is the element of vicarious travel, exotica if you will. Even the great literary door-openers, Solzhenitsyn, Márquez, Rushdie, Mahfouz, Gordimer, Kundera, owe their charm, or what charm they have, to that singular fact: you can travel to them, as you could travel to Naipaul, without leaving your seat.

That is not the chief quality of what I'm trying to define as "international." The international novel I'm thinking of defines national problems that have international application. They defy the monolithic response of the American, or European, reader. They are curiously familiar, they all have their analogues in our own literature, as they must, they are not anomalies to their time and place, not inexplicable eruptions from an unprepared sterility. In the three authors represented here today, Beatriz Escalante, R. Raj Rao, Victor Pelevin, there are traces of course of the Márquezes (or Fuenteses), of the Rushdies, of the great Russian voices, but there are also traces of feminism you won't find in Márquez, and the lives of the gay Bombay you won't find in Rushdie, and of a Russia so luridly transformed it never occurred to Solzhenitsyn, and would have been self-censored if it had. A world curiously like our own, Victor mentioned to me, a parodied America.

What we miss, if we don't seek it and demand it of our publishers, is the continuity of cultures themselves. It is that continuity that must be nurtured, lest we continue in our own well-intentioned ignorance. The rest of the world watches the daily ebb and flow of American life with fascination and of course disgust and amazement through our movies, CNN, and, Lord, even our novels, but we receive from the rest of the world only the punctuated moments of their greatest drama, or shame, and ongoing, inexplicable suffering. That is not the way the world is, not the way those countries are.

This page intentionally left blank

Rushdie as Novelist, Rushdie as Critic

1. *Midnight's Children*

THE LITERARY MAP of India is about to be redrawn. The familiar outline – E.M. Forster's outline essentially – will always be there, because India will always offer the dualities essential for the Forsterian vision: the open sewer and the whispering glade, Mother Theresa and the Taj Mahal. Serious English-language novelists from India (often called Indo-Anglians), or those from abroad who use Indian material, have steered a steady course between these vast, mutually obliterating realities; hence the vivid patches of local colour provided by the timeless south India of R.K. Narayan's novels and the cool pastels added by the later fiction of Anita Desai. The Indian novels of Paul Scott and Ruth Jhabvala also fall comfortably between those two poles. For a long time it has seemed that novels from India write their own blurbs: poised, witty, delicate, sparkling.

What this fiction has been missing is a different kind of ambition, something just a little coarse, a hunger to swallow India whole and spit it out. It needed a touch of Saul Bellow's *Augie March* brashness, Bombay rather than Chicago born, and going at things in its own special Bombay way. Now, in *Midnight's Children*, Salman Rushdie has realized that ambition.

If I am to do more than describe my pleasure in this book, if I am to summarize and interpret, I would have to start by saying that *Midnight's Children* is about the narrator's growing up in Bombay between 1947 and 1977 (and about the thirty-two years of his grandparents' and parents' lives before that). It is also a novel of India's growing up; from its special, gifted infancy to its very ordinary, drained adulthood. It is a record of betrayal and corruption, the loss of ideals, culminating with "the Widow's" Emergency rule. As a growing up novel with allegorical dimensions, it will remind readers of *Augie March* and maybe of Günter Grass's *The Tin Drum*, Laurence Sterne's *Tristram Shandy*, and Céline's *Death on the Installment Plan* as well as the less-portentous portions of V.S. Naipaul. But it would be a disservice to Salman Rushdie's very original genius to dwell on literary analogues and ancestors. This is a book to accept on its own terms, and an author to welcome into world company.

The "midnight's children" of the title are the 1,001 children born in the first hour of Indian independence, August 15, 1947. Two of these babies are born in the same Bombay nursing home on the very stroke of midnight: a boy born to wealth and a boy born to the streets. And, of course, a nursemaid switches babies: a street singer cuckolded by a departing Englishman is given the aristocratic Muslim infant and names him Shiva; a wealthy Kashmiri-descended family, the Aziz/Sinais, is given the "cucumber-nosed" English-Hindu and names him Saleem. Shiva and Saleem (the narrator) are destined to be mortal enemies from the stroke of midnight.

Saleem receives all the attention. His birth is celebrated with fireworks, and Prime Minister Nehru sends a letter saying that his fate will forever be entwined with that of India. Growing up on a Bombay estate, he bumps his head one day while hiding in his mother's laundry hamper and discovers a gift for telepathy. From the age of nine, he can enter other lives at will, see through walls, plumb all secrets, including the secret of his true parentage. But his telepathic gifts bring death and destruction and very little happiness. He discovers that every one of the midnight's children is miraculously gifted; only Saleem is telepathic but some can travel through time (and even report that India is destined to be ruled by a "urine-drinking dotard") and one can change sex at will. The extravagance of Rushdie's inventions will call to mind the hovering presence of Gabriel García Márquez; call it a tropical synchronicity.

The midnight's children are the hope of the nation, and they await Saleem's calling of a "midnight parliament." The only thing inhibiting Saleem from embracing his political destiny arises from his fear of the murdering street tough Shiva, whom he knows to be the rightful inheritor of all his privileges. And so, because of Saleem's fear and guilt, the gifts of the midnight's children are never pooled. When they do finally meet, it is during Mrs. Gandhi's "Emergency." Because of the threat they pose to the Only True Succession, the 581 surviving midnight's children are sterilized, and then treated to an even deadlier procedure: they are *sperectomized* – drained of hope.

(Perhaps you wondered about the *real* reasons for the Emergency, the various Indo-Pakistani wars, the deaths of certain Indian and Pakistani political figures? Simple: to destroy Saleem, the Sinais, and the gifted extended family of midnight's children. The plot of this novel is complicated enough, and flexible enough, to smuggle Saleem into every major event in the subcontinent's past thirty years. Saleem the Nose – variously called Snotnose, Stainface, Baldy, Sniffer, Buddha, and Piece-of-the-Moon – knows.)

The complex plotting of the book can be gauged (and its playfulness appreciated) by observing how closely an old seer's prophecy is followed. Of Saleem, it is predicted shortly before his birth: "'A son [. . .] who will never be older than his motherland – neither older nor younger. [. . .] There will be two heads – but you shall see only one – there will be knees and a nose, a nose and knees. [. . .] Newspaper praises him, two mothers raise him! Bicyclists love him – but, crowds will shove him! Sisters will weep; cobras will creep . . . [. . .] Washing will hide him – voices will guide him! Friends mutilate him – blood will betray him! [. . .] Spittoons will brain him – doctors will drain him – jungle will claim him – wizards reclaim him! Soldiers will try him – tyrants will fry him . . . [. . .] He will have sons without having sons! He will be old before he is old! *And he will die . . . before he is dead.*'"

As a Bombay book, which is to say, a big-city book, *Midnight's Children* is coarse, knowing, comfortable with Indian pop culture, and, above, all, aggressive. Salman Rushdie assumes that the differences between Colaba and Chembur are as important, and can be made as interesting, as the differences between Brooklyn and The Bronx. "We headed north," Saleem notes, "past Breach Candy Hospital and Mahalaxmi Temple, north along Hornby Vellard past Vallabhbhai Patel Stadium and Haji Ali's island tomb [. . .]. We were heading towards the anonymous mass of tenements and fishing-villages and textile-plants and film-studios that the city became in these northern zones [. . .]." Its characters speak in many voices: "Once upon a time there were Radha and Krishna, and Rama and Sita, and Laila and Majnu; also (because we are not unaffected by the West) Romeo and Juliet, and Spencer Tracy and Katharine Hepburn." Much of the dialogue (the best parts) reads like the hip vulgarity – *yaar*! – of the Hindi film magazine. The desiccated syllables of T.S. Eliot, so strong an influence upon other Anglo-Indian writers, are gone. *Midnight's Children* sounds like a continent finding its voice.

How Indian is it? It is slangy, and a taste for India (or a knowledge of Bombay) obviously heightens the response. Here is a description of a café where Saleem's mother goes secretly to meet her dishonoured first husband: "the Pioneer Café was not much when compared to the Gaylords and Kwalitys of the city's more glamorous parts; a real rutputty joint, with painted boards proclaiming LOVELY LASSI and FUNTABULOUS FALOODA and BHEL-PURI BOMBAY FASHION, with filmi playback music blaring out from a cheap radio by the cash-till, a long narrow greeny room lit by flickering neon, a forbidding world in which broken-toothed men sat at reccine-covered tables with crumpled cards and expressionless eyes." Very Indian.

Of course there are a few false notes. There is a shorter, purer novel locked inside this shaggy monster. A different author might have teased it out, a different editor might have insisted upon it. I'm glad they didn't. There are moments when the effects are strained, particularly in the early chapters, when an ancient Kashmiri boatman begins sounding like the Two-Thousand-Year-

Old Man. On a more serious level, Rushdie at first has a difficult time endowing the villains of Indian politics with mythic stature (Grass's Germany made it so easy); petty household intrigues seem more momentous than the misaffairs of state (Márquez's Latin America made it easy too). But with Ayub Khan, the Bangladesh war, "the Widow" and her son, the later pages darken quite handsomely. The flow of the book is toward the integration of a dozen strongly developed narratives, and in ways that are marvellous to behold, integration is achieved. The myriad personalities of Saleem, imposed by the time, place, and circumstance of his extraordinary birth ("'So much, yaar, inside one person,'" remarks a Pakistani soldier, of the Saleem then known as Buddha, the tracker; "'so many bad things, no wonder he kept his mouth shut!'"), are reduced to a single, eloquent, ordinary soul. The flow of the book rushes to its conclusion in counterpointed harmony: myths intact, history accounted for, and a remarkable character fully alive.

2. *Imaginary Homelands: Essays and Criticism 1981–1991*

SALMAN RUSHDIE is an author in the grand manner, arguably the most interesting younger novelist now working in the English language. This generous new collection of seventy essays, interviews, and book reviews is his earned withdrawal from a decade's capital of occasional and commissioned journalism. His fans – less numerous than his recent sales but more ardent than many reviewers – now have the opportunity to trace the patterns and developments that underlie the three great novels of the eighties on which his reputation rests: *Midnight's Children*, *Shame*, and *The Satanic Verses*. This addition to the Rushdie shelf, though somewhat random and mercenary in origin, is playful, profound, and provocative, in much the same ways as his fictions.

If Philip Roth had not already used the title *Reading Myself and Others*, it might have served Rushdie as slightly more diagnostic than the one employed here. Here we have Rushdie on a wide range of his contemporaries. When engaged, he is a sympathetic and illuminating critic. The sympathies are extended, in moving tribute, to Bruce Chatwin and Raymond Carver. Morally and politically, one feels Rushdie's special debt to, and affection for, "the snail," Günter Grass. Intellectually and artistically, he seems most in awe of Italo Calvino.

The voice that comes through, in Rushdie's best reviews, is a muted "me too." Without mentioning himself, or his own work, he nevertheless suggests a comparison: with Grass's political engagement and Calvino's controlled fantasy, with Carver's humanity and Chatwin's effervescent curiosity. (He's not always so restrained; when overt parallels to his own situation intrude, the Rushdian voice often turns flippant.) Rushdie engages books with love, or with love-turned-sour; with expectation or disillusionment. He is never less than instructive. He holds nothing back.

On a recent American novel, for example, he begins with this ironic celebration of the national imagination: "The idea of the Star, of the human individual who radiates celestial light, is a quintessentially American one, because America is in love with light; just listen to its national anthem, star-spangled banner, dawn's early light, twilight's last gleaming, rocket's red glare, was there ever such an ode to illumination? But if America sees itself as the Light Incarnate it knows, too, its Darkness, and loves its dark stars also, loves them all the more because it fears them so: Al Capone, Don Corleone, Legs Diamond, and the demon-god of E.L. Doctorow's *Billy Bathgate*, the barbarian Arthur Flegenheimer, who stole a dead man's name and became Dutch Schultz."

In analyzing the decline in V.S. Naipaul's fictional power, he notes, "There is one word I can find nowhere in the text of *The Enigma of Arrival*. That word is 'love', and a life without love, or one in which love has been buried so deep that it can't come out, is very much what this book is about; and what makes it so very, very sad." In the same essay he declares, apropos of Naipaul, but certainly also of many others he finds wanting, "when the strength for fiction fails the writer, what remains is autobiography."

Rushdie, by that definition, is a strong writer, a postmodernist in his deliberate fragmenting of narrative, his inclusion of the non-literary and demotic, his elevation of jingles and movies and the vox populi of vagabond English to the plateau of high art; Naipaul, on the other hand, is the last of the old-line Modernists – dry, distanced, chaste, an aged eagle spreading his arthritic wings in the inherited and largely unearned voice of T.S. Eliot. No wonder – apart from their radically opposed politics – Rushdie should find so little of value in the later work of England's "other Indian." (Neither, of course, is "Indian," except in the eyes of a racist society.)

Race and society, religion and immigration: these topics bring out Rushdie's rage, and his love. The core of *Imaginary Homelands* is his longer essays: on English society (particularly its racist aspect), on India, and, inevitably, on his own precarious situation as the world's most bizarrely persecuted author. "Outside the Whale," "'Commonwealth Literature' Does Not Exist," "The New Empire within Britain," and "In Good Faith" are classic essays, employing the full Rushdie arsenal.

"The New Empire within Britain" (1982) scores British society for never having "deimperialized" itself in the way, for example, that German authors at least attempted linguistic de-Nazification. The historical models for subduing unruly colonials therefore became internalized as institutional racism, ways of marginalizing immigrant and second-generation minorities. "We have, in Britain today," writes Rushdie with dry scorn, "judges like McKinnon who can say in court that the word 'nigger' cannot be considered an epithet of racial abuse because he was nicknamed 'Nigger' at his public school [. . .]."

The essay closes with an observation applicable to America, where the slippery word "multiculturalism" is beginning to gain respectability. "In our schools," he writes, "this means little more than teaching the kids a few bongo rhythms, how to tie a sari and so forth. [. . .] Multiculturalism is the latest token gesture towards Britain's blacks, and it ought to be exposed, like 'integration' and 'racial harmony', for the sham it is." The trouble with all these "multis," whatever their passing appeal to politicians and guilty liberals who wish, usually for consumer purposes, that they'd never lost their grandparents' steerage language, is that the mainstream never sees itself as part of the equation, as one of the "multis." The pot itself never melts, only the ingredients as they get chopped up.

The last fifty-seven pages of the book are a record of Rushdie's own spiritual journey back to Islam, and for this – an obviously painful and, in fact, unique literary document – a certain amount of specialized knowledge is required. Rushdie, as he is careful to describe, grew up in a secular Muslim Bombay family. He detested (and continues to detest) the "Muslim" state of Pakistan, to which his family migrated. He lost his faith in England as a teenager and became a secular Cambridge socialist, "Muslim" in a social sense that many Catholics and Jews will recognize.

The problem – and it is an enormous one – is that Islam does not recognize the lapsed Muslim, the principled agnostic. In preparing an article on Rushdie last year, I interviewed his major antagonist within the faith, one of the "mullahs" of Bradford who organized the celebrated book-burning. For him, the growing community of secularized Muslims (embodied in Rushdie and many others) is an agonizing theological dilemma. That abstract problem became Rushie's personal nightmare. Before the twentieth-century diaspora of Muslims to Britain and elsewhere, Islam had never dealt with the problem of survival in a secular climate of political impotence. Permanent minority status is not part of the Islamic vision.

Rushdie trusted the size, strength, and loyalty of his special, disaffected, but still connected secularized community to support *The Satanic Verses*. The character of Saladin Chemcha is a brilliant and compassionate group-portrait. Tragically, and for reasons in part peculiar to British racism – Muslims' desire to grab the media spotlight to publicize their own grievances, rather than join with "white" liberals at Rushdie's side – the hoped-for debate between the secular and the fundamentalist elements in British Muslim society never happened.

"My real safety, I have long believed, lies in the attitudes of the Muslim community at large," Rushdie states at the close of *Imaginary Homelands*. And indeed he is right – if, that is, he can appeal to the faithful, and gain their tolerance, over the heads of the political obscurantists in Iran and India who manipulate the faithful for partisan ends. In a way that Rushdie never foresaw, he is an avant-gardist of the faith as well as of the literature; the tragedy is that the faithful are not as tolerant of new thinking as are book reviewers.

Salman Rushdie is eloquent in defending *The Satanic Verses* against bigoted attackers, but of course he can only defend his book by defending his imagination, his liberated, thoughtful, fanciful genius. And his subversive imagination is the very thing the mullahs want extinguished.

This page intentionally left blank

Exile and Memory

I F I MAY, I would like to take advantage of this rare opportunity to speak in Mexico and begin with a few personal observations on the role of immigration in my own life and how it might apply to similar situations along today's Mexican-American border. It might seem bizarre to see parallels, but I think of the history of the French-Canadian people, with whom I am identified, as being another variant of the "Latino" if not quite "Chicano" experience. We, too, constitute a distinct identity in North America, abandoned by the colonial nation (France), defeated by English-speaking conquerors, and isolated for two hundred and fifty years while the rest of the continent surged ahead.

French Canadians, or Québécois, were a monolingual, parish-based, 100% Catholic community, living in a church-driven, priest-ridden, intellectual backwater, a joke even in France (*"Qu'est-ce que c'est le Canada? Cent arpents de neige."* i.e., What is Canada? A hundred acres of snow. – Voltaire). When my father was born there in 1905, it could be said that the Province of Québec had not overtly changed since the early 1600s. He was the youngest of eighteen, eventually nineteen, children – another brother was born five years later – and, as the seemingly last-born son, the *donné*, given to the priesthood. That experiment lasted about six years. The revolution that changed Québec did not occur until the mid-1960s. It is known as "the Quiet Revolution" (*la révolution tranquille*) and when it was finished, only one person had died and the culture had been transformed from top to bottom. Today, Québec has to import its priests and nuns from Haiti and the Philippines; it has the lowest birth rate on the continent, and is a truly progressive society built on the Scandinavian model.

When I talk about the history and adventures of (French-) Canadian immigration into the United States, I'm often met with incredulity. People ask if there is even a shade of difference between the two countries, if a transfer from Canada to the United States can even be dignified, or complicated, by the term "immigration." (Lurking behind the skepticism is the low-status word "migrant," with its suggestion of illegality, transitory residence, poverty, unskilled and backbreaking labour.) For most of the history of Québec, its workers were seasonal, off-the-books migrants in the American agricultural, construction, textile, and shoemaking industries.

Mexicans might recognize the parallels I'm trying to sketch. Immigration between adjacent cultures as close as the two I've been describing, with shared languages and cultures, with families living on both sides of an easily crossed border, deserves a special name. I'd call it "repatriation," that is, repopulating-by-return, a kind of sociological and psychological refusal to accept boundaries that cut across a larger sense of homeland. A hundred years ago, New York newspapers were calling for the expulsion of French Canadians from northern New England. Massachusetts labour leaders, fearing the arrival of low-salaried French Canadians who kept the entire textile industry operating, called them the "blue-eyed Chinese." Sound familiar? The American southwest was Mexican; Florida was Spanish; interior North America and northern New England were French. It is a global phenomenon, as we are learning about Kurds and Pashtuns. Cultural homelands are very difficult to fence off.

New World societies like Mexico, Canada, and the United States have historically expanded their cultures in three important ways (apart from repatriation): by accepting immigrants, exiles, and expatriates. Enough has been written about immigration to relieve me from the need for much reiteration here apart from offering a brief definition. I am assuming that immigration is an unforced option based on economic or quasi-economic calculations. When my father crossed the Québec border for Lewiston,

Maine as a seven-year-old child labourer, he became an immigrant (an "undocumented alien") to the United States. He traded 25¢ a day in a lumber camp for a dollar a day as a "bobbin boy" in the spinning mills.

Similarly, when I returned to Québec after my first twenty-five years in the United States, I became an immigrant to Canada, not to enjoy economic advantage, but out of artistic and psychological necessity. The immigrant is seeking a better life (however defined), a safer life, and a more interesting or challenging life. My father came for survival; I went for fulfillment.

Whatever the immigrant's secret motive, he signs an implicit contract and accepts certain terms of submission. The final goal is assimilation. The immigrant bows to a new authority, salutes a new flag, learns a new language and knows that his children and grandchildren will be estranged from him and the original home-land. I was a good immigrant; I became Canadian just like my parents and all my relatives. My parents, however, despite twenty-five years of "Green Card" status in the United States, never went through the process of naturalization. They were immigrants who stopped short of assimilation. My mother, in particular, never gave up her core-identity as a Canadian and went back and died in Canada. She was an expatriate-in-immigrant's-clothing. My father, whose core was more malleable, after five marriages died in the French-Canadian ghetto of Manchester, New Hampshire.

My wife came to the United States from India for post-graduate study. She immigrated to Canada with me; we returned to the United States fourteen years later when Canada turned hostile to so-called "Third-World" immigration. The choice I made to make my life in Montreal and her choice to leave India to study in the United States (where we met, in graduate school), were totally voluntary. We went with the idea of contributing everything to the new country, to submitting to its codes and becoming functioning and productive Canadians, which we did (and are). The question that haunts me still, now that I am re-established in the country of my birth and upbringing, is: *What am I?* Am I an immigrant to the

United States, as I was to Canada? I was an immigrant to my parents' country, but when I returned to the United States, I became an immigrant to the country of my birth. Like many Mexican-Americans, I'm a "native" of both countries. I often feel like an expatriate American – living in my own homeland.

"Exile," on the other hand, has a clear definition. It is forced expulsion. The "sin" of the exile is that his/her politics, learning, passion, orientation, race, or religion demonstrates too deep an attachment to his homeland and too shallow a regard for the powers that govern it. An exile abandons his homeland and seeks asylum for the preservation (or free exercise) of the most vital aspect of his life. In this demand, he occupies a middle ground between the *immigrant* who voluntarily leaves his native country in anticipation of bettering his conditions, and the *expatriate* who voluntarily quits his original homeland and takes up life in a new one, aiming to enjoy the benefits of both without excluding an allegiance to either. The expatriate keeps an imaginary chateau in his homeland and an apartment in the new country of his choice.

Exiles and expatriates, whose numbers are never large, exert enormous influence on their adopted countries. Immigrants arrive by the millions, but it usually takes a generation or two for their presence to be felt. Among the categories of dislocation, the exile is tragic, the expatriate is regal, and the immigrant remains anonymous and déclassé.

There are nuances in any definition, but I would count Russian writers as diverse as Vladimir Nabokov and Aleksandr Solzhenitsyn as classic exiles. Today, Norman Manea and Andrei Codrescu from Romania, Wole Soyinka from Nigeria, Ariel Dorfman and Isabel Allende from Chile, and hosts of Hungarians, Poles, Chinese, Palestinians, North Africans, Cubans, Colombians, Argentines, and Chileans have found refuge and second homes in Canada, the United States, and Mexico. American culture has been enriched beyond any conceivable measure by the thousands of exiles from every area of the arts, sciences, and professions who re-established themselves in the universities, in Hollywood, in studios and laboratories in the wake of Fascist and Nazi threats. My own university education and my continuing attempts at self-education remain dependent on the pioneering work of European exiles, seventy years after their flight from Europe. For the most part, exiles abandoned their mother tongues and transferred their expertise to the study of New World conditions.

On the other hand, it seems to me that distinguished authors like Milan Kundera (from Czechoslovakia to France), Imre Kertész (Hungary to Germany), Samuel Beckett (Ireland to France), T.S. Eliot, Ezra Pound, Henry James (from the United States to England or Italy), Wilson Harris (Guyana to U.S.), W.H. Auden and Christopher Isherwood (U.K. to U.S.), and, in our own day, Michael Ondaatje (Sri Lanka to England and Canada), V.S. Naipaul and Derek Wolcott (Trinidad to Britain), Salman Rushdie and Chinua Achebe are, to one degree or another, expatriates. Not to make light of the difficulties they've faced and overcome, or the mental anguish of separation, they were not served with the same expulsion orders as most exiles. They can, and often do, return to their homelands. Their work often reflects their continuing commitment to the culture (the imaginary chateau) they left behind. When I called the expatriate position "regal," I'm merely emphasizing the great prestige that attaches itself to the category. The Nobel Prize committee seems especially fond of the expatriate as representing the most refined and cultivated of sensibilities.

Many of the most interesting American writers of the present moment are foreign-born, or the children of immigrants. They write in the long tradition of immigrant literature in this country, starting with the sturdy Germans and Scandinavians, up through the generation of Jews, Italians, and Greeks. Even a French Canadian, Jack Kerouac, enlivens that history. Now it's the turn of the Latinos, the Africans, the Asians, and the Caribbeans. Their literary concerns are, quite properly, focused on the strains of assimilation. Jhumpa Lahiri, Ha Jin, Edwige Danticat, Amy Tan, Chang-Rae Lee, Bharati Mukherjee, Cristina García, Sandra Cisneros, Junot Díaz, Aleksander Hemon – the list is already endless and growing by the week. At this time in American literary history we are experiencing an outburst of expression unparalleled in our history, much of it fed by the clash of cultures, and the triangulation of works by exiles, expatriates and immigrants.

I remember my first teacher, Bernard Malamud, once (correctly) assuming my political position as liberal Democrat. It was 1964; I was in my early twenties. His wife cautioned him, "Bern, think of his feelings – he might be a Republican," and Bern snapped back, "Don't be silly." In the world of my youth it was unthinkable that a young artist could be anything other than "liberal" (that is, an enthusiastic partisan of the New Deal and the Great Society), and automatically an opponent of the war in Vietnam, a strong supporter of civil rights and an enemy of any candidate or idea deriving from the Republican Party.

Today, I know I could not make the same confident assumption about the political affiliation of any of my students. In my youth, I could safely assume that any writer I encountered would be a child of Depression-era or immigrant parents, or would have received an education at the hand of European exiles and that they would share a set of political assumptions that put us in a camp that we considered mainstream but which would be called today "left-wing extremist."

These days I suspect that a great percentage of my student-writers, if they bothered to vote at all, would be Republican. They are egalitarian as to race and gender; ecological and pacifistic by nature. In other words, they have no conventional political commitment, except, perhaps, a general revulsion to conventional partisan politics. These years, the "rebel" or anti-establishment position is more closely identified with the rhetoric of libertarian Republicanism than with the multiple advocacies of the liberal left. The left is old; it's your grandfather's politics. And they're probably correct.

One important reason for this transformation, I think, can be laid to the dynamics of exile. Most exiles of the first half of the last century were fleeing right-wing oppression, especially, of course, Nazi Germany. From their tragedy we learned about ourselves. We learned to distrust the mask of mere culture. Many of my teachers were first-generation German and Russian Jews. Their political positions can be defined as secular, socialist, and pacifist. They saw the political aspect in the aesthetic and the aesthetic component of the political. In the American cultural hierarchy, we can identify them as Hannah Arendt, Irving Howe, Lionel Trilling, and Alfred Kazin. Or Erich Fromm, Bruno Bettelheim, and Herbert Marcuse. Or Edward Teller, Albert Einstein, and Enrico Fermi. Or Billy Wilder, Ernst Lubitsch, and Douglas Sirk. Politically and socially their guidance joined populist protest (from labour, civil rights and anti-colonialism) with Marxist analysis. For a generation or so, the sensibilities of working-class immigrants and racial minorities were fused with the vigour of the exiled European intellectual. I was a college student then, and a young professor in their final years.

In the past few decades, however, many of the "new" exiles have escaped from left-wing tyrannies in central Europe, Asia, or Cuba. Their politics necessarily gravitate to free markets, capitalism, and individualism. The current gubernatorial candidate in California, Arnold Schwarzenegger, boasts that his form of Republicanism derives from a reaction against his "socialist" upbringing in Austria. The same etiology applies to the very conservative Cuban-Americans in Florida. Just as an earlier generation of exiles had seen Nazism as the essence of state-sponsored horror, the later exiles see Communism and even socialism and liberalism in the same way. Many of the so-called "neo-conservatives" that today drive American foreign policy are children of the original left-wing exile-immigrants who began changing their views when they could not support anti-Vietnam protest, or the personal-liberation upheavals of the sixties, then with liberal inattention to threats against Israel, and finally with the deliberately anti-democratic assumptions behind affirmative action, i.e., privileging racial identity over objective merit. (That same perception is also driving Asian-Americans into the conservative camp.)

My liberal friends call these new right-wingers opportunists (following the example of another European exile/immigrant, Henry Kissinger, who broke with tradition and serves the conservative cause; his successors, Zbigniew Brzezinski and Madeleine Albright, retained their core-liberalism); I'd prefer to see it as a tide of history that is larger than the merely individual. An exile, I would say, has the strength of thousands in the passion of his ideas; he has the unique ability to change the course of history. That's the reason they were expelled from their homelands, and the reason they achieve heroic influence in their adopted countries.

I apologize for this too-brief summary of the lingering effect of exile in the contemporary United States. Exiles have been with us long enough and have left a deep enough impression to have fostered their own counter-revolution, a kind of generational revolt that might have confirmed the theories of another old central European exile, Sigmund Freud.

American Fiction

I WANT TO TAKE this opportunity, at the outset of these lectures, to extend my gratitude to the Office of International Programs here at Meiji University, and to the Department of English for its invitation and various kindnesses. I know that whatever dim light I may be able to shed on literature in my country, my various countries, will hardly compete with all that I hope to learn from my stay in this country.

I have titled these lectures, collectively, *Here, There, and Everywhere* to capitalize on a well-worn cliché which usually expresses a kind of exasperation with uncontrollable growth, the unorderly exuberance – as though books and literatures were a kind of weed-garden that had grown beyond the bounds of all comprehension. Indeed, in the case of American publishing, with its annual production of more than fifty thousand titles – a hundred and fifty trade titles a day, seven days a week, fifty-two weeks a year, with at least ten thousand of them, perhaps thirty a day, designated as works of trade fiction – the image of weeds, of literal asphyxiation, is not too exaggerated. What can possibly be said of such a mountain of separate books? Surely the consideration of even a dozen titles, which is far too ambitious for a brief address, is a futile gesture in the face of such abundance.

Whatever statements I can make, whatever books I choose to discuss, must first of all be seen as reflective of my own prejudices, and of my own selectivity based on my own set of priorities, which might easily be seen as biased in favour of social realism, class, ethnic and racial consciousness, and regional specificness. Cultural critics, not to mention post-feminists and post-colonial Marxists, and of course deconstructionists, might see my selections as reflective only of my age, sex, race, sexual orientation, profession, and cultural background.

The most agonizing question facing American literary criticism at the present moment is simply this: who speaks for American writing? In a nakedly deconstructionist age, who dares to speak with any authority for anything apart from one's own narrow subjective focus? What is judgement, who has the right to judge, to select, to comment upon anything that he or she has not personally validated through life-experience? What is the pose of objectivity, what is the assertion of value but the admission of prejudice?

I will return to those questions at other times in these lectures. For the moment, I'll try to glide over such strained and unanswerable objections with a simple disqualifier – the confession of my own self-awareness. I am aware, in other words, that great harm has been done to the variety of literary forms and literary expression by generations of white males in positions of authority. The literary canon – often referred to as the collective works of Dead White Males – has been used to suppress heterogeneity, much in the way, to cite a familiar example, the suffocating authority of T.S. Eliot in the thirties through the fifties rendered all counter-positions immediately suspect.

I should also note that speaking in Japan to a Japanese audience means that many of the most agonizing questions in American society and American literature have little or no equivalent in Japan. (At least, this is what we understand of Japanese culture in the United States: that it is, relative to any standard we understand, homogenous, with minimal differences of race, class, or region.) Viewed from a Japanese perspective, the struggle to assimilate or to preserve one's difference, the profound class and regional disparities, the continuing cultural segregation of America's minority populations, its intellectual sexual apartheid, its social and sexual fragmentations, its pervasive violence, all inhibit the possibility of a shared response between lecturer and audience.

This being said and, I hope, always borne in mind, I'll neverthe-less attempt to stake a very small claim on a very small selection of contemporary American fiction. I'll start with the deaths of four major American novelists in the 1980s. All four were male, three were New Yorkers, two were recovered alcoholics, all were white, one was religious, one was self-consciously "ethnic," and each restricted his fiction to a particular, self-identified subculture that earned him devoted readers and imitators. Their work is, in fact, so highly inflected by their own cadences of style and obses-sive themes and recurrent characters that their names have been changed into adjectives, much in the way of a Kafka becoming Kafkaesque, or a Faulkner Faulknerian.

The authors I'm referring to are John Cheever, Bernard Malamud, Raymond Carver, and Donald Barthelme. It is a sign of the profound fractures in American culture that it is inconceivable that a character in the fiction of any one of those writers could have appeared in the fiction of any other – they would seem as strange as unicorns. Malamud's characters are urban, East-Coast, first- and second-generation Jews, uneasily assimilated into portions of American society as shop-owners or academics or writers. Cheever's are East-Coast suburbanites or New England "Yankees" from Protestant, Anglo-Saxon backgrounds, outwardly successful and inwardly desperate. Carver's are small-town, West-Coast, lower-middle-class vagabonds, marginally employed, tormentedly married, drug- and alcohol-dependent, yet doggedly devoted to some larger, elusive design or promise. Barthelme's are overtly metafictional constructs, owing more perhaps to European and Latin-American models, not "characters" or even "stories" in a tra-ditional manner, but sly allusions to previous creations, references to pop culture, to myth, to history. He was our American Calvino, our Borges.

The reason I've cited these authors is for the glory of their work, and for the legacies they have left behind them. The world of John Cheever neatly opens onto the work of John Updike, of Ann Beattie, Michael Chabon, even of the Canadian Alice Munro –

worlds in which a promise of Eden and of resurrection is fatally
interrupted by uncontrollable urges, by sexuality, by melancholy,
greed, or intolerable restlessness. The suburbs of Cheever's work,
"Shady Hill" and "Bullet Park," are the last believable Edens created by the last descendants of Puritan America. They excluded all
minorities, Catholics were suspect and Jews were barred, and of
course African-Americans could only appear as servants.

To remark on their racial exclusiveness is to emphasize not
their narrow fortressing, but their fragility. They live by codes as
elaborate as at the court of Versailles. As with the character of
Neddy in "The Swimmer," perhaps Cheever's single most famous
story, the suburban construction is a psychological allegory, a place
tolerant only of the young, the rich, the beautiful, the "right sort."
One false step, one blunder, one failure, and the artificial world
begins to slip. Horrible, disfigured loneliness and death is the fate
of Cheever's failures; they are charming monsters in the final analysis. In the corrupted romances of Cheever, it seems to me we have
the inheritor of Hawthorne and the world of the New England
Transcendentalists, couched in the musical language of that other
great celebrant of life's excess and regret, F. Scott Fitzgerald, except
that the old Transcendentalist faith has faltered.

The barricaded world of the lily-white suburb, fed by commu-
ter trains filled with gin-swilling executives downing two or three
quick martinis before getting off in Westchester or Connecticut and
returning to their ex-debutante wives and well-exercised children
and a night of more partying, more drinking, some flirtations, perhaps an adultery, perhaps even house-breaking and murder, followed by regret, headache, and incrimination, is a vision of an
American Hell, a secular version of the Puritan sermons.

What makes Cheever's characters memorable and compas-
sionately-drawn is their Fitzgerald-like blind faith that they can
outrun death and decline, that their youth and attractiveness and
athleticism and money will cling to them always. That their dark
secrets, their bad habits, will not do them in. In this way, it might
even be said that Cheever's characters allegorize more than just

the ruin of houses and families in New England and the New York suburbs; there is something touchingly, pathetically American about their faith in appearances, and their helpless decline in the world.

About Bernard Malamud, whose physical world abutted Cheever's in the way that the midtown office towers of Manhattan where Cheever's characters presumably worked look down on the lower east side and the Brooklyn ghettos across the bridge where Malamud's characters actually lived, Cheever had absolutely nothing to say. Nor did Malamud ever create a Cheeverian character although the two authors were good friends and very admiring of one another's work. Bernard Malamud, I should mention, was my first teacher, and remained for the next twenty-five years a very close personal friend, the father that I never had. For those reasons, I'm not the best person to discuss the relative merits of his work – that is, to argue Malamud's place relative to Saul Bellow, or Philip Roth, as they are commonly linked ("the Hart, Schaffner, and Marx of American Jewish writing," Roth once called them).

Bernard Malamud gave voice to a community of writers, primarily but not exclusively Jewish, who have come to their maturity as authors in an era that I, and they, would term "Malamudian." Cynthia Ozick, Grace Paley, Harold Brodkey, Lynne Sharon Schwartz, Hilma Wolitzer, Leonard Michaels, Herb Gold, Woody Allen, Philip Roth, Joseph Heller, have all directly benefitted, in the cultivation of their own literary voice, from the inflections of Malamud's stories, especially those collected in *The Magic Barrel* and *Idiots First*, and the early novels, particularly *The Assistant*, *The Natural,* and *The Fixer*. It was Malamud, and of course Isaac Bashevis Singer, who brought the resources of Russian Yiddish storytelling, the folk-epic, to English and to the American experience. One need only read such classic stories as "The Magic Barrel," "Take Pity," "The Jewbird," or "Idiots First" to realize the artistry that went into the creation of so apparently a "natural" communal voice. Until Malamud and Bellow, Jewish writers in America had been caught up in the immigration dilemma of Henry Roth's *Call It Sleep*, in which *Yiddishkeit* and the memories of the Old World necessarily lost out to pressures of conformity to the American ideal; or, they reflected the Jewish political experience of New York radicals of the 1930s, as in the work of Daniel Fuchs and Michael Gold. Malamud built an American fiction that implied its roots in a different world, without ever stating it. Jewishness was everywhere, in the style, the outlook, yet nowhere explicit.

One should not overlook parallel developments in the field of literary criticism. When Malamud was working out a personal, storytelling aesthetic in the early 1940s, reading American literature in the New York Public Library while attending City College of New York and teaching night classes in a Brooklyn High School, his CCNY classmate Alfred Kazin was doing the same thing, and daring to bring out *On Native Ground*, a ghetto-reading of so-called classic American texts that had been, until that time, the preserve of Harvard-trained Protestant blue-blood Bostonians. (As a gloss to this phenomenon, one might read Diana Trilling's *The Beginning of the Journey*, her recent autobiography, for its account of her husband Lionel Trilling's fight for acceptance at Columbia University. It could be said that in the 1930s, for a Jewish intellectual, the longest twenty blocks in America lay between 137th Street, home of CCNY, and 116th Street, the gates of Columbia.)

After the generation of Malamud, Trilling, and Kazin, and just after them, Irving Howe, Seymour Krim, Delmore Schwartz, Isaac Rosenfeld, and Norman Podhoretz, upper-class notions of politeness, breeding and good taste as necessary credentials for literary commentary disappeared from the American academy. Ideas, passion, and commitment counted. Freud and Marx counted. Sex mattered. The *Partisan Review* crowd – Philip Rahv, Dwight Macdonald, Mary McCarthy, Hannah Arendt – took over, bending literature to a social agenda, undermining the New Critics' apolitical, asocial aesthetic. Implicitly, the anti-semitism of a T.S. Eliot was the enemy. No one "owned" the literature of this country anymore, in the way that, say, British critics like F.R. Leavis defined and exercised proprietorial rights over the so-called Great Tradition in Britain. The only exception was the so-called "Fugitive" Movement, centred on the campus of Vanderbilt University in Tennessee, where certain Southern-born, intensely loyal sons of the South and all its twisted institutions tried to define and defend an agrarian tradition of Southern yeomanry in American letters, against the liberalizing, assimilating, non-Christian, racial integrationists of the North.

Raymond Carver, who died of lung cancer in 1988 at the age of 49, is commonly regarded as the most influential short-story writer of his (and my) generation. We were classmates at the University of Iowa, so once again, as with Malamud, it is difficult for me to see quite beyond the personality and affection I felt for the man, into a pure assessment of his work. Ray came from so-called "Okie" stock, familiar to anyone who's read Steinbeck's *Grapes of Wrath* – the families whom the Great Depression forced off the ancestral land of the South and Plains, out to the greater promise of jobs on the West Coast. They were America's great rural proletariat: Anglo-Saxon, fundamentalist Christian, uneducated, poor, isolated, victimized and victimizers, in the sense that they were, for a very long time, the vociferous supporters of many of the South's worst racial-exclusion laws.

Whatever the justice or injustice of that perception, it is certainly true to say that Raymond Carver's people, and the world he writes of, is a place that no right-thinking American wants to visit. It lacks education, vision, taste, comfort, ease, money, sophistication, and a progressive attitude. We've read of them before, in Faulkner, in Flannery O'Connor, still in their native South. They are easily patronized as "hillbilly," or "redneck." The men are given to fighting, liquor, and spousal abuse; the women can probably hold their own in most fights, or in most drinking-contests. Carver modernized them, universalized them, added drugs to the liquor supply, put them in shopping malls, on the Interstates, in dead end jobs, in tract housing and trailer parks. They remain what they always were, stubborn folks with codes of honour, alternately passive and rebellious, resistant to outside help, suspicious, in fact, of nearly anything or anybody posing as a social worker, politician, or welfare-giver.

This easy characterization overlooks the psychological and cultural resources that have enabled them to survive in America for the past three hundred years. Like the African-Americans to whom they bear a great (if unacknowledged) resemblance, they have created a separate subculture in America, marked by music, by survivalist skills, by clanship, by religious and family cohesiveness, and by a defensive deflection of most attempts at a forced integration into an educated, commercialized, professional mainstream. Such resources enrich the literary gifts of the rare children in either black or Appalachian culture who dream of writing, and who manage to find books to nurture the inclination to write. The urgency of their material, its obvious pain and the price tag in sheer human misery that it seems to carry on the page, its elemental qualities of rage, of confusion, of loss, underwrite its power. In the case of Raymond Carver, it linked up with the spareness of Hemingway, the moral earnestness of John Gardner, the plainness of non-literary northwestern speech (Carver was from Oregon, and despite the years he spent as a professor at Syracuse University, most of his work is set in the small towns of Oregon and Washington or northern California) to create the essential "Carveresque" voice. A lonely man meditating at night on things gone wrong, with a drink and cigarette in his hand, children wheezing from asthma on the sofa, cold wind seeping through the cracks, his wife asleep, the bills unpaid, out of a job.

From Carver and those who've shared his vision if not precisely his life, has sprung a contemporary school of writing called at times "Minimalism" and at other times "Dirty Realism." Richard Russo, Joy Williams, Bobbie Ann Mason, Richard Ford, Denis Johnson, Charles Baxter, Tim O'Brien, Joyce Carol Oates,

Richard Price, Carolyn Chute, Russell Banks, E. Annie Proulx, to playwrights like David Mamet, and literally dozens of others of both sexes have found their lives mirrored, and their voices liberated, by Carver's example. There are "Carver Look-Alike" contests to accommodate the flow of sincere imitations that flood into magazines. The voice has become so imitatively successful that the novelist Diane Johnson, a veteran judge of literary contests, recently wrote in a piece published in *The New York Times Book Review* (April 10, 1994):

> Reading a trove of books inevitably gives you an overview of trends and tendencies that might not emerge from weekly browsing in the book reviews. A few years ago, I found that I often could not distinguish among a sudden rash of minimalist short-story volumes; differences among these (mostly young) writers were lost in a kind of universal Carveresque competence.

Russell Banks's *Continental Drift*, set in New Hampshire and Florida is perhaps the longest and most successful example of modern doomed realism hearkening back to Stephen Crane and Theodore Dreiser. These works share an earned and difficult eloquence about a stubborn American reality: survival without hope, violent aimlessness, self-destructiveness, with dim prospects of futurity. Certainly the ascendancy of Carver's vision in the past several years, leaving behind us the bittersweet alternative visions of Cheever and Malamud, speaks directly to a national uneasiness whose only redemption is in the style of its presentation, the stoic beauty of its own despair.

Donald Barthelme was the American master of an essentially European form of collage, of metafiction, of sophisticated allusion, of vast learning, irony, wit, and compression. Calvino, Kundera, Kafka, all have left their traces; John Barth and Robert Coover, Steven Millhauser, would all bear a kind of witness to his achievements. His works are intellectual puzzles waiting to be solved, a reminder perhaps that the over-determined urban worlds most of us live in – not Malamud and Carver characters, however – is composed of familiar second-hand fragments of information, patterns and compulsions made predictable by overexposure in books, movies, and advertisements. The opportunity for originality in such a vision is extremely narrow, and when it fails, it merely accents its cleverness. A variant of the same world was explored by Thomas Pynchon in *The Crying of Lot 49* and *V.*, puzzle-books of even more complicated and self-referential parody, collapsing into a vortex of paranoia. Paranoia and solipsism are adjacent responses to American commercialism, violence, and replicated abundance; the true sons of America very often go mad. When it works, however, in the way that absurdist drama works, or Kafka works, the moments of heightened authenticity pushing against manic inventiveness or against tired academic or commercial jargon can be startling and poignant. One begins to see patterns; Barthelme was our great order-giver, the geometrician of American polylogorrhea. Needless to say, Barthelme's vision has been passed on to dozens of writers, to the cyber-spacers and speculative whizzes, to pattern-makers, to ironists and historical allusionists. Don DeLillo, Richard Powers, Allen Kurzweil, Nicholas Baker, Jay Cantor, all strike me as working the Barthelme end of the literary spectrum.

The reason I've spent so much time building up a sense of the American culture having lost four giants, four anchors, in recent times – comparable to the loss of Hemingway and Faulkner within a few months of one another in the early 1960s – is to spend the rest of this lecture assessing the current scene which is so very different just five to ten years after their passing. It seems to me that the 1980s marked the end of a coherent literary culture. The fissures in contemporary American society have once again erupted – as they last did in the confrontational 1960s. We are now a society of victims and victimizers, mutually hostile and mutually suspicious.

Who speaks for America today? Separate, non-communicating subcultures today generate excellent books in great profusion, but the phenomenon of "crossover appeal" – that is, of female authors appealing to men, or vice-versa, black to white, immigrant to mainstream, gay to straight, is rare. The contemporary American literary situation is perfectly postmodern in affect: many voices, many focuses, many mutually-unintelligible worlds cohabiting the same physical space. Critical commentary from outside the authorizing community is all too often considered intrusive, unwelcome, and certainly irrelevant. Would I dare to write on women's, or on African-American experience? – not on your life. Exploring an alien consciousness, as in a male writing in female voice, white in black, is considered "voice-appropriation," a kind of literary imperialism. Male writers can be called to account for their age-old sexual obsessiveness, their single-minded sexual longing. This "objectifying" treatment of women characters – descriptions of their sexual attractiveness to the diminishment of other qualities – is enough to destroy a book's credibility, as certainly it should be. But there is no time-moratorium on this form of deconstruction; very few male writers of the past can stand up to this new scrutiny – Hemingway, as an obvious example, can be laughed off a syllabus for his obvious misunderstanding of women. More seriously, Faulkner, O'Connor, and Eudora Welty can be censored, along with Mark Twain, for injudicious use of offensive racial epithets, even when the word, usually "nigger," is clearly the character's, not the author's, usage. Students at Berkeley recently demanded that Flannery O'Connor's story "The Artificial Nigger," written forty years ago, be changed to "The Artificial African-American," or else be dropped from the short-story course.

To spread the blame around, however, males can find little but parodies of themselves – as egocentric, self-pitying buffoons, helpless, cold, silent, driven adolescents – in many feminist books. In a recent review I find the following summation of complaints about a well-received novel by a successful and highly-praised young novelist:

It would also help if there were even one likable, independent man in their midst. . . . she might have saved her story had she created a male character who was as sensual, complex and interesting as the women she has given us in the past.

Unfortunately, the smorgasbord of men – and women – in [this novel] is fairly unappetizing. Among the former we find only Alan, balding and insensitive; Dale, pretty, charming and "vague"; David, intellectual but about as sexy as a plate of mashed potatoes; and Eric, good in bed, but "an anal-retentive jerk" . . .

It might be argued that men are getting paid back for the generations of failure to understand the complexity and needs of women, when "frigid bitch" summed up a man's comprehension of the phenomenon of rejection. Sexism is only the beginning. Racism, nativism, heterosexism, ageism, classism, regionalism, are charges that can be levelled against nearly any author perceived as coming from a "privileged" (i.e., white, male, straight, middle-class, educated) background. Echoing some of the charges of Foucault, there is even an alert out against so-called "Enlightenist" thinkers who would dare to place too much confidence in the Cartesian consciousness or rationality itself.

Who speaks for America?

The Dirty Realists, Raymond Carver's sons and daughters, brothers and sisters, speak from a layer of alienated America, but they also speak, predominantly, as men, as white men, as rural or small-town heterosexual white men, as alienated, under-employed, relatively unskilled and inarticulate white men, usually with a few bad habits, and the relevance of their message is coded in precisely those terms. Because their lives are blank, their language spare, their experiences confusing and repetitive, the stories are sometimes called "minimalist." Readers must be prepared to fill in the blanks, which means they must have shared some of the same experiences, or passed through the same wastelands. What can such stories say to women, to immigrants, to blacks, to Hispanics, to gays, to urban intellectuals, to readers wishing to see their urban, affluent, and fragile successes in some way mirrored? Carver is influential, but hardly universal.

The immigrant literature, which has, over the past ten to fifteen years, become a vast and engaging part of a new American consciousness – witness the works of Amy Tan, Oscar Hijuelos, Cynthia Kadohata, Cristina García, Bharati Mukherjee, Maxine Hong Kingston, Meena Alexander, Ruth Prawer Jhabvala, Jessica Hagedorn, Isabel Allende, among many, many others – would seem, at first glance, to follow from the niche carved out by earlier waves of European immigrants and their children, the Bernard Malamud position. But this is not necessarily the case. America itself has been deconstructed since the time of the first-generation Jews. America, rather than being the safe haven, the promise of freedom, is in many ways identified as the source of other countries' misery. A naive Jewish reading of America's role in the Second World War would see America as the saviour. A more sophisticated reading shows that American foreign policy could have saved millions of Jewish lives, or perhaps even stopped the Holocaust, but for anti-semites in high places. And both readings conflict with the Japanese-American experience of war-time concentration camps.

The agenda of the new wave of Asian- and Latin-American writers has therefore been to cling to the differences that separate them from "white" or "Anglo" America. Implicitly, their books deal in the forms of victimization, or indictments, with the pain of leaving a homeland and nostalgia over returning, and the bruising at the hands of an uncaring and largely hostile host-society whose presence is rendered only sketchily.

In other words, the various crises in American culture of the present time are being mirrored, as they should be, in our literary responses. Confidence in the collective virtue of the American experience has been lost. We have entered a New World Disorder, suspicious of objectivity, hostile to traditional standards of excellence, engaged in the active deconstruction of all assumptions until their naked political agendas are revealed. The literary canon is not a standard of excellence; it is an enforcement of white, male, heterosexual, Enlightenment, Anglo-Saxon Protestant hegemony. The early twentieth-century assumption that one's condition of birth conferred only temporary limitations to be ameliorated by education, personal effort, a benevolent government, an expanding economy, and appeals to the Constitution, as well as the basic goodness of the American character, has been under attack since the sixties, with its exposure of political expediency, racial intolerance, and militarist adventurism. Thanks to the legacies of Presidents Reagan and Bush, faith in government intervention is at an all-time low. America's competitive position, its educational standards, its self-confidence, all have perceptibly tumbled. The failure to eradicate poverty, violence, and racism has engendered cynicism, and a surrender of the argumentative high ground to skeptical and communal forces.

There is a racial and generational divide still unresolved between those whose experience of poverty and intolerance in America was seen as part of an inevitable process of absorption, and those for whom the harsh conditions of the present time seem permanent and not even worth resolving. For them, belonging to a larger society may never happen. We are living today in a culture of separate communities and with rare exceptions this holds true for our literature as well.

Speaking out for America as a collective experience has become an unpopular, even suspicious position. Deconstruction, as a prime example, rivets itself to the unexamined hypothesis, revealing the hypocritical or chauvinist base to nearly any attempt at synthesis. Self-identified affinity groups have become so ghettoized, in many cases, proudly self-ghettoized, that the word "assimilationist" can be hurled as a curse by the immigrant community itself to members, by birth, of the same group. This has happened to Salman Rushdie in Britain, to Bharati Mukherjee and

Richard Rodriguez in the United States, and to any number of writers assailed as black-on-the-outside, white-in-the-middle "Uncle Toms" or "Oreo Cookies," or yellow-on-the-outside, white-on-the-inside "bananas," or red-on-the-outside, white-on-the-inside "apples." The fear of group ostracization and snide disapproval encourages pugnaciousness, a picket fence, if not barbed wire, around communal experience.

Speaking personally, I must acknowledge the fragmenting effects of the past twenty years on my own reading habits. Because I have grown wary of commenting on work by women for fear of revealing more prejudice than understanding, I have come to read fewer and fewer novels by women. When I do, I often find the characterization of males shallow and unconvincing – much in the way feminist scholars attack the stereotypical and "objectified" treatment of women in the entire canon of male writing. At present, I find that writing by gay males, whose work in the past I had turned to for its so-called wit and sparkle, now shows, because of a grounding in mortality that no other group in the society can possibly know, a higher level of passion, commitment, self-assurance, candour, and compassion than any other community in our literature. They are trying to reach out. The two greatest American novels written in my lifetime are by black writers: Ralph Ellison's *Invisible Man* (1952) and Toni Morrison's *Beloved* (1988) both achieve greatness because of their mastery of a communal experience, wedded to a universal voice.

Look, I want to say – I *know* men are self-centred and insensitive, I *know* whites are repressive and racist, I *know* straight men are uptight and violent. I know these things because great books have shown them to me, and I have tried to adjust my behaviour and to overcome the prejudices of a typical American boyhood to be worthy of them. Some of those great books I've already talked about today. Where do I *now* find the novels that acknowledge growth and change, novels and stories that deal maturely with marriages and love affairs, or with social and racial interactions that reflect the change of consciousness we've all gone through in the past generation, and do so without reducing one side, or both, to parody?

My formula for a great American literature in the time of contemporary doubt and fracturing is to write from the heart of one's community, from the centre of one's isolated experience, and to reach for the conscience, the soul, of an alerted, conscious mainstream. The great writers know that we are all red, not white on the inside, and interchangeable, not immutable. We are watermelons, whatever our outside shape or colour; red and pulpy and juicy on the inside with seeds of black and white.

American literature carries a special burden in the world: it is multinational and multicultural. It cannot assume, as European and Asian literatures can, the universality and homogeneity of its audience, even though, until about thirty years ago, it comfortably did precisely that. I have been describing today literary response to a time of heightened, often angry, and always confrontational self-awareness, and the reaction against two hundred years of smug self-confidence. American literature can never be European, for the same reason that American music and cinema can never be either. We are open to too many influences, appealing to too broad an audience with diverse tastes. But, I feel, serious literature, which is not a popular art, must find a way to reach over the fences and trenches that separate us. I am looking for works that dare once again to be social instead of communal, books that take us beyond the familiar divisions in our culture and presume to speak maturely, not generically, for larger numbers. "Who knows," the unnamed, allegorical narrator of Ellison's novel asks at the end of his experience, "but that, on the lower frequencies, I speak for you?"

This patient audience has surely caught on to my own dilemma by now. I am a white, middle-class, heterosexual, middle-aged male who has spoken about other white male writers more or less like himself, although to my thinking I may have more in common with some women or homosexuals than I do with characters from

Cheever or Carver. I, too, come from a particular community, one which I will talk about in my next lecture, but which for purposes of today's lecture I have suppressed. Today I have posed as an Anglo-Saxon, white American male, talking of other Dead White Straight Males. Doing so, I have perpetuated the marginality of everyone else. There must be a way around this dilemma.

I want to end this lecture on a positive note – I'm trying – despite everything I have said about an imploding literary culture, and about mutually-deafened communities who refuse to listen to each others' work. I find it difficult to be optimistic. Publishing houses are finding it even more difficult. Editors are losing their jobs, famous publishing houses are merging, or being closed down. A hundred and fifty books a day – who has time to read them? We are witnessing a split in American readership, between motivated, aggressive sub-groups with "designer" book-tastes, and those who are catered to by the large publishing houses with their built-in audiences for the off-the-rack generic titles. Occasionally, the big houses profit from a crossover surprise like Amy Tan's *Joy Luck Club* (immigrant) or Terry McMillan's *Learning to Exhale* (black, female), but for the most part the big houses ignore the specialized market, and the specialized market ignores them.

There are two or more literary markets in America. One is in New York, still churning out the titles and selling to the chain bookstores. The other is in dozens of towns and cities, selling through the mail or private bookstores. The era of the mass reading public is over (as much as I regret it), for I too was raised with the dream of a young author speaking for all America – Wolfe, Mailer, Kerouac, Hemingway, Fitzgerald, Saroyan – walking down the street and seeing his book piled in the bookstore window, beautiful women dropping their drinks when he entered the room, going to Paris, or living in New York on the proceeds of book sales alone.

All that is over. It belongs to myth. More than likely, he will go to Iowa, get a degree, and teach. His first book will not be followed by a second, at least not at the same publishing house, and not with the same editor. Maybe his editor will go to Iowa and get a degree. If he has earned a niche in the publishing world with a special appeal to a loyal sub-audience, he might survive to write a second or third book, for far less money with a much smaller press. Very, very few authors in America earn enough money through their writing to live solely from the work.

As for the mature reader, he or she is likely to find him/herself reading where he/she doesn't feel welcome, as though they'd wandered into a church where they're only vaguely aware of the pieties and rituals, listening to a sermon that doesn't really apply to their sins, or speak to their salvation. People around them are shouting "Hallelujah!" It seems disrespectful to leave. They drop a small contribution into the plate and sneak out. The old uniform Latin mass is dead; the universal Church is gone. We're in the age of a hundred vernaculars.

Some Thoughts on Canadian
and Australian Fiction

I LEARNED ONLY on arriving in Tokyo that Meiji University is a sister-school not only of the University of Iowa, where I currently teach, but of York University in Toronto, where I used to teach. I am doubly-related to Meiji, or, the world which I think of as uniquely my own already exists in the computer banks of Meiji. Many of you have probably taken the same trip I have taken, or will do so in the future.

The value of maintaining Canadian and American ties is readily apparent to you, whereas it is still considered frightening in North America. The struggles to pass NAFTA, the North American Free Trade Agreement, last year in the United States and three years before that in Canada exposed both countries to internal pressures that they had never before experienced. All three countries, including Mexico, had to ask themselves if they were psychologically prepared to admit the dreaded "other" to a kind of equality with themselves. For the modern Canadian, the Other is the American; for the American he is the Mexican, for the Mexican he is the generic Gringo, the Yanqui.

In earlier times, however, "the other" also has had an aboriginal component. Australian novels like Thomas Keneally's *The Chant of Jimmie Blacksmith* or David Malouf's *Remembering Babylon*, or Patrick White's *A Fringe of Leaves*, take the historic encounter between colonial culture and the Aboriginal Australian as their primary story. Canadian writing has far less to say about coming to terms with its native population – perhaps the best Canadian novel on Indian themes was done by the Irish-born Canadian,

Brian Moore, in *Black Robe*, which focuses on French-Jesuit conflicts with the Hurons in the seventeenth century. (To add to its
already burdened international pedigree, the book was successfully filmed by the Australian – naturally – director, Bruce
Beresford.) In general, portraits of Indians in Canadian writing are
sentimental, or comic, as in the case of W.P. Kinsella's stories, and
do not render the tragic story of the North American Indian with
the elegiac tone of a Faulkner, or the uncanny entry into sympathy
of the Australian. Of course there would be no Mexico, and no
Mexican literature, without the absolute integration of Indian and
Hispanic cultures.

Where Canadian writing has been historically eloquent is in
its treatment of the immigrant. Today, therefore, I'm going to con-
centrate on literary encounters between white and aboriginal in
Australia and between Anglo-Canadian and immigrant in Canada. All of the books I'm looking at are by contemporary authors,
but none of the books is set later than 1945, and most of them much
earlier than that.

Today's choice of topic – Canadian and Australian fiction – is
dictated by my two nationalities. I happen to be, or to have been, a
Canadian, although I have spent most of my life in the United
States. I might say that I have a sociological grip on American life,
and a psychological understanding of Canadian. For the past several years, I have concentrated my reading on books from the
so-called British Commonwealth of Africa, India, the Caribbean,
Australia, New Zealand, South Africa, and Canada.

I was born in the United States in 1940, on the Canadian border, but I didn't live for an extended period in Canada until I was
in my twenties. (I know the whole question of "borders" must
seem exotic to an island nation.) Canada was already at War in
1939, when my parents left. They'd wanted to save me. I spent
most of my childhood in the American Deep South in the 1940s –
Faulkner country – when the South was relatively unchanged from
the time of the Civil War eighty years earlier. Canada was the place

my French-speaking father never wanted to see again and my English-speaking mother would always call home. It did not exercise a great fascination over me.

Yet I realize that Canada was all over those small Southern apartments we lived in. It was in the British-style food we ate – crunchy, undercooked vegetables (in the South, vegetables are boiled until they are brown and soggy) and liver and kidney and tongue and heart, parts of the animal given in the South only for pet food, or used to bait a fishhook. Canada was in the progressive social and racial attitudes I was raised with by my socialist mother, so at odds with the vicious racism of the segregated Deep South. It was in the maps she hung on every wall, and memorization drills I put myself through, learning the world, collecting stamps, memorizing capitals and rivers and mountains with a kind of helpless absorptiveness.

I'm reminded of my own map-obsessed childhood every time I read Canadian writing. Here is Michael Ondaatje, early in his novel *In the Skin of a Lion*, describing the midnight passions of his nine-year-old hero, Patrick Lewis:

> He longs for the summer nights, for the moment when he turns out the lights, turns out even the small cream funnel in the hall near the room where his father sleeps. Then the house is in darkness except for the bright light in the kitchen. He sits down at the long table and looks into his school geography book with the maps of the world, the white sweep of currents, testing the names to himself, mouthing out the exotic. *Caspian. Nepal. Durango.* He closes the book and brushes it with his palms, feeling the texture of the pebbled cover and its coloured dyes which create a map of Canada.

I want to say, speaking as a Canadian, but not as an American, that I understand the chemistry by which maps become friends, how they speak, how maps take on personality. When I was a child, I lived in more than two places at once. I was living in central

Florida, in the town of Tavares, a place that tormented me, and I was living inside the radio that pumped baseball games from the North and radio dramas and comedies from Los Angeles and New York. I was living inside my stamp collection, and in the coins my mother had saved from pre-War Europe, where she'd been a student. I was living in the Canadian magazines we still received every month, with their long features on the British royal family. But most of all, I was living the Canadian life of intense *not-being*. I was memorizing lists of French and English kings, of Popes, of Holy Roman Emperors, Russian Czars, fish, birds, animals, baseball statistics, presidents, along with the most minute geography my mother's atlas could provide. My mother's old school atlas, which was the basis of all my geographical knowledge, had been published before World War I! In fact, it was probably the same school atlas that young Patrick Lewis was studying in 1920. It still contained maps of Austro-Hungary and of the Ottoman Empire.

By 1946, when I was six and beginning to learn the world through maps, the British Empire that lit up her atlas like the red neon glow of Tokyo was already vanishing. India would soon be gone, and the protectorates of Palestine and Cyprus and the Sudan, then South Africa and Nigeria and east Africa. I was learning the names, and the cabinet officials, of countries that had long disappeared, while her world still flared red with the British Empire, Green with France, Purple with Portugal. Parts of interior Africa, of Brazil and Australia and central Asia, were featureless plains marked "Unexplored." The southwest of the United States in her atlas still did not acknowledge the states of Oklahoma and New Mexico and Arizona – that was "Indian Country." China was still spotted with various western concessions.

Of course, they had been explored by 1946 – but I was holding a heavy, authoritative, Canadian book that said they hadn't! In her atlas, the past was still alive, and the present was long in the future. The present might never be. I was learning my mother's nineteenth-century world intact, a world she probably still lived by. Europe's Jews were still alive. The Russian Czar still sat on his throne. King Zog and King Michael and all sorts of improbable royalty still ruled the world. I had faith in the book, even as I knew its fallibility. But I preferred its assurance to the more accurate post-World War II maps that my mother took from *National Geographic* and tacked to my walls.

Now, I say this is an allegorical "Canadian" life, even though it was led in the most remote part of the United States. It is not just an introverted young American's life because of the prevalence of that same topus – maps, desperate knowledge about lives anywhere but here – in much Canadian writing: *Life is not here*, it teaches. *The past is still alive, it will always remain Indian Territory, or Unexplored. Be prepared for travel. When you grow up, if you have any ambition you'll be living under a different flag. It's more important to know their world, England or the States, than ours. They'll never learn ours anyway. Don't complain about it.*

One of the great ironic gifts of a Canadian sensibility is the sense of absurdity it carries with it. Canada would not exist except as a continuation of British institutions. Canada is best defined negatively, as that part of North American that is not Mexican, or American. It is the great Not-America. And once you begin to absorb the lesson of not-being in a not-country, you begin to understand the advantages of invisibility and the great charm of non-achievement. Canadians are therefore seen, by Americans (which, after all, is the only way they can be seen, since they cannot see themselves), as being just like Americans, only nicer. Americans consider being just like them a compliment. Toronto is seen as being just like Chicago (skyscrapers along a lake) but cleaner, and maybe forty years earlier. So not only do Canadians and Canada not exist, they are yet to be born – forty years, after all, is a long time ago.

For Americans, Canada is a vacation land. Its greatest charm is that it is a safer and cleaner version of the United States. A Canadian begins to understand early that he is a version of something else, or someone else, and while all the adjectives applied to him are both complimentary and condescending – nicer, cleaner, safer, quainter, simpler – this can only make him want to become nastier, dirtier, and more complicated. He yearns to be as nasty as the French and as dirty as the Americans, and as complicated as, say, the British. He'd love to be inscrutable.

This may seem a long preface to my topic, which is Canadian and Australian fiction, yet being part of a place and realizing that the place doesn't really exist in the eyes of the world, or never existed, or disappeared long ago, or exists only as an oddity or as an anachronism, suggests in part an ability of some writers from those two countries to insert themselves into times and places and consciousnesses that clearly are not their own. These authors are appropriators of foreign voices, alien countries, different skins, and they are, in the most serious sense of the word, time-travellers. If there are autobiographical elements in their own novels, I have not been able to detect them. Their experiences did not "authorize" them to write their lives.

Michael Ondaatje was born in Sri Lanka, of an old mixed-Tamil and Dutch Burgher family well established on the island. At least to this date, 1994, Ondaatje's fiction has not made use of his Sri Lankan background. He has written an entertaining and instructive memoir of his eccentric family, *Running in the Family*, almost as a foreclosure against using it for autobiographical fiction. As with many of the writers I have already discussed, and will mention today, he is a close friend of long standing. This should be kept in mind whenever Canadian writers talk of each other's work. We are all, in a sense, talking about ourselves. He came to Canada at the age of nineteen for university, and he has remained there ever since, living in eastern and western parts of Ontario and, for many years now, in Toronto.

I mention these autobiographical facts only to emphasize their total estrangement from his fiction. His first two novels, *The Collected Works of Billy the Kid* and *Coming Through Slaughter*, both deal with nineteenth- and early-twentieth-century American themes, characters, and settings: the frontier, and New Orleans jazz. The city of Toronto informs his third novel, *In the Skin of a Lion*, set in the 1920s and 1930s during the building of the water viaduct over the Don River, and the setting of the intake-pipe far out into Lake Erie. But to cite those engineering details is to misidentify the novel, like saying Hemingway is about bullfighting.

In the Skin of a Lion is one of the great immigration novels, about the Macedonians, Greeks, Finns, and Italians who built the viaduct, and it is about labour, and the misuse, abuse, and rebellion of labour. Mainly, however, it is about transformation: the physical transformation of a city, the metaphorical transformation of immigrants and therefore of the country, and the transformations of individual bodies and souls. And beyond that, I think Ondaatje is interested in continuity's support of transformation, the traits that survive the enormous upheavals of love, of madness, of violence, of war, and of an altered nature. In other words, he has an epic imagination.

In his next novel, the Booker Prize-winning *The English Patient*, the setting is World War II Italy, in a bombed-out villa north of Florence. At its centre is a burned, unidentifiable flyer whose identity is assumed to be English. Serving his needs is Hana, a twenty-year-old Canadian nurse. It is 1945, the war in Europe is nearly over. They are joined by two other survivors: an Italian-Canadian thief in his forties named Caravaggio, and a twenty-six-year-old Indian (Sikh) sapper, or bomb-deactivator. On a simple-minded political level, then, the heroic English aviator is helpless – scarred beyond recognition, but marvellously articulate, quoting Herodotus's *Histories*, evoking detailed memories of intricate paths through the desert, or artifacts and paintings in every Italian monastery and museum, and exquisitely painful memories of a love affair conducted just before the war with the wife of a young British explorer – and being cared for by a motley assortment of Commonwealth subjects. I suggest this "political" reading only to reject an absurdity: the book is not an allegory, and not political in any normal sense. The "English" patient, we learn, in fact, is not even English. If anything, *The English Patient* is a delicate sequel to *In the Skin of a Lion*, set just four years after the close of the first book. Hana (the nurse) is the daughter of Patrick – the boy who was reading the maps – and the thief Caravaggio was a family friend, all back in Toronto in the 1930s.

Ondaatje is a very careful assembler of facts. His books are steeped in obsessive reading about arcane subjects: turn-of-the-century New Orleans jazz and the Louisiana madhouses, Toronto engineering accomplishments and immigrant labour societies of the 1920s, bomb-removal manuals, Herodotus's *Histories*, Libyan Desert exploration of the 1930s and 1940s, and proceedings of the Royal Geographical Society. He is one of the great anti-auto-biographers currently writing fiction. And this, too, is a part of the Commonwealth literature I'm describing: communal biography replacing the author's autobiography. Henry James might well call it an unstable point of view. The point is, these authors have easy access to more than one mind; they have the confidence born of a more homogeneous society. We will see it again in the works of David Malouf and Thomas Keneally.

American fiction is rooted in conflict and confrontation. Its great scenes are those of crisis, violent encounters often ending in death. American literature seeks a definitive conclusion. (It's difficult imagining Ahab returning from the sea to take up a domestic life in retirement. Or Moby-Dick, seeing the odds were against him, deciding to sound at the crucial moment.) In Ondaatje's work, however, there is no such ending, or else, the ending that he provides is far more inclusive than anything I know in the U.S. At the close of *The English Patient*, for example, it is 1959, fourteen years after the end of the plot. The lovers, Hana and Kirpal Singh, have long separated and returned to their native countries, Canada and India. The Indian is now a doctor, he is married, with small children. I want to quote the last three paragraphs of the book, because they show, in ways I cannot, a deliberate fracturing of plot and expectation that most of us bring to a novel:

> During the evening meal he watches his daughter strug-
> gling with her cutlery, trying to hold the large weapons in her

small hands. At this table all of their hands are brown. They move with ease in their customs and habits. And his wife has taught them all a wild humour, which has been inherited by his son. He loves to see his son's wit in this house, how it surprises him constantly, going beyond even his and his wife's knowledge and humour – the way he treats dogs on the streets, imitating their stroll, their look. He loves the fact that this boy can almost guess the wishes of dogs from the variety of expressions at a dog's disposal.

And Hana moves possibly in the company that is not her choice. She, at even this age, thirty-four, has not found her own company, the ones she wanted. She is a woman of honour and smartness whose wild love leaves out luck, always taking risks, and there is something in her brow now that only she can recognize in a mirror. Ideal and idealistic in that shiny dark hair! People fall in love with her. She still remembers the lines of poems the Englishman read out loud to her from his commonplace book. She is a woman I don't know well enough to hold in my wing, if writers have wings, to harbour for the rest of my life.

And so Hana moves and her face turns and in a regret she lowers her hair. Her shoulder touches the edge of a cupboard and a glass dislodges. Kirpal's left hand swoops down and catches the dropped fork an inch from the floor and gently passes it into the fingers of his daughter, a wrinkle at the edge of his eyes behind his spectacles.

I feel that it's right to be presenting these ideas in a Japanese context, because there is something Haiku-like in the idea that the tipping of a glass, or the dropping of a fork, is the same as the shifting of continents, World War II and the Atomic Bomb, spies, exploration, heroic pain and sacrifice. All of the skills that young Kirpal Singh had learned, and the ideals he had put into practice, in saving thousands of British lives from unexploded Nazi bombs had been wiped out in one terrible event, and he'd returned to India, not gone on to Canada, to live his life, Yet, their lives are bound together in a single sentence, in her hair, in Canada, knocking over a glass, and he, at the same time on the other side of the world, catching his daughter's fork before it touches the floor.

Ondaatje's method of composition avoids plot, avoids confrontation. It is a very discreet, very quiet, perhaps very "Asian" way of organizing the events in people's lives. (We might note here a short list of other Asian-born authors bringing a different aesthetic to western traditions, like Kazuo Ishiguro, Salman Rushdie, and Bharati Mukherjee, all of whom have, in a brief time, climbed to the pinnacle of their adopted national literatures.) At the close of *In the Skin of a Lion*, for example, Patrick's long swim up the uptake pipe from Lake Erie, through the filtration system, laden with bombs for the purpose of blowing up the water works, is described with breathtaking accuracy. Yet when he gains entrance, and confronts the Chief Engineer, the man responsible for many workers' deaths in the execution of his ambitious plans, nothing happens. Patrick does not kill the engineer. He does not trigger the blast. The engineer does not shoot him, nor even arrest him. The rebel does not die, as he would almost have to in an American novel. (Gatsby does not return to North Dakota and open up a hardware store.) Everyone backs off. Patrick is allowed to leave, and then to enter, off-stage, *The English Patient*, and to die in a dovecot somewhere in France early in the War.

All of Ondaatje's books are strung together by vivid scenes, events linked in a wondrous chain of revelation, by vision, not by plot or character. A man stands up in the desert from a burning plane, his head on fire. A young Sikh deactivates a bomb hidden in a chalk horse. A statue of the Virgin rises from the sea. The Sistine Chapel is illuminated by kerosene lamp. A thief steals a camera from the bedroom of a Nazi making love to his mistress. A thief joins the nurse in the bombed-out villa, but they do not become lovers. The young Sikh joins them, and he and the nurse do become lovers, but there is no jealousy, no duels over the woman. It is not that kind of book.

It takes something very powerful to break up the nurse and her Indian lover – the most powerful thing in the world. Of all the wires in this book that can blow people and cities apart – because the book is about booby-trapped bombs and wires leading everywhere from innocent traps – it is the *wireless* that destroys their Eden. The news on the radio of the Atomic Bomb dropping on Japan realigns everyone. Suddenly, the Indian realizes he is Asian, his ideals have been betrayed. The Canadians are part of a new alliance with the Brits and Americans. The new world of racial and ethnic politics has dawned.

David Malouf is a poet, novelist, and librettist. His ancestry is Lebanese, though his family has been in Australia, Brisbane, for over 100 years. There is very little, overtly, to link his work to that of Michael Ondaatje except for the fact that both are poets as well as novelists, both explore realities that might be thought of as sociological, or historical, in order to strip them of documentation and restore them to a dream-like state of pure language.

Remembering Babylon, Malouf's latest novel, is set in Queensland in the 1840s. A Scottish settler family, the McIvors, stumble across a miraculous boy, Gemmy Fairlie (again, a historical character), a white boy raised by aboriginals. He barely remembers a few words of English, and, though white, is in all other ways – talents, knowledge, bush lore, body language, smell – aboriginal.

There is a long tradition of such writing in all cultures. In the United States, "captivity narratives" had long focused on white children kidnapped, or raised, by Indians. There is of course, Kipling's *Kim* and *The Jungle Book*, there is Faulkner's *Light in August*, and there is Malouf's earlier novel, *An Imaginary Life*, which restages the final years of the Latin poet Ovid, in exile on the shores of the Black Sea, being served by, and devoting himself to, a feral boy. But in *Remembering Babylon*, Malouf has gone a step further. The boy, Gemmy, is not really the focus. Malouf is interested in the legacy of Gemmy on the various McIvors, and on the community that will, inevitably, move to exclude him. Transformation and continuity, again. It is also part of the tradition of the "mixed-blood" narrative that there will be every shading of communal response to the presence of an unplaceable alien in their racially-structured midst. There will be religious tolerance, scientific curiosity, level-headed reason, and racist violence. Eventually, all intercessors will fail, for what is usually missing is love.

This is the case with Gemmy. But rather than using the case to indict racism in Australia, which it well could, Malouf's interest is clearly elsewhere. He is first of all investigating the power of language itself: "Could you lose it?" the settlers wonder, looking at Gemmy. "Not just language, but *it*. *It*." By which they mean whiteness, civilization as they know it. By which they mean something else entirely: if he, born a white boy, could lose it in the bush, could they?

What Malouf has done, in choosing an ancient story from Australian history, is to go back to the last moment when, as the narrator says,

> Most unnerving of all was the knowledge that, just three years back, the very patch of earth you were standing on had itself been on the other side of things, part of the unknown, and might still, for all your coming and going over it, and the sweat you had poured into its acre or two of ploughed earth, have the last of mystery upon it, in jungle brakes between paddocks and ferny places out of the sun. Good reason, that, for stripping it, as soon as you could manage, of every vestige of the native; for ringbarking and clearing and reducing it to what would make it, at last, just a bit like home.

"The other" and "the unknown" resonate with the same power as the nostalgically remembered "home" of England and Scotland. Malouf has rediscovered the moment of supreme energy in his country's saga, when the aboriginal world and the colonizing world stared at each other in mutual fear and horror. Within a few years, by the time of Gemmy's death, the decline of the aboriginal was already irreversible. There would be occasional uprisings (such as the one in 1900 described by Keneally in *The Chant of Jimmie Blacksmith*), but nothing that armed force would not eventually destroy.

While I've only had time to discuss, briefly, three novels, I want to cite a number of others from the shelf, if you wish, of English-language writing that draws upon the same sense of cultures in confrontation. In Chinua Achebe's *Arrow of God*, a Nigerian village headman is thrown in jail by British authorities for what they term cheekiness; he had gone to seek an explanation for a minor civil servant's having slapped his son. The old man languishes in jail, "to teach him a lesson," in the minds of the British. Meanwhile, because he, the headman, is not able to preside over a religious ceremony in his village, the life-sustaining yams are not planted. The village starves. He loses his position, the animist religion dies, and a Christian Missionary, trained in the British school, takes over spiritual authority. All because of a slap on the road.

In Timothy Findley's Canadian novel, *The Wars*, the subject is Canada's coming-of-age in World War I. It is a story that Canadian writers can tell because of the national trauma "The Great War" (my mother's atlas-war) had – far more than World War II – on an entire generation. World War I, for Canada and for Australia, was the unthinkable intrusion of the outer world on what had been a dream of isolation. Findley finds in the War madness and absurdity, but it is not the ironic farce of Joseph Heller's *Catch-22*, nor is it the stoic heroism of Hemingway. Findley's hero goes mad, frees the horses; there is nothing noble or redemptive in the experience, except – and this is the exception that links it to Malouf and to Ondaatje – while the soldier dies, his mother, his sister, the doctors and nurses who treated him live on. Findley's interest is transformation, and continuity. In the same way that an Indian doctor catches a falling fork from his daughter's hand, they have been touched, they have been transformed by one man's madness. The story rests with the community of survivors, not with the doomed individual.

Malouf's interest in the story of Gemmy is really an interest in the civilizing force of so-called savagery. It is the humour, the innocent knowledge of Gemmy that will in later life motivate all the McIvor children to take an extra caution with truth, with knowledge, even with love. Janet McIvor, who loved Gemmy most, withdraws from the world to become a nun and a keeper of, and student of, bees. She'd learned apian culture from Gemmy. Lachlan Beattie, the boy who first encountered Gemmy, becomes a minister of the crown, and, briefly, futilely, defends a German immigrant in World War I deported on trumped-up espionage charges. In the great matters of state, perhaps, nothing too extraordinary. But without the example of Gemmy, there would have been nothing at all.

The fate of Gemmy is left for the final pages, stuck off in a corner of the narrative, in a distant memory of the now-old Lachlan Beattie. He remembers:

> It involved a 'dispersal' six years before by a group of cattlemen and two native troopers, too slight an affair to be called a massacre, and no newspaper had got hold of it. The blacks had been ridden down and brought to earth by blows from a stirrup iron at the end of a stirrup leather – an effective weapon, when used at a gallop, for smashing skulls. The remnants of the clan, including the young woman who gave him his facts, had scattered and been absorbed into a larger group. The bones of the victims, eight or nine in all, men, women, two small children, they had carried with them and disposed of in the usual way, in parcels in the forks of trees.
>
> The story already had elements in common with others he had heard up here, which when he tried to track them down had proved elusive. Perhaps they were all one story. Whether this one had happened, as the woman claimed, six years ago in her own lifetime, or in her mother's, or last year, it had

been gathered now into the dreamtime of the land itself, a shadowy realm where the bones of facts had already drawn around them the skin of rocks, of beasts, of air.

What have we, then, in this brief selection of Canadian and Australian novels? A different sense of history and of community, I feel, a different narrative possibility from that which drives American fiction. No less prejudiced to outsiders, no less narrow-minded, but more reluctant to use violence to solve its problems, and with a longer communal memory. The authorities, be they members of parliament, soldiers, or chief-engineers, turn out not to be scoundrels; rebels and outsiders are not necessarily major heroes. In many ways, the equivocal nature of heroism, which is under study in all three of these books, is also what motivated Thomas Keneally to take up the convoluted character of Oskar Schindler in *Schindler's List*. It is extraordinary, but I hope understandable, that an Australian Catholic like Keneally would be the man to bring that essentially Jewish and European story to life.

The authors looked at today (and I have been forced by time-constraint to ignore Thomas Keneally's *The Chant of Jimmie Black-smith*, his evocation of, and reflection upon, an aboriginal uprising in 1900, and to do no more than mention his world bestseller, *Schindler's List*) build their narratives around history as opposed to autobiography, around group consciousness rather than the individual. They rush to occupy with sensuality and imagery the vacuum of history and of landscape that they had perhaps once encountered on maps or in the blank unexplored area that was their national consciousness.

Of course there are exceptions to everything I've just said, and I'm well aware of the traps that await any critic who would attempt anything so dated as national thematics. Terms like "Canadian," "Australian," or "American" are never binding or proscriptive, any more than Murakami and Mishima might be linked because of the accident of a common nationality. The work, for example, of two prominent Canadian writers, Margaret Atwood and Alice Munro, is at times strikingly autobiographical and ahistorical.

What I've taken you through is a reading of two authors, Michael Ondaatje and David Malouf, who, I feel, have tried to take us to a place in their history when things could have turned out differently, to "being," as Malouf writes, "in a place that had not revealed all its influences upon them," when alien forces confronted one another and briefly held the power to destroy one another once and for all. We know of course how tragically history turned out. But these authors show a time when for some reason the forces of instant destruction turned their backs instead.

Portrait of the Artist as a Young Pup

M ONTREAL HAS a certain genius for spawning poetic move-ments – from poets like A.J.M. Smith, Frank Scott, and A.M. Klein in the 1920s, down through Louis Dudek and Irving Layton a poetic generation later. And while individual novelists had always existed there – Hugh MacLennan, John Glassco, Brian Moore, and Leonard Cohen – it was my privilege to be associated with the only conscious *gathering* of English language Montreal prose writers in the century.

Time and doctoral dissertations seem to bestow inevitability and distinctive colouration to such groups, as though internal affinity accounts for literary alliance. We were five prose writers in the same city at the same time; we had similar critical standards and very different literary tastes. And in late 1970, under the guidance of John Metcalf and Hugh Hood, we – Hood and Metcalf, Raymond Fraser and Ray Smith and myself – became The Montreal Story Teller Fiction Performance Group. We're now a footnote in the larger history of Canadian literature, but we rate a few paragraphs in the history of contemporary Canadian fiction. The Story Teller is yet another instance of synchronicity and serendipity at work: contemporary Canadian literature was just being born; and we were in a time and place, and possessed the energy and vision, to assist in its delivery.

Montreal is a cultured city with many writers. The problem, in those first few years, was with me. The only young writer I knew in town was Jerry (C.J.) Newman. Hood was around, of course, but teaching in another world, l'Université de Montréal. I'd been writing in a vacuum, except for Jerry's critiques, and nearly all the stories I was publishing – despite their Canadian setting – were still being placed in the United States. Nevertheless, I felt hurt and resentful when John Metcalf, another local story-writer I'd never met, published the first significant anthology of new writing – *Sixteen by Twelve* – and left me out.

(How a pompous young pup can howl!)

I was still discovering the city, or, more precisely, discovering parts of myself opened up by the city. I was respectful if not worshipful of all its institutions. I defended its quirks and inconsistencies as though defending myself against abuse; I was even charmed by things I would have petitioned against in Milwaukee like separate Catholic and Protestant schools, Sunday closing, and male-only bars. "The Frencher the Better" was my motto to cover any encroachment on the aboriginal rights of the English.

I was writing very openly, in the late sixties, of Montreal. The city was drenched with significance for me – it was one of those perfect times when every block I walked yielded an image, when images clustered with their own internal logic into insistent stories. A new kind of unforced, virtually transcribed story (new for me, at least) was begging to be written – stories like "A Class of New Canadians," "Eyes," "Words for the Winter," "Extractions and Contractions," "Going to India," and "At the Lake" were all written in one sitting, practically without revision. I'd never been so open to story, so avid for context. I was reading all the Canadian literature I could get my hands on, reading Canadian exclusively; there was half a continent out there to discover. My literary community was more on the page than in the flesh. Jerry Newman, George Bowering for a few years, Margaret Atwood for one year, and the poetry readings at Sir George Williams and the parties after them – those were my only contacts with the raucous, boozy, quick-witted writing life I'd known, and depended on, at Iowa.

Those, then, are the pre-Story Teller facts. I knew of Metcalf from the Clarke, Irwin 1969 volume of *New Canadian Writing*. (He'd appeared with Jerry Newman and Doug Spettigue; I'd appeared a year earlier in the same series with Dave Godfrey and David Lewis Stein.) Of course I knew Hugh Hood's work – he went all the way back to my Iowa days when I'd read *Flying a Red Kite* in Dave Godfrey's hand-me-down review copy. Ray Smith I knew through his "Cape Breton is the Thought-Control Centre of Canada" story in *The Tamarack Review* – one of the breakthrough stories in our writing. I particularly remembered it because until its appearance I'd thought my *Tamarack* story "The Mayor" (later retitled "The Fabulous Eddie Brewster") was a shoo-in for The University of Western Ontario President's Medal as best Canadian story of the year. That "The Mayor" actually *did* win is a testimony to the innate conservatism of the judging process.

I know how this must read: I was a posturing little pup – a typical product of American alienation, mixed with Canadian sentimentality. (The portrait of Norman Dyer in "A Class of New Canadians" is my own ironic self-portrait.) I considered myself an heir to the Two Solitudes, the uncrowned princeling fated to write the books, discover the new talent, script the movies, teach the secrets, that would move Canadian literature to the cutting edge of the world's consciousness. Canada's duty was to exploit its twin heritage of English and French, its twin tensions of America and Britain. I was ambitious, ruthless, selfish, vain, and arrogant. I was also hard-working, observant, anxious to learn, and even humble.

Then Metcalf called. How he got my name, I never asked. He mentioned the group: himself (whom I resented), Smith (whom I feared), Hood (whom I admired) and Ray Fraser (whom I didn't know). None of us, I suspect, knew that Literary History was knocking – the moment when one's lonely individual efforts have suddenly passed a critical mass and begun to set off other writers' alarms.

Our purpose was admirably eleemosynary. We would charge two hundred dollars a performance – forty dollars apiece. Twice the amount paid by *The Fiddlehead* for my stories "Eyes," "A Class of New Canadians," and "Words for the Winter." The Protestants wouldn't have us. (I had assumed, until reading the full story in Metcalf's "Telling Tales," that the Protestants had rejected us because Hugh was so dreadfully Catholic.) But the island was even richer in Catholic schools, and they were agreeable to trying us out.

Money, then, was the first goal. Hugh, as a matter of principle (everything with Hugh is a matter of principle), insists on top dollar for any creative work. John and the two Rays were living hand-to-mouth as freelancers. Ray Fraser epitomized the word, and the consequences, of "freelancing." He raised it to an art while writing characteristically Fraseresque stories for the local tabloid, *Midnight*, in the Maritime tall tale genre touched with a bit of the Montreal macabre: DAD RAPES INFANT SON; SERVES HIM FOR DINNER.

Our second goal was a bit more combative. John was tired of the bloody poets getting all the readings and recognition. It seemed to us that the league of warblers had enjoyed their monopoly on the stages of the country quite long enough. Prose was intrinsically more interesting and easy to follow than poetry. There was no reason why stories, if limited to fifteen minutes, should not move, delight, and instruct any audience – and still not betray our own high standards. This, it seemed to me, was a battle worth joining.

The third, and most altruistic, goal was to prove something to, and for, Canada. John had taught in the high schools and knew the attitudes of the boards and most of the teachers. Chesterton and Kipling as moderns. Morley Callaghan or Hugh Garner thrown in just so the students could thrill to seeing descriptions of familiar Toronto landmarks in print. Just think what *we* could do – living, young, funny, sexy, bold, dirty, Montreal writers. We'd begin that great reaming out, the great scouring of all those corroded pipes. We'd have the rarest of all literary privileges – that of creating our audience.

I remember those drives through unfamiliar but very Catholic parts of the island – a jolly band of prose-troubadours in my car, or Hugh's. We were a hit from the beginning; I couldn't understand it. The bookings were coming three and sometimes four times a week. Every now and then I'd wince at our collective arrogance, inflicting all this shameless puffery, this elevating slobber, on immigrant youngsters whose English needs were for something more rudimentary and whose experience of literature was utterly virginal. And a second later I'd think (like the appalling Norman Dyer) what a splendid, noble thing we were doing. Those kids were our perfect audience, uncorrupted by ghastly good taste, analogues to our purest intentions. Didn't we want to communicate the real, the actual, the tangible *montréalitude*? Didn't we want to present ourselves as serious writers who were also living, imperfect Montreal presences? Didn't we pride ourselves on the accessibility of our stories, that anyone could appreciate them? Our proudest boast was that unlike Chesterton or Belloc or who-ever-the-hell, *we were in the phonebook*! Look us up, call us, talk to us. We drink, we fart, we get horny, we make fools of ourselves, our lives are usually in a mess, we're afraid of cops and taxes, and we're not ashamed to show it. Like kindergarten kids with finger paints, we wallow in it! We make art of it!

In a typical reading, John and I did two voices from a segment of his novel *Going Down Slow*, in which a high-school teacher is so drunk, rude, and honest that he gets thrown out of a bar. I then read my story "Eyes," about a man who watches Greek butchers popping calf testicles in their mouths, and sucking. Big Ray Smith read a chapter from *Lord Nelson Tavern*, a monologue on the pathos of having been a tall girl in the cutie-pie fifties, with such intensity that he ended up in tears while the audience laughed. Hugh's "Socks" was about an immigrant from southern Italy who ends up working on snow removal in wet socks. And there was Ray Fraser's unpredictable and never-repeated routine, tall tales of mounting disgust, teetering over a pit (one suspected) of imminent intervention from a hardly-amused administration.

Despite all that (and of course because of it) we became legitimate. We grew out of the ghetto of Catholic schools, to the junior colleges and university classrooms. We were featured in the second issue of the *Journal of Canadian Fiction*. (My two tales in that issue, "Is Oakland Drowning?" and "The Voice of the Elephant," were inspired purely by our ensemble readings, the need for levity, brevity, and surreality. I wanted to be as precise as Metcalf, as witty as Smith, as various as Hood, as irreverent as Fraser.) We read at the conventions of the Protestant teachers. We popped up in Fredericton, Saint John, and Ottawa. We got to be polished, convincing, and even successful in all three of our initial goals.

We were clearly an idea whose time had come. We were a new generation of Canadian fiction, arriving all at once, in all parts of the country. The first book of the movement was Hugh Hood's *Flying a Red Kite*, then Alice Munro's *Dance of the Happy Shades*. There were the two Clarke, Irwin collections, plus the early House of Anansi books – collections by Dave Godfrey and Ray Smith. Peggy Atwood was busy revising *The Edible Woman* during her year at Sir George Williams. Jerry Newman wrote *A Russian Novel*. Then came *Sixteen by Twelve,* the first national collection. Then the Story Teller, the first national performance group in fiction.

We were, however, a group very much of our time and place and class-interests: no French, no women, no unseemly minorities. When I think of our work – as distinguished from Alice Munro's, for example – I see a line of continuity with the typical French language Montreal *conte*. Our work had a similarity to that of Carrier, Vigneault, Ferron, and Tremblay, though we in no way consciously emulated them. (Carrier and I have both written about hockey sweaters.) It was merely that the structures we accepted – a dramatic appeal to a tangible audience, a firm sense of place and voice and readership, a political and aesthetic intention – differed from those of the printed page. We were performers. We were moving toward compression. We have all written long prose fictions by now, but I wouldn't call any of us as successful in the novel as we have been in our stories. It took me an inordinately long time to write my first novel (if indeed I ever have); John (I suspect) is most at home in the novella form, and what can any of us say about Hugh Hood's giant opus? It seems to me he is writing *one* enormous novel, not twelve separate ones. Or that *The New Age* is the world's longest short-story collection.

(I should acknowledge here the influence of Hugh on my work. His ease of delivery, the way he wraps allegorical signifi-cance around the keenly-observed realistic core, the variety of his styles and voices, left me feeling one-dimensional. It was Hugh who offered the title for, and could easily have written, "He Raises Me Up"; and it was with Hugh in mind that I attempted my own "Socks"-like casual memoir, "I'm Dreaming of Rocket Richard.")

The Story Teller is now a part of Canadian literary history. For me, it was the public manifestation of inner maturing. I learned in the group that I still needed an ensemble; despite my immodest flights of fancy, I wasn't yet ready to stand alone. I always had the sense that of the five, I was the one the audience hadn't heard of, and I was the one they had to endure after the famous Hugh Hood and the sexy Ray Smith and the satiric John Metcalf and the whack-o Ray Fraser. So I learned to tame myself, to wait.

We are now at the age of the rock stars of the sixties; we've had to change, or run the risk of becoming absurd. The easy work is all behind us – that fire and passion – but I have to feel our best work is yet to come. We're a little too grey and cranky to give collective readings. We've already proven that prose readings are interesting and profitable; we've succeeded in stuffing Canadian literature into most crannies in the curriculum. But, I fear, we've lived to demonstrate the applicability of Murphy's Law to literary fund-ing. Official money and government money will drive out private money. Bureaucracy will replace individual choice and initiative. The magic, the sense of occasion, the mystery of having a writer in your presence, of words made flesh – that is now taken from our students. The budget for such an extravaganza has all been lost. In the way of benevolent bureaucracies, everyone gets something – a lot *less* of something – and the intangibles that provided a context, and much of the authentic pleasure, have disappeared.

We have lived to see a dangerous corollary to our hardest-won battles. It goes like this: if you're in the phonebook and if you give readings, let's call you up and ask you to read. I've had calls from high-school teachers a thousand miles away, asking if I wouldn't mind flying out and addressing a tenth-grade class. I've been at Canada Day and I've had my ticket punched down at Harbour-front in Toronto. Right now, in the fall of 1983, on my first long trip back to Canada in three years, I'm being allowed to give more than my upper limit of eight "senior" Canada Council supported readings. I enjoy it. It's part of the whole fabric of Canadian life; it's what I dreamed; it's the literary equivalent of the CBC's own national mandate. But.

But this. Thirteen years ago our Sir George Williams poetry series had an equal mix of Canadian and American poets; now (I'll wager), if it has a series, the writers are all domestic. Very few colleges in Canada have anything but Canadian readings. We've all been everywhere, usually more than once. We used to have a two thousand dollar budget for our readings; we even budgeted our after-reading parties at seventy-five dollars for booze, breads, and meats. I remember the big pre-reading dinners at the best restaurants, and I remember the packed auditorium. I realize times have changed. I'd forgo the big dinner and the catered party. But I fear now no one would really *care* to eat with the writer or go to a party after his performance. The "less is more" philosophy does not work at all in the matter of public readings.

This year I'm giving my readings at one o'clock in the afternoon, in classrooms. At many, with no lunch, no announcements, no audience. I remember the weeks it used to take, designing posters, arguing over layouts, cajoling for colours, picking them up at a printer's, and then distributing them to Montreal's bookstores and cafés. Now there is a Xeroxed nine-by-twelve sheet of typing paper with a Magic-Marker announcement of my reading, taped to the door and pinned to a cluttered bulletin board. There are thirty students for my reading – the same attendance as the regular class. It *is* the regular class. The last well-attended reading I've given, significantly, was not at a university, but at the Jewish Public Library in Montreal. What does it all mean? Simply that the general public will no longer come out at night for a Canadian reading.

And, I fear, we suffer too much exposure of too much Canadian talent. Alice Munro is an estimable writer and probably only second to Mavis Gallant as a writer of prose, but it's wrong that she alone should be the model for all short story writing by women in this country. When I teach writing in Canada all I need are her books, Atwood's novels, and maybe works by one of two others (Kroetsch or Wiebe) depending on the region. There's something wrong when a Chinese-Canadian woman has never heard of Maxine Hong Kingston, or, perhaps even worse, when a Jewish-Canadian woman concerned with her background has not plunged beyond the sensibility of Mordecai Richler because she has not discovered the larger world of Jewish *women* writers.

I once had the bizarre experience of being told that I could fly Audrey Thomas – a writer I admire greatly – to Montreal from Vancouver at Canada Council expense, but couldn't offer John Gardner a fifty-dollar busfare from Bennington, Vermont. By that time, you see, Sir George Williams had given up its private budget for other exigencies, and the Canada Council was picking up the tabs, and the Canada Council cannot fund anyone from outside of Canada.

Good sense and maturity will eventually triumph. Excess is never a cure for deficiency, and a less-charged time will permit both generosity and cosmopolitanism. Our little revolution of the sixties needs to be protected from too much success. Canadian literature should not substitute for world literature. We need to redirect a fraction of the honoraria and travel expenses now paid to keep a hundred or more Canadian poets and fiction writers constantly airborne, and give it to the dozens of world-stature authors out there in Europe, Asia, the Caribbean, Latin America, and the United States who would be excited by the prospect of reading in Canada and instructing our students. Otherwise, our little revolution will die of boredom.

This page intentionally left blank

Notes on the 'Canadian' Short Story

1. At Home in All Voices: Leon Rooke

YOU REMEMBER the old Storyland Limited? Half an hour, there and back. Little stops along the way, quaint stations, scenery like a picture postcard, friendly passengers, velvet banquettes, polished mahogany trim. Redcaps always helpful, conductors who knew their business, announcing the stops in plenty of time, taking your elbow as you edged out the door – remember that? You felt good after every trip, relaxed, respected.

Then the Twentieth-Century Express roared into town. They cut the staff, ripped out the upholstery and left a blind old man in blue rags behind, who cursed as he punched the tickets. No more porters. No more little stops. Washed-out scenery too – just the backs of tenements where, approximately, lonely men in shirt sleeves flicked the butts of loosely-rolled cigarettes into the dust swirls left by retreating winter ice, exposing the brownish clumps of dying grass feebly fed by the anemic turds of sullen pets.

After the bankruptcy came the Great Reorganization. Sleek wagons of vinyl and plastic – amazing what they can do with old cattle cars. But confusion reigns. Computers prove whimsical. So many conductors, so many uniforms. Sometimes they help, mostly they babble snatches of poetry and philosophy mixed with lyrics of old dog food commercials. You've got to be sharp to make any sense at all. I end up taking tickets or wearing a red cap and *shlepping* (how did I even learn that word?) heavy bags. No one knows where we are, or the names of towns. Acrylic posters block the windows. The ticket destination reads only: THERE.

Which brings me, approximately, to Leon Rooke, at home in all conventions, in all uniforms, all voices. Twenty-one stories are reprinted in Oberon Press's *The Love Parlour* and Fiction Collective's *The Broad Back of the Angel* (both published in 1977); with inevitable overlaps the thirteen stories in the Fiction Collective selection reduce to ten not available in the Oberon Press selection. *The Love Parlour* has a "modern" bias; *The Broad Back of the Angel* is more "postmodern," a little zingier, and more American in feel. If you like Leonard Michaels, Max Apple, some of Russell Banks, some Barth and Barthelme, give the Fiction Collective selection a try. Both are bargains.

I'm slightly biased towards the Oberon selection. I'm predisposed, as is Rooke's friend and selector-of-stories, John Metcalf, to the ominous landscape, the single apt detail ("The sun, obscured though it might be, was hot on the side of her face and a fly was crawling on her neck – or perhaps it was sweat."), and I like the voice of untethered consciousness as it shuffles and deals – I like those things more than incessant wit and parody. (The three "Magician" stories and the two "Friendship" stories in the Fiction Collective selection are sometimes funny but I didn't reread them. Clear them away and there's still more honest *fiction* than you're likely to encounter in any book of stories currently on the market.) The Oberon selection, by contrast, has only one story I'd remove – "If Lost Return to the Swiss Arms" – which, despite its O. Henry Award some years back, seems to have been conceived in a pre-modern idiom. The rest of the book is gold.

I'm much taken with the Mexican-set "For Love of – " (" – Madeline, Eleanor, and Gómez") series of stories and Oberon reprints all three. With the Fiction Collective selection you get only two panels of what is obviously a triptych: two of the three is a mutilation. Fiction Collective, however, will give you a scary, deadpan gem called "Wintering in Victoria," which is available in Canada only in an Oberon annual. It should be permanently gathered in this country, with the best of his work.

Even as it stands, I judge the Oberon collection of Rooke's short fiction to be the most technically accomplished, most perfectly realized, and easily the most psychologically sophisticated ever published in Canada. I only wish Oberon had a way of distinguishing this book from the dozens of drab, perfunctory efforts they've published in the past. And should a Fiction Collective editor be reading this, it's only fair to point out that he/she did something far worse: in "Dangerous Women" (known as "Call Me Belladonna" in Canada) a character's perfectly reasonable allusion to Watergate ("Here it was 1973 . . .") has been . . . what, freshened? . . . to "Here it was 1977 . . ." thus transforming a sluggard into a catatonic.

What should be emphasized is this: in both collections there is more than one masterpiece. Fiction Collective's title story would qualify, plus "Wintering in Victoria"; Oberon's little volume is a feast. "If You Love Me Meet Me There" and "Memoirs of a Cross-Country Man" are so intense, so perfectly implanted as *voice* (postmodernism's victory over modernism) as to be unparaphrasable.

One doesn't "enter" such stories in the conventional sense. Instead, they enter you.

2. Reading John Metcalf

YOU CAN READ a collection of stories as you might a novel – only more so. The hero will have a dozen names and faces (or eight, in the case of *Standing Stones*) instead of one, and multiple traumas of birth and growing up. Like all mythic heroes, he is something of a self-made man; he realizes early he is not destined to stay where he was born or to accept the definitions that birth placed upon him. He defies his origins, which are mendacious and mincing. His earthly parents and their gods are abandoned early; he seeks new masters. They steal, they drink, and they burn. Even in prison their freedom is alluring, a freedom that blasphemes the system. He yearns to violate standards he already despises, to get a tattoo, to behave irresponsibly, to get roaring drunk, sleep in and bail out. Throbbing American jazz and joyless English Methodism intersect in bluesy ways.

Montreal seems inevitable.

He can't rebel, of course, not then, or there – not in an England so spiritually crimped, so grim and War-pocked. If he stays, he's more likely to stew in his juices than subvert the system. He's not yet heard the Flaubertian advice to write like the devil but live like a bourgeois. From that agonized compromise, in fact, he will construct his life's body of work, but it will take a few moltings before getting there.

So far, the formula sounds familiar. Most anyone born into genteel poverty, castrating repression, and Non-Conformist orthodoxy (the worst kind) will worship at the shrine of alternate gods. Why do Catholics in general, American Southerners, and British Protestants in particular – at least those who survive – make such good writers? They carry the memories, the smell of the censer, the biscuit tins and flowered wallpaper, and their scabbarded antidote – the language (and, in the case of Britain, the paintbrush as well) to confront it.

Our hero will be married here, divorced there, sometimes at rest but usually in need. He was born here, or over there, he has a few children, or none, boys or girls, and he has had wives and girlfriends and years alone wondering if there will ever be marriage again. He finds her; she dies. She finds him; he escapes.

Heroes change continents but never leave home. They remain in their core connoisseurs of small, private spaces, the oxymorons of triumphant disappointment. Their heroes are scourges of bad food, spiritual poverty, hypocrisy, tarnished language, and fraudulent claims. Even at their lowest, they will not yield to tasteless convenience. From multifarious assaults on their dignity they construct their prayers: Dear Lord, never let me forget. Give me the strength of memory, do not take from me the shank of shame, the wrath, the small triumphs, the secret victories, the glossary of vindication.

John Metcalf's work is a jeweller's art. Of course he loves the short story (and has done more for its celebration and preservation than anyone in Canada). Of course, his own potential novels are distilled into long stories, like "Polly Ongle," "Private Parts," and "Girl in Gingham." Unlike Rupert Brooke, he *is* "magnificently prepared for the long littleness of life."

Metcalf worships. He just had to find *his* church.

His worship is the deployment of language, the meticulous placement of words. In the honourable tradition of British empiricism, he is suspicious of all grandiloquence, all theories leading to grand synthesis. Fraud reveals itself in flaccid language; flaccidness inflates to cant and bombast. Or, as Yeats put it, "Words alone are certain good." Words arranged as paragraphs, paragraphs shrunk to single words. He reminds me of a friend who once declared, "How hard it is to find something *plain*!" Plain is honest. Plain is good.

Words deployed like cut diamonds on black velvet trays.

Metcalf's worship asks us not to look to the altar or attend to the preacher. It directs us, rather, to the stained glass, the slants of colour and arrangement of shards separated by lead as though they were (and are) radioactive. A word like "dottle," say – crumbs of tobacco dribbling from a pipe onto a vest or jacket – evokes (for me, at least) a vanished, cloistered, unselfconscious eccentricity, a pre-industrial, cottage-bound, self-contained life; who ever knew it? A pre-*Depend*, pre-*Shout*, pre-*Nicoban* world. When "dottle" vanishes, so does a shelf of history; so does a wondrous life-form. Where else but here have I ever read it?

What separates Metcalf from nearly any stylist I know is that his "new" words are *old*. They relate to worlds that were; they are the rivets that align the visible with the remembered. No neologisms, no linguistic stretch marks.

You wouldn't know it, revisiting the miseries of bachelorhood and marginal employment in 1960s and 1970s anglophone Montreal as presented in these stories, but those were magic times in that city and John Metcalf is their guide. The Québécois barely exist; the exotics are more likely to be Jews. One problem we young writers in Montreal faced in those years was our ambition to scoop it all up, to get it all in, against the ribbed crabbiness of the genre itself. The models of our beloved form were derived from Chekhov and Joyce and Hemingway, but the scope of our ambitions was novelistic at the very least. We were all packing for the long trip. Palpable and teeming, that was the life we knew and saw. A French-language novel of that same era, Réjean Ducharme's *L'avalée des avalés* (*The Swallower Swallowed*), captures that thirst. In English, only Hugh Hood with his twelve-volume *roman fleuve*, his collected stories, and *Around the Mountain* managed to get it all in, the old-fashioned way. Metcalf was luckier than most of us. My model was Faulkner, but rattling around in the back of *his* head was the entire British literary canon, Milton to Wodehouse, Leavis and Connolly and the Angry Young Men.

Especially Wodehouse. What delicious sentences!

We can still revel in the echo of those decades. Alice Munro, a frequent visitor to Montreal in those years, and John Metcalf are the prime saboteurs of the conventional short story in Canadian writing. Time and again, their stories seem to end, that is, to approach the formal end of what could be a normal story but the narrative voice won't let go. The voice still pleads for new understanding, for forgiveness and one more chance to get it right. It's the voice, not the form, that *is* the story. It's the voice that kidnaps the ending, that violates and compromises all that is neat and expected. "Polly Ongle" ends in Metcalf's longest sustained monologue, an address to the statue of José de San Martin in an Ottawa park. "Single Gents Only" concludes with a reading of *The Wind in the Willows* to a drunken roommate in a cold room under dreadful wallpaper. Or, most nakedly (without giving away the concluding sentences), at the close of "The Eastmill Reception Centre":

> You don't understand, do you, what it means for me to make these confessions? To *have* to make these confessions, to face the death I feel inside myself?

Let me try to put this in a different way. Let me try to find words that perhaps you'll understand. Words! Understand! Good Christ, will it never end, this blathering!

It's the voice endlessly reflecting on the defects of its own storytelling, pulling it out from the fire while it's still plastic, as a glassblower or smith might, reshaping it before it hardens. There are writers who prefer the oblong, the slightly wobbly, the plain and honest if not quite perfect, and . . . well, the *dottled*. The voice is never satisfied, it carries the story forward, or laterally, or backward at the last moment. The narrative is like a river plodding its way to the sea and the story-form is the ancient riverbed it effortlessly follows. But when the burden of meaning is too great, the voice punches out a new channel and the story spreads to become a delta.

You float down the river and come out in a different place, in a different time.

3. A Stunning Glare: Alice Munro

FOR MORE THAN fifty years, the stories of Alice Munro have been appearing, first in Canadian periodicals, then in *The New Yorker* and other prominent American magazines, and gathered in twelve generous collections. Her work has been translated into numerous languages. The most recent collections are *The View from Castle Rock* (2006), *Runaway* (2004), and (my choice for closer inspection) *Hateship, Friendship, Courtship, Loveship, Marriage* (2001).

Her artistic home is in a form honoured by literary history and loved by its practitioners, but often ignored or indulged by commercial and critical interests. She has never written in any form other than short fiction (despite her publisher's early attempt to market the linked stories of *Lives of Girls and Women* as a novel); she has kept the form evolving, much in the way that John Cheever and Ann Beattie did in the 1970s and Raymond Carver in the 1980s. There are truths that get lost inside a novel.

I'm reluctant to call the typical late-phase Munro product a "short story" since it departs, often radically, from the defining characteristics of the genre as handed down to us by Chekhov, Joyce, Hemingway, and so many others. Pick up nearly any story in a literary magazine, or nearly any well-received collection, and the contrast with Munro is immediately apparent. They lack her sense of lived-in naturalness. They seem forced, programmed. Most stories labour at the outset to establish their reality; most ground the reader in a fully realized setting and introduce characters in a timely fashion. There are no authorial intrusions, no violations of point of view. Flashbacks will be introduced sparingly, and flash-forwards not at all. In most stories, something is hidden and must be revealed; once exposed (the so-called epiphany), the story is over.

Munro breaks all the rules. She does not trade in orderly precision; there are profusions of characters. It's difficult, at times, to know exactly *whom* the story is about. In fact, I would say Munro's great achievement is to free us from the very questions of "whom" or "what" the story is "about." Like life itself, her stories are about the shadows at play *between* characters and events. "Floating Bridge" moves through a series of epiphanies, leading a character from anger to compassion, death's door to a renewed sense of adventure, for the time remaining. In the title story, the linkages between the girls' nasty pranks, old Mr. McCauley's anger, the peregrinations of Ken Boudreau and the determined, redemptive figure of Johanna Parry manage to encapsulate the entirety of human longing. It's a small-town-Ontario *Casablanca*. Nearly any detail one might choose to isolate is as "important" as any other. (In yet another story, she can endow a term like "post and beam," an architectural style, with moral ferocity.) Minor characters, off-stage, might deliver the clinching verdict, as in the Latin quotation that finishes the title story. A Munro story like "Hateship, Friendship, Courtship, Loveship, Marriage" can have multiple heroes, many endings, and quite a few beginnings. Her stories engulf the reader; they open casually and build with apparent randomness, sliding backward from present action, or leaping to future visions.

These stories are longer than "short" stories, some verge on being novellas, but I think the word that most defines her form, particularly in later years, is "the long story" like Flaubert's "Un coeur simple." (In fact, the Flaubert story is a fair model for many of Munro's: an easily overlooked central character, an odd angle on history and power, a modest setting, plain people with a stubborn resistance to glamour who nevertheless exert a steady, mysterious presence.)

An eruption from plainness – "a stunning glare" – (as she describes an ordinary Ontario August day), I would say, marks her style. Her plots, settings, and characters all seem at first glance "plain," reflecting a Protestant suspicion of ostentation. The tight social strata of Southwestern Ontario and Vancouver-suburban British Columbia are delineated with all the care of a late-born Jane Austen: country people, town people, city people, educated or not, artistic or not. Yet, all characters are extraordinarily endowed with the ability to surprise, even to astound. While there's a communal disapproval of too much finery, underneath, even solid citizens yearn to experience the radiant, or the forbidden. And for the most part, they do. There's as much adultery in Munro's stories as in any modern writer's, but the adultery is rarely planned, and never harshly judged. It's part of life, yet another inexplicable gift to be factored in.

There are now so many Munro titles (individual and collective) that readers are bound to have personal favourites. The general quality of her work is so distinctive, however, that one's stated preference is likely to appear entirely subjective.

This page intentionally left blank

How Stories Mean

1. To Begin, To Begin

> Endings are elusive, middles are nowhere to be
> found, but worst of all is to begin, to begin, to begin.
> —Donald Barthelme

THE MOST interesting thing about a story is not its climax or dénouement – both dated terms – nor even its style and characterization. It is its beginning, its first paragraph, often its first sentence. More decisions are made on the basis of the first few sentences of a story than on any other part, and it would seem to me after having read thousands of stories, and beginning hundreds of my own (completing, I should add, far fewer), that something more than luck accounts for the occasional success of the operation. What I propose is theoretical, yet rooted in the practice of writing and of reading-as-a-writer; good stories *can* start unpromisingly, and well-begun stories can obviously degenerate, but the observation generally holds: the story seeks its beginning, the story many times *is* its beginning, amplified.

The first sentence of a story is an act of faith – or astonishing bravado. A story screams for attention, as it must, for it breaks a silence. It removes the reader from the everyday (no such imperative attaches to the novel, for which the reader makes his own preparations). It is an act of perfect rhythmic balance, the single crisp gesture, the drop of the baton that gathers a hundred disparate forces into a single note. The first paragraph is a microcosm of the whole, but in a way that only the whole can reveal. If the story begins one sentence too soon, or a sentence too late, the balance is lost, the energy diffused.

It is in the first line that the story reveals its kinship to poetry. Not that the line is necessarily "beautiful," merely that it can exist utterly alone, and that its force draws a series of sentences behind it. The line doesn't have to "grab" or "hook" but it should be striking. Good examples I'll offer further on, but consider first some bad ones:

> Catelli plunged the dagger deeper in her breast, the dark blood oozed like cherry syrup . . . .
> The President's procession would pass under the window at 12:03, and Slattery would be ready . . . .

Such sentences can be wearying; they strike a note too heavily, too prematurely. They "start" where they should be ending. The advantages wrested will quickly dissipate. On the other hand, the "casual" opening can be just as damaging:

> When I saw Bob in the cafeteria he asked me to a party at his house that evening and since I wasn't doing much anyway I said sure, I wouldn't mind. Bob's kind of an ass, but his old man's loaded and there's always a lot of grass around . . . .

Or, *in medias res*:

> "Linda, toast is ready! Linda, are you awake?"

Now, what's wrong with these sentences? The tone is right. The action is promising. They're real, they communicate. Yet no experienced reader would go past them. The last two start too early (what the critics might call an imitative fallacy) and the real story is still imprisoned somewhere in the body.

Lesson One: As in poetry, a good first sentence of prose implies its opposite. If I describe a sunny morning in May (the buds, the wet-winged flies, the warm sun and cool breeze), I am also implying the perishing quality of a morning in May, and a good sensuous description of May sets up the possibility of a May disaster. It is the singular quality of that experience that counts. May follows from the sludge of April and leads to the drone of summer, and in a careful story the action will be mindful of May; it must be. May is unstable, treacherous, beguiling, seductive, and whatever experience follows from a first sentence will be, in essence, a story about the May-ness of human affairs.

What is it, for example, in this sentence from Hugh Hood's story "Fallings from Us, Vanishings" that hints so strongly at disappointment:

> Brandishing a cornucopia of daffodils, flowers for Gloria, in his right hand, Arthur Merlin crossed the dusky oak-panelled foyer of his apartment building and came into the welcoming sunlit avenue.

The name Merlin? The flourish of the opening clause, associations of the name Gloria? Here is a lover doomed to loneliness, yet a lover who seeks it, despite appearances. Nowhere, however, is it stated. Yet no one, I trust, would miss it.

Such openings are everywhere, at least in authors I admire:

> The girl stood with her back to the bar, slightly in everyone's way. (Frank Tuohy)
>
> The thick ticking of the tin clock stopped. Mendel, dozing in the dark, awoke in fright. (Bernard Malamud)
>
> I owe the discovery of Uqbar to the conjunction of a mirror and an encyclopedia. (Jorge Luis Borges)
>
> For a little while when Walter Henderson was nine years old he thought falling dead was the very zenith of romance, and so did a number of his friends. (Richard Yates)
>
> Our group is against the war. But the war goes on. (Donald Barthelme)

The principal dish at dinner had been croquettes made of turnip greens. (Thomas Mann)

The first time I saw Brenda she asked me to hold her glasses. (Philip Roth)

The sky had been overcast since early morning; it was a still day, not hot, but tedious, as it usually is when the weather is gray and dull, when clouds have been hanging over the fields for a long time, and you wait for the rain that does not come. (Anton Chekhov)

I wanted terribly to own a dovecot when I was a child. (Isaac Babel – and I didn't even know what a dovecot was when I started reading.)

At least two or three times a day a story strikes me in the same way, and I read it through. By then I don't care if the climax and dénouement are elegantly turned – chances are they will be – I'm reading it because the first paragraph gave me confidence in the power and vision of the author.

Lesson Two: Art wishes to begin, even more than end. Fashionable criticism – much of it very intelligent – has emphasized the so-called "apocalyptic impulse," the desire of fiction to bring the house down. I can understand the interest in endings – it's easier to explain why things end than how they begin, for one thing. For another, the ending is a contrivance – artistic and believable, yet in many ways predictable; the beginning, however, is always a mystery. Criticism likes contrivances, and has little to say of mysteries. My own experience, as a writer and especially as a "working" reader, is closer to genesis than apocalypse, and I cherish openings more than endings. My memory of any given story is likely to be its first few lines.

Lesson Three: Art wishes to begin *again*. The impulse is not only to finish, it is to capture. In the stories I admire, there is a sense of a continuum disrupted, then re-established, and both the disruption and re-ordering are part of the *beginning* of a story. The first paragraph tells us, in effect, that "this is how things have always been," or, at least, how they have been until the arrival of the story. It may summarize, as Faulkner does in "That Evening Sun":

> Monday is no different from any other weekday in Jefferson now. The streets are paved now, and the telephone and electric companies are cutting down more and more of the shade trees . . . .

Or it may envelop a life in a single sentence, as Bernard Malamud's often do:

> Manischevitz, a tailor, in his fifty-first year suffered many reverses and indignities.

Whereupon Malamud embellishes the history, a few sentences more of indignities, aches, curses, until the fateful word that occurs in almost all stories, the simple terrifying adverb:

Then.

Then, which means to the reader: "I am ready." The moment of change is at hand, the story shifts gears, and, for the first time, *plot* intrudes on poetry. In Malamud's story, a Negro angel suddenly ("then") appears in the tailor's living room, reading a newspaper.

Suddenly there appeared . . . .

Then one morning . . . .

Then one evening she wasn't home to greet him . . . .

Or, in the chilling construction of Flannery O'Connor, there appeared at her door three young men:

> They walked single file, the middle one bent to the side carrying a black pig-shaped valise.

A pig-shaped valise! This is the apocalypse, if the reader needs one; whatever the plot may reveal a few pages later is really redundant. The mysterious part of the story – that which *is* poetic yet sets it (why not?) above poetry – is over. The rest of the story will be an attempt to draw out the inferences of that earlier upheaval. What is meant by "climax" in the conventional short story is merely the moment that the *character* realizes the true, the devastating, meaning of "then." He will try to ignore it, he will try to start again (in my story "Eyes" the character thinks he can escape the voyeurs – himself, essentially – by moving to a rougher part of town); he can't of course.

Young readers, especially young readers who want to write, should forget what they're taught of "themes" and all the rest. Stories aren't written that way. Stories are delicate interplays of action and description; "character" is that force which tries to maintain balance between the two. "Action" I equate with danger, fear, apocalypse, life itself; "description" with quiescence, peace, death itself. And the purest part of a story, I think, is from its beginning to its "then." "Then" is the moment of the slightest tremor, the moment when the author is satisfied that all the forces are deployed, the unruffled surface perfectly cast, and the insertion, gross or delicate, can now take place. It is the cracking of the perfect, smug egg of possibility.

2. The Cast and the Mold

WHEN WE truly *apprehend* something from a story, when, years after we've read it, we are suddenly struck by the *appropriateness* of a word or an image or a character, it's often because we've gone beyond simple comprehension (comprehension is what they teach in schools), well beyond anything deliberately in the story or consciously provided by the author. It is because we have finally grasped the *world* of the story and have found ourselves suddenly viewing the surface of the story from precisely the same angle as the author. And instead of a shimmering reflection – beautiful, undeniably – we've suddenly seen far below the surface. We see structure and purpose and meaning and metaphor and we see the hidden nine-tenths of everything superficial in the story. We see, in fact, that the story was only a single example of something much larger, more diffuse, and practically unnamable. We may even return to that story ("I must go back and reread that Cheever story . . .") – and be disappointed by it. Was it really there? Or did we over-endow it? It's only when our own experience in some way unites us with the same meaning that the story (or the poem-painting-movie-or-music) will take on dimension, become permanent and living in our own imagination. Until that happens, art is cold and attractive and perhaps even admirable, but it remains basically an intellectual exercise. It's not yet *true*, and it's not haunting enough to be beautiful.

That cold, attractive entity we call a story is often a casting, something plastic poured into a mold, allowed to set, and then extracted, polished, and exhibited. The plastic is event; the mold is something akin to impulse, a trigger, an urgency to set it all down. A hall of castings is a book, like this one. And what of that shaggy, disreputable, rusting, unlovely thing called a mold? That larger, encompassing, all-embracing *world* that contained all the delicate flutings within its heavy, iron-or-clay shell? Usually it's lost to us, smashed open by the artist as he extracts his finished product. And yet, I would argue, it very often *is* the story; it contained the story and gave it form and guided that molten flow in a thousand invisible ways. But once the flow had hardened, its purpose was served. It disappeared.

The reader's job, like the archaeologist's, is to reconstruct that mold, re-imagine it, to admire both the hand (the story) and the glove, that crumpled world that once contained it. No writer is comfortable confronting his theme head-on; it's practically impossible to say precisely what you want to say *and* to gain the effects you want to gain. That's a job for salesmen. But because the artist's message is mindful of so many things (including its own futility), the message is necessarily coded, textured, qualified. The writer trusts instead to the diligence of the reader and to time itself being on his side; time which will resurrect his work because part of his work – the mold of his work – always resided in time-lessness, slightly beyond and above the story.

My stories "Broward Dowdy" and "The Fabulous Eddie Brewster" are "war stories" or stories of a separate peace. "Broward Dowdy" contrasts the squalor, intolerance, poverty, and brutish-ness of central Florida with a certain nobility of character, humility, and fundamental human decency. Two boys confront each other over the gulf of literacy and the all-important determinant of class. The narrator's family has temporarily fallen (due to the War), and that fall enables the narrator to glimpse a life he would otherwise have dismissed. The War – an event that Broward knows nothing about, can know nothing about – has brought them together. Squa-lor and dignity can co-exist; the war is not confined to unnamed islands in the Pacific – the last image in the story conveys strongly the possibility that Broward Dowdy will also be a casualty.

"The Fabulous Eddie Brewster" is, of course, more comic; more of a "tall tale." It assumes a certain similarity between central Florida of the 1940s and Vichy (Nazi-occupied) France during World War II. A man of many disguises who could prosper during one régime should do well under the other. And Etienne-Eddie manages very well. But I was also, consciously, talking about Can-ada and the French-English conflict, about losers and survivors, those who hang back (from moral scruples), those who dream but can't really act, and, finally, those who can take The Big Plunge, no matter what the consequences. I rather like the character of Eddie Brewster – sure he's a hustler and a cheat and a collaborator – he's not terribly admirable, but he's also around to establish a dynasty in his second, perhaps even his third, country. The *story* is about an immigrant hustler with a blot on his record; the *mold* (to me at least) is about extending oneself, from never leaving Regina, to never leaving the French-speaking ghettos of New England, to not taking the final plunge (in backing the brother with a little money), to plowing ahead like some force of nature, starting over rather than yielding to bitterness, envy, or self-pity. Resistance, semi-transformation, and utter collaboration are all under scrutiny in this story (and they are the terms of our national dilemma); they were all attractive notions in my parents' generation, and that's what this story is about.

3. On Ending Stories

STORIES BEGIN mysteriously but end deliberately. A writer can't really *will* a story to open, but, in the act of writing, the appropriate ending (event, tone, revelation, effect) will probably suggest itself. Most endings arise in the act of writing (a few stories "arrive" so fully formed that the ending is as mysterious as the opening; the writer is rarely so fortunate), and they all share a single purpose: to give a final emphasis to a particular aspect of the story. Literally, it's the writer's last word on the subject: he'd better choose those words carefully. The opening anticipates the conflict. The ending immortalizes the resolution.

There are only two kinds of endings: those that lead you back into the story, and those that lead you – gently, or violently – away. I associate the first kind of ending with de Maupassant and Chekhov, and with modernists who adapted those stories for their own purposes – Hemingway, Joyce, James. Of authors who lead away from the story, who wish to emphasize the artifice of the story, or wish to address the reader directly, I associate dozens of our contemporaries. Impatience with art is as old as faith in art; the choice of ending is the battlefield for those particular feelings.

You are aware of stories that end with a letdown. "That's it? It's over?" you ask yourself. There's a Hemingway story (there are many Hemingway stories like it) that ends, "Bill selected a sandwich from the lunch basket and walked over to have a look at the rods." That's an ending? Norman Levine can fade out in the same way. It's subversive, of course, a subversion of the expected neatness of closure, the gathering up of narrative and thematic threads, the welling-up of music, the frozen gesture that summarizes *the whole meaning of the story* .... We realize that the short story initially paid its debts to theatre, or to fable; audiences expected a big payoff at the end. When it didn't happen, it was revolution, it was art. Chekhov subverted the expectation dramatically: his vision of a static, purposeless society required the destruction of climax and resolution; the lack of an expected ending makes us feel the lack of resolution, vitality, movement. It preserves tension. You can read that last paragraph, then go back in a circular fashion to the first sentence, and *it almost makes sense*. Joyce adapted the Russian vision to the Irish reality, seeing in that paralysis and indecision an opening to unconscious inhibitions. The so-called "epiphanies" that end his stories are merely the revelation of the subconscious exerting mastery over the blighted, conscious lives. Joyce's stories end when the buried life is suddenly manifest. In their separate ways, James and Hemingway and a number of other modernists and their followers have done the same: sunk the ending deep in the story's texture, forced the reader to dig up the whole story in order to resolve its tensions. The author is not overtly helping the reader: the story *is* its ending.

I think of these endings as the most disturbing. They hit a glancing blow at the reader, but generally ignore him. By approximating the most casual of voices, they manage (in the hands of masters) to sound most urgent. By ignoring us, they speak to us directly. What remains unresolved and undisclosed becomes inviting and forbidding. They offer us no way out of their bland circularity; thus, they linger with us. For me, they are the saddest stories. (Certainly a mastery of that kind of openness, and that kind of "dropped" ending, accounts for the remarkable power of the American author Ray Carver – a very contemporary Hemingway-like voice.)

Endings that lead us away from the story can do so gently or abruptly. The most traditional kind of ending is the one that serves as a prose equivalent to the theatrical last scene, the rising of music and receding of the camera, as lights go out, one-by-one, and characters fade off together in a figurative sunset. Such endings announce a faith in continuity, order, harmony – no matter what particular horrors may have been investigated in the story. They are sophisticated and traditional ways of updating the old "happily ever after" ending so familiar from the fables. Even if the endings are thematically "sad," they are formally (or cosmically) "happy"; they lead us away from the specific exemplum (the story) to a generalized harmony. They are religious in form, if not in content.

How can you detect such an ending? Well, they *sound* like endings. From Eudora Welty we get, "Outside the redbirds were flying and criss-crossing, the sun was in all the bottles on the prisoned trees, and the young peach was shining in the middle of them with the bursting light of spring." From Margaret Laurence's first collection, "The sea spray was bitter and salt, but to them it was warm, too. They watched on the sand their exaggerated shadows, one squat and bulbous, the other bone-slight and clumsily elongated, pigeon and crane. The shadows walked with hands entwined like children who walk through the dark." Again, from Laurence's second volume of stories, "It seemed to me now that in some unconscious and totally unrecognised way, Piquette might have been the only one, after all, who had heard the crying of the loons."

Such endings strike me as reassuring, reconciling. A writer with a disturbing, alienated vision probably would not employ such an ending (and, indeed, individual authors hold a number of endings in their repertory; as I said earlier, it all depends on the effect desired from any particular story). These endings, however, are "safe," and they grow out of essentially recollective experiences; they are mellow, and they are the kinds of endings that self-conscious writers have instinctively subverted.

There are other endings to be discussed: they are violent or playful; metafictional or accusatory. In some stories, I think of the image of a trapdoor – Cheever does this well – in which the last paragraph is so *utterly* at odds with the material that has come before that an entirely new, last-minute interpretation is forced

onto the whole story. (Why not? Anything that works is legitimate.) Cheever himself seems particularly fond of the ending to
"The Country Husband" (he even mentions it in the foreword to
his *Collected Stories*). It goes like this:

> "Here, pussy, here, poor pussy!" But the cat gives her a
> skeptical look and stumbles away in its skirts. The last to
> come is Jupiter. He prances through the tomato vines, hold-
> ing in his generous mouth the remains of an evening slipper.
> Then it is dark; it is a night where kings in golden suits ride
> elephants over the mountains.

A rhetorical flourish, then – the opposite of the stoical close of
Hemingway and friends. An impulsive reaching out; the tension
between the dreamer and the fouled dreamland is always present
in Cheever (it has its terse side, too; the ending of "O Youth and
Beauty!" reads, "The pistol went off and Louise got him in midair.
She shot him dead."); Cheever's endings never slide off the page,
and if they close with the music welling up, it's a full symphonic
number.

I must confess to my own fondness for this kind of close – as
though the full possibility of the story did not occur to the author
(or to me, since I often use it) until the last minute. In both stories
selected for the anthology *Making It New*, I used variants of this
ending: in "How I Became a Jew" choosing to close the nightmare
of a Cincinnati school-day with questions about the promised
land, and in "A North American Education" rounding off the tale
of generational conflict, sexual discovery, disillusionment (all that
stuff that won't let go of me) with a deliberately skewed vision
taken from a different time and place, emphasizing the titanic force
of connectedness, on the one occasion it had indisputably happened. (As Hemingway said in a different close, "It was a good
thing to have in reserve." And as he said in another one, one that
also won't let me go, "Seems like when they get started they don't
leave a guy nothing.")

There are other endings: the interrogative, ending with an accusing question that throws the whole story up in the air, but aiming it for the reader's heart. There are Judgemental endings, such as Flannery O'Connor's: "The tide of darkness seemed to sweep him back to her, postponing from moment to moment his entry into the world of guilt and sorrow."

All I would leave a good reader with is the injunction to look at endings as urgent, final communications. They are the cords we have bitten (sometimes only raggedly chewed) in the act of giving birth.

This page intentionally left blank

The Craft of the Short Story

D OWN ON the family tree of utterance, where drama and prose first split from song, dance, and poetry, we have to account for story, a form that is brief as a poem, stirring as a drama, but not quite a *Homo habilis* or *erectus*. They would be novels, or journalism. Stories are a little like the footprints left by an elfin *afarensis*, our earliest ancestor, a diminutive apelike child, known not by her bones but footprints she and her family left on the mud of a Rift lake shore, fleeing a volcanic eruption. A volcanic eruption is a novel. Fleeing it is a story. The death of the dinosaurs is a novel; discovering it through the presence of unnaturally large deposits of iridium in underlying rocks is a story.

Anyone here today knows the Ten (or Twenty or a Hundred) Commandments of story-writing, even if she or he has yet to internalize them in practice. She knows the difference between *scene* and *narration* and when to use it. He understands the implication it holds for controlling *pace*, for delaying gratification, for racing ahead. You're acutely attuned to the slightest violations of *point of view*. You know that the short story is a *dramatic* form, but one that is focused on *revelation*, not reconstruction. It being dramatic, you know that *timing* is essential and that perfect timing in a story – when to introduce material, when to withhold, what to provide, what to suppress – is as essential on the page as it is on-stage.

Perhaps it's unnecessary to add that all practitioners of the form feel the short story is still an undefined and under-appreciated genre. We know that it is not just a compressed, squashed-up novella, but for some reason the famous pronouncements on the craft of fiction, by Percy Lubbock, E.M. Forster, Henry James or books by Sartre, Günter Grass, and

Vargas Llosa, apply only to the novel. That snub makes us all
the more dedicated.

You perhaps remember the stories of Ann Beattie that first
started appearing in *The New Yorker* in the 1970s. You can probably
parody them quite successfully, as indeed a great many have without acknowledging their debt. The first paragraph generally introduced a WASPy collection of loosely related friends, siblings, lovers, ex-lovers, ex-spouses, children, and cleverly named pets,
going about the summertime business of picnics or boating in a
rented old house close to the shore. They're generally educated
and vaguely arty; they haven't done great damage to themselves
or others, but they still long for something. Some sort of disillusionment has fallen across their lives, severing a vital connection
they once felt, but we don't know what it was about. They seem
prematurely old, mysteriously exhausted, defeated.

You could go crazy with Beattie's first paragraphs, thinking it
necessary – as in a conventional story – to sort out the degree of
alienation or lingering affection, and keeping the names straight
before going on. We had to retrain ourselves to read Beattie, which
is a way of saying Beattie retrained us to read, and to write, stories.
We had to exclude the word "why?" from our list of demands.
Why are they unhappy? Why did things not work out? That training went by the name of minimalism.

Or you are in the world of Raymond Carver's characters
where, for some reason, a wife (usually) is leaving or has just left,
maybe for good, and the husband can't quite muster the energy or
focus to reel her back. Or he's thinking of leaving himself, or moving on, or both of them are thinking of it and almost getting around
to doing it. They seem amiable enough, despite rough talk and
rough patches brought on by drink, drugs, or poverty. That, too, is
WASPy minimalism. Psychic minimalism we might call it.

Or Richard Ford's characters, forever moving, pulling up
stakes and getting out, being abandoned.

In other words, the local volcano is smoking, and getting
ready to blow. Gather the children, don't look back, head for the

shore, man the life rafts. The writers, and readers, are looking at fleeing footprints. They've seen something, they've smelt the sulphurous fumes, they're setting out while they can. Pompeii is a great short story. Look at what we've read from those dishes, those cups, those bodies arched in their beds.

The point I'm getting at is the essential short story gesture, as opposed to the novel's. We are not in the business of establishing any of the *whys*. The preconditions are fine where they are; they were built by another civilization, carved out by different glaciers and hurricanes. Novelists like those things, journalists can deal with them, memoirists need to get to the bottom of them. The story traces what lingers after the whirlwind, after the fracture. Or before it. We're not in the business of establishing the reasons, social, historic, economic, psychological, why things happen. They've already happened. As a character in Malamud's "Take Pity" says, "How did he die?" and the answer comes back, "Broke in him something. That's how." "Broke what?" "Broke what breaks."

That is why the dominant mood of most stories is one of unfulfillment: of longing, hoping, loss, yearning, regret, and disillusionment. It's a mood we call Fitzgeraldian, Hemingwayesque, Cheeverian, Carveresque. By turning away from the need to explain too much, to create, construct, and establish, the story opens a space that is not available to the novel. It is the story's signature space of tethered ferocity, the eruption of gesture and repression, the accountant of the unconscious presenting his bill, the Joycean epiphany. It is the reason I call the short story an expansive form, and the novel, contrary to most opinion, contractive. The story says the most that can be said about a restricted moment in time and space. The novel says the least about a great many more.

I'll offer one observation that probably has only a tangential place in this talk. American novelists are generally at ease with writing stories, and have been from the beginning. Hawthorne and Melville have given us some of our greatest novels *and* stories, as have Jack London, Faulkner, James, Hemingway, O'Hara, Oates, Malamud, Ford, Fitzgerald, Paley, Cather, and Flannery O'Connor – an endless list. This is less common in other cultures. I'll mention some famous story-writing novelist-exceptions only to show I'm not entirely clueless: Turgenev, Gogol, Tolstoy, D.H. Lawrence, Mansfield, Kipling, Joyce, Calvino, Mann, Tagore, Kafka, and Márquez. But novelists in the rest of the world generally write poetry, not stories. The pure story-writers like Alice Munro, Grace Paley, Lee K. Abbott, and for the most part, Mavis Gallant, don't bother with novels. (My friend Lee Abbott who has written nine volumes of stories has never written a novel. Nor did Ray Carver. Lee told me, "I never found anything big enough that couldn't be said in under twenty pages.") Even in our cultural neighbour Canada, novelists like Atwood and Ondaatje and Bowering and many more made their reputations as poets, and the same is true in New Zealand and Australia. For some reason, though, it's extremely rare for American prose writers to establish any kind of reputation in, or to attempt, poetry. It's a curious self-segregation we practise. There was, again, Melville, with mixed results. On the contemporary stage there's Marge Piercy and Raymond Carver. Joyce Carol Oates has published a great many poems, Lynne Sharon Schwartz is a first-rate novelist, story-writer, essayist, translator, and now poet, but the paucity of names, and the relatively pale status of their poetry, more or less makes my point. The short story is the American novelist's delectable poem.

Robert Reeves spoke of these craft lectures as nuts and bolts discussions of writing within our areas of expertise. So here comes the plumbing. Every detail your story needs, the fuel, is there from the beginning, lying low, like a small, neutral-looking Band-Aid, not calling attention to itself. The stories I write, for instance, are bundled in the first paragraph, but it takes the story's full length to unwrap them. On first encounter, that inoffensive Band-Aid is just hiding one of life's little nicks, reinforcing the notion, perhaps, that your character is no porcelain deity, but someone who gardens or chops tomatoes. Band-Aids are sturdy icons of self-reliance, comforting in their way. So we take in the information very early in the story, the mildly interesting detail of a small Band-Aid, remembering it in the generalized, non-inventoried way readers remember details in a story. But you, sneaky writer, have introduced it for a reason. It's a prop you've paid for, and it's there when you need to reach back for something extra. Timing is all: the fact of the Band-Aid should be introduced but the suggestion of its meaning should be delayed. You can't use the Band-Aid late in the story if it wasn't there at the beginning. You can't stumble over furniture in the dark if you didn't describe the low Danish tables in the afternoon.

Details introduced early, or characters alluded to or making fleeting appearances, are part of the story's census. They are active ingredients, because nothing in a story is inert. It is, remember, a dramatic form. Every prop, every detail, every character will be used and used again; if they're not reused you might think seriously of eliminating them in the first place. I think of them as having had their hands stamped, like the wandering attendees at a rock concert. They've paid, they may go out for a smoke or whatever, but *they'll be back*. Similarly, you know that providing too much fuel in the way of explanation and background can clog a story just as skimpiness of preparation can cause it to starve. As with the space shuttle, too much fuel is as dangerous as too little.

Knowing all this, how does anything get written? How do we return to a state of innocence that allows us to suspend all the rules and simply follow our instincts like the innocents we were, before the first fatal workshop? Forty years ago, my first writing teacher, Bernard Malamud, offered a definition that works for me, even today. He called stories "the dramatization of the multifarious adventures of the human heart." It sounds so simple.

"Drama" is tricky. Like pornography it's hard to define but you know it when you see it. Drama is motion, story details are offered in movement, and they are tied to character. You learn to look askance at your own draft and ask yourself, *is this sentence doing everything it can*? Let's say an old tree grows in a yard. But this is a story, not a novel. You're not just *setting a scene*; your scene is already there. The story is moving faster than such a smug, self-satisfied detail as an old tree growing in a yard. You don't have the time or space to construct a mini-history or society; you're catching reflections off a pre-existent reality and fully living characters. That work has already been done.

Story details work in ways that are fundamentally different from those in a novel. They have to work on several conflicting levels, leading to character revelation. So let's say it's a two-hundred-year-old oak tree on the south lawn, which, again, is doubly irrelevant. A two-hundred-year-old oak tree on the south lawn with a rope-tire swing on its lowest branch, and whose top branch casts a shadow across the upstairs bedroom window where, on this bright May morning, behind the screen and fluttering curtains, motion is detected . . . you get the idea. Maybe the sentence is now *too* impacted, too burdened, trying to do too much, so you break it up, or cut it back. But *who* is causing the motion behind the curtain and screen? Who is watching? Change the time-flow, move from omniscience to first-person: *I remember the tree that used to grow, now a table-wide stump:* possibly. How to get at the dramatic truth, the heart's adventure? The rope-tire swing is abandoned, and suddenly the shadow that falls across the bedroom window, obscuring the face within, is eloquent. The family is in trouble.

Was it *your* family? Are you the face behind the curtain, is it your bedroom? Or are you the watcher? Were *you* the child swinging that day when some indescribable, Flannery O'Connor-style horror pulled up at the curb? (Three young men, one carrying "a pig-shaped valise," as one of her stories relates.) Or is the horror locked inside as you furiously swing? The tree stands for something – is it security, nature's benevolence, eternity, or is it diseased, aged, and mortal? We don't know yet, but it has worked its way into the story; therefore it belongs. The shadow on a bright morning, it too signifies. Whose face is looking out the window?

I'm feeling the tug of possibility. My heart is filling, ready to break. The delicate interplay between creation and revelation – how much to put in, and how much to chip away, and when to begin – is one of the great attractions and challenges of the short-story form.

Your workshop experience has left you with a nervous relationship to the word *epiphany*, like a lapsed Catholic passing a church. You know epiphanies when you see them, you're respectful of them, but after a hundred years of worshipful admiration, can't we avoid them? Must every story close on one, lead to one? Haven't we earned freedom from the pitiless glare of those masters of the form who can find epiphanies in a grain of sand? Perhaps your taste runs more to speculative abstraction, from Borges through Kafka and Calvino, or to voices from the *shtetls* and the Holocaust, or minority and immigrant voices, Asian and African voices – do the same rules apply? Are the rules of psychological realism, based in bourgeois probabilities with American inflections, universal? Haven't we learned new formulas from Magic Realism, oral narrative, and tribal griots? Can't we finally riff on the story, jazz it up, break with convention, and find our voice within?

Where, in short, is the sacred thread, the umbilical cord that ties together the universal fascination with brief utterance?

You know how formally demanding the short story is and how perfectly the great stories conform to theoretical templates. Not a sliver of light sneaks through. Why can't you match it? And so you've come to the conclusion that writing a short story is not just about form, it's not tennis or golf or a ten-metre dive. Excessive consciousness of craft can get in the way of a good story (and as we know from Billy Collins, it's bad for your cholesterol). No great story was ever written purely as an exercise in form, but many, I fear, have been lost for its lack. If there's craft and no passion or energy, the short story is little more than an ultimate academic exercise. But you are here to learn something from this lecture, and it should be something that will help you learn the craft – and words like passion and energy have no equivalence in form and theory.

My advice is for you to learn the craft, internalize it, so that you can banish your inhibitions and free your energies. Master the form so that you can ignore it. Understand the theory behind the form, because form and theory are your corrective lenses. They're meant to help you see more, see farther, and see clearer, that's all. Just as morality is the enemy of justice – and by the way I think story is about the dealing of the highest imaginable justice – so can form for its own sake be the enemy of energy.

Finally, what we're all seeking is the control of, and the release of, energy. Form is the graphite rod in the fissionable pile. Energy is anarchic, represented by style, by bursts of invention, by non sequitur, by cuts and leaps, twists of plot, and madcap antics. Think of voice as the nozzle through which the energy flows. Think of the great story-writers, those whose characteristic voice moderates the release of energy: Flannery O'Connor, Hemingway, Carver, Cheever, Malamud, Beattie, Munro, Gallant, and why stop there? Think of Borges, of Joyce, Kafka, and Babel.

Stories are attractive, beloved of writers and some readers, because each time we start the writing or the reading, perfection seems possible. The novelist, unless he's French, doesn't entertain such a notion – isn't the novel defined as "a flawed narrative of over 50,000 words"? We write stories not for money or the fame they will bring to us, but for the respect we can bring to them.

I don't have time to comment on everything, so I'll leave the stage with some brief observations. I've already noted a few: stories are energy, stories are expansive, stories are like fireworks going off, or, as a Beckett might say, like a fart. They get and hold our attention, they linger a while, they vanish with nothing but a smirk.

Stories are perennially youthful. They are of course often the work of the young, but they remain young. They keep defining what youth feels like, or felt like, even as we age. The reason seems simple enough; they are about youthful subjects: longing, hope, disappointment.

Stories are the membrane we sling around discontinuity and chaos, the whole insolence of a universe that does not respond to cause and effect, or consequence, and antecedent. They are the voice we give to chaos, anonymity, quotidian derangement.

Story is the permanent avante-garde, it can draw its immediate inspiration from art, technology, philosophy, myth, newspapers, sports, a letter, an overheard scrap. Some blessed souls can write novels on little more, but novels are about resolution and completion. Story is about destruction, the slipping away.

We shouldn't worry about the permanent threatened status of the story – it is the canary in the mineshaft, and as such it is the first challenged genre in any time, any place. In a bloated culture distracted by shoddy goods, stories are an invaluable commodity. Stories are handcrafted gems; they reflect the expertise and experience of their maker. Stories finally survive because of the passion of the story-writer.

So, the issue in the world of short story is really only that of zealously maintaining a small space in which it is permitted to flourish. In times of change and crisis, story will have to be written. We know that each new generation is guaranteed to be more discordant and confused and speeded up than any previous generation (this has been going on since the beginning of the Industrial Revolution), and after the music has been played, the stories will be written.

It is a transparent membrane, so that readers can see it work, like a jellyfish, like an IMac. The process of destruction and incoherence is going on in plain view.

I am struck by the numbers of times we say, "Ah, but his finest work is to be found in the stories, not the novel." Hemingway, Porter, Welty, O'Connor, O'Hara. We might add, Turgenev, Gogol. Even as I write this, the *New York Times* daily review declares Kipling's finest work to be his stories.

I think we realize that novels cannot by their very nature sustain energy, the collisions and incoherences. Stories are like smashed atoms, and the tracing in nanoseconds of an evidence that something is there, or was there, but it disappeared in the very act of discovering or describing it. Schrödinger's Cat; Heisenberg's Uncertainty; they were thinking like story-writers.

We want to be in that blessed state while writing, in which the world exists for the completion of the story, everything fits, all experiences are aspects of your story, not the other way around. After a certain point in a story, the world conspires to complete it.

The Justice-Dealing Machine

P ASSIONATE READERS of short stories, if that is not a redun-
dancy, should have no trouble agreeing to a few stipulations.
First, the short story and its related subgenera – the sudden fictions, the story-byte, the flash, or even its stately auntie, the
novella (but not the novel) – are the hot literary forms of our inter-
millennial age. The energy and furious activity sucks us in. So
much friction, so many collisions, inside a confined space. A
related stipulation: word-count considerations aside, stories are
the expansive literary form of our age; novels the condensed.
Stories say the most about a very few moments. The novel says the
least about a great many more. When filmmakers "adapt" a novel
for the screen, they're really turning a novel into a short story. A
third stipulation: every story should end (and every great story
does end) on the curtain-dropping note, the intent (or the shadow
of the intent), struck by Frank O'Connor at the close of "Guests of
the Nation": "And anything that ever happened me after I never
felt the same about again." If not those words (and who would
dare be so bold to state them now, although John Updike echoes
them at the close of "A & P": "and my stomach kind of fell as I felt
how hard the world was going to be to me hereafter."), they leave
us with the feeling that something profound has been attempted,
and often achieved. This is the reader-writer short-story contract: I
will never feel the same way again (about whatever), after reading
this story. Why begin reading a story (or writing one), if not for the
expectation that perfection is achievable, and that this one might
just blow the reader's (or the writer's) socks off? The same note is
sounded at the close of Flannery O'Connor's "A Good Man Is
Hard to Find" ("'She would of been a good woman,'" The Misfit

said, "'if it had been somebody there to shoot her every minute of her life.'"), which recapitulates Chekhov's "Gooseberries" ("The rain beat against the window panes all night.") and Joyce's "The Dead" and "Araby" ("Gazing up into the darkness I saw myself as a creature driven and derided by vanity; and my eyes burned with anguish and anger.") and ironically in Mann's "Disorder and Early Sorrow" as the narrator gazes upon the ruin of his culture, and his family: "Heaven be praised for that!" In fact, there's not a successful story I can think of that does not rephrase, or adapt, the same Frank O'Connor sentence. Either the central character, the narrator, or the reader will be moved, literally, and never returned to the space he or she had been inhabiting. He or she will be lifted up and transported and set down in a different place by whatever the author shows them. And I'd suggest a fourth stipulation, which is the one I want to linger over in the next few pages. Stories trace a fundamental change of heart (emphasis on *fundamental*), a change that is so deep that it transcends the normal, rather sentimental association of the word "heart." It shakes the pillars of consciousness ("nothing would ever be the same"). It stops, temporarily, the stars in their courses. The question is, how does a story do that?

In the summer of 1961, I was blessed to study with Bernard Malamud, whose description of a "story" (one day in class) was "the dramatization of the multifarious adventures of the human heart." On its most engaging level, Malamud's "The Jewbird" is touching and moving. It can be read as a tall tale, a comic whimsy. It can also be seen as a version of the eternal conflict between social duty and the awakening of personal responsibility. The short-story contract promises that the final product will blow our socks off and earn a line like Frank O'Connor's. In Malamud's working: "Who did it to you, Mr. Schwartz?" asks the child, looking at the talking, tortured, expelled crow, now dying. "Anti-Semeets," the Jewbird answers. How do we explore, fundamentally, the human heart in ten pages or less?

Flannery O'Connor once quoted from Catholic theology: "the

roots of the eye are in the heart." That's a beginning (and was there ever a clearer eye than Flannery O'Connor's?); the heart does inform our speech, our seeing and hearing. But how to get to the heart – can the senses alone deliver us there? Clearly, there's a place for plot and setting and character, for concrete details, pertinent overheard dialogue, and all the other devices learned in workshops. But even when all the techniques and senses are developed perfectly, will we get to those "multifarious adventures," or to Frank O'Connor's moment of conversation? Not without a deeper commitment.

I'm suggesting a fifth stipulation. Short fiction is a justice-dealing machine. The extra level of intuition that lifts a story to greatness is its deployment of "justice," not in its legal, but in its literary sense. And what is the enemy of justice? For lack of an obvious word, I'd say "morality." Justice dares to challenge the difference between morality, which represents the "proper" and the popular, and the lonely, unwelcome discovery that we are truly alone, separated from society, religion, family, or any other code to sustain us. All the burdens fall on our flesh, unprotected. In other words, it is a special understanding of the meaning of justice that delivers us to the Frank O'Connor moment.

Literary justice derives in myth from the story of the baby Achilles, dipped in the river that provides him immortality. He has only one vulnerability, the heel by which he'd been held. Any testing of Achilles must involve the exposure of his hidden vulnerability. The character of Achilles can be read, apart from his heroism, in his need to hide that same vulnerability. Any story concerning Achilles is incomplete until (however indirectly and improbably) an arrow finds his heel. Let that moment stand, then, for everything we want to hide, every weakness we've spent a lifetime disguising, and for every indirection and sophisticated technique of short-story writing. The short story is the straightest line to the best-hidden secret. Relentlessly, short fiction drives to the stripping away of all defences, the exposure of the one thing we had always repressed.

Literary justice has nothing to do with ethics or morals or public standards of right and wrong (and, especially, not with "correctness"). Patricia Highsmith, author of *The Talented Mr. Ripley* and a number of other morally complicated, justice-dealing novels, wrote in *Plotting and Writing Suspense Fiction*: "I find the public passion for justice quite boring and artificial, for neither life nor nature cares if justice is ever done or not." ("Public justice" is what I'm calling "morality.") "Justice" is quite properly terrifying; God is just, Allah is just, and Thomas Jefferson feared God's justice for the young republic's embrace of slavery. The reason that morality is boring and artificial is that morality is merely the approved collective behaviour and beliefs of a majority at any given time and place. Morality is poll-driven, V-chipped, and has nothing more than a gossipy interest in revealing flaws and secrets.

In "Guests of the Nation," morality, in the form of IRA honour, demands the execution of British prisoners, but justice declares it cold-blooded murder. In "The Jewbird," justice confers no special degree of righteousness to a family of poor Jews who use and then expel the ghost of their cultural past, the unwelcome, unkempt, feathered visitor. In "A & P," an act of righteous defiance gains neither advantage nor gratitude. The mass-killer Misfit of "A Good Man Is Hard to Find" is out there, and your car will pop a tire just a few feet from wherever he's hiding. The Misfit represents blind and pitiless justice. The family, with its clichés, its Bible, its innocent grandmother and children, is moral to its core.

When I was beginning my career as a literature professor, I was invited to testify for bookstores and publishers against the city of Milwaukee's ban on the open sale of Terry Southern's *Candy*, as well as *Tropic of Cancer* and *Lady Chatterley's Lover*. In preparing for trial, it was necessary to decide what the claim of moral values (i.e., "community standards") versus artistic freedom might be. Morality is nothing more profound than the beliefs of the majority, as interpreted by the police and D.A., and, if it comes to that, a jury of our peers. The designated enforcers of social values knew that the majority, anywhere in the country, could be counted on to suppress "obscene" works, and they knew obscenity when they saw it. I was reading my D.H. Lawrence, George Bernard Shaw, and Wayland Young (*Eros Denied*), all of whom drew vivid distinctions between changing standards of "morality" and what has endured from antiquity as "justice" in the literary pantheon.

As societies evolve, they grow more accepting of "obscene" images and excluded (usually sexual) minorities. That plasticity is the proof that morality has nothing to do with the immutable canons of justice. Fortunately, it was 1964, one of those moments in cultural history when moral standards were molting. The times were a-changin', and the city attorneys understood that as well, and dropped the case before trial. It would have been impossible for me, as a twenty-four-year-old, to say then what was on my mind, namely that justice is the enemy of morality. Moralities are social contracts that reflect the collective beliefs of a given society at a particular stage of its development. Stoning adulterers is moral, clitorectomies are moral, capital punishment is moral. In "Guests of the Nation," it is the moral imperative of war (an eye for an eye) to execute enemy prisoners, even if justice tells us that killing men we've gotten to know and even to like is premeditated murder. In "A & P" it is moral to make a sexual goddess ashamed of her beauty, to banish her from the store and force her to dress according to company standards so as not to discomfit the submanager's sense of propriety, or cause a reassessment of his own repressed sexuality.

The problem that Highsmith addressed is how to understand the uncomfortable complexity of justice. The career of her special Misfit, Mr. Ripley, slices through the layers of morality. Because of her special relationship to justice, and contempt for high-minded public morality, Highsmith's Ripley (like Flannery O'Connor's Misfit) remains mythically disturbing. If I were asked to testify in a case similar to Milwaukee's today, I might try to suggest that justice is inherent in form, not in content. Great writers cannot rest until they have performed the arrow's duty, flying through unprotected flesh to expose the core of justice that generates any valid conflict. Without the writer's understanding that every character has an Achilles' heel, there is no story. Without the demonstration that a character is somehow and somewhere vulnerable (but only in a way, and in a place, that a story can discover), the story is unfinished, or unsatisfying. Not to show any disrespect for my great teacher, perhaps I could say, whimsically, that stories explore the multifarious adventures of the human heel.

A Delayed Disclosure

M Y MOTHER was thirty-seven years old in the bleak, wartime spring of 1940 when I was born. I assume it was bleak because it was Fargo, North Dakota, in early April, and I know it was wartime because my parents had just left Canada to escape it. Other pregnancies followed but none were carried to term. Doctors said she was too old. They said I had survived – barely – because I was the first, before my mother had built up antibodies against my father. What that meant, exactly, was never fully explained, but in my childhood, competing "Rh-positive" and "Rh-negative" blood factors were popular explanations.

Antibodies seemed plausible; the notion even carried a whiff of censure for the late-in-life, beneath-her-class, "interracial" status of the marriage itself. There was something culturally as well as genetically incompatible between my parents. My father was an uneducated village Quebecker and a lapsed Catholic; my mother was a Manitoba-born Anglo and anti-Catholic in an almost North of Ireland way, and the city in which they'd met and married was Dark Ages, 1930s Montreal. She took the doctors' admonitions to heart. She'd been vain, she'd defied her destiny as a "bachelorette," and there was something trashy about carrying a baby at a grandmother's age. Hers was a poisoned womb.

In those years, doctors operated on the Sherlock Holmes principle – once you've exhausted the probable, the impossible must be considered. I was a weak, impoverished thing, didn't walk, didn't talk, didn't sit up; my parents were extraordinarily strong, athletic, "physical specimens." By rights, I should have been a eugenic marvel. I should have benefitted from hybrid hardiness, like Manitoba wheat. And so, there must have been a psychological component. (Psychoanalysis was also in the air.)

Sixty years ago, women – those frigid, castrating, smothering wives and mothers – were blamed for most inexplicable and insidious family disasters. Fathers might be ne'er-do-wells or alcoholics or abusive, but those were known, pre-absolved failings with predictable outcomes, especially in the province of Québec.

"Failure to thrive," however, as we'd say today, required more subtle analysis. How to explain bed-wetting? Spastic colon? Sissiness? Juvenile delinquency? The answer, in the words of the bestselling pop-essayist Philip Wylie, was middle-class, American "momism." Freudian analysis added heft to the argument. "Moms" were modern witches. Obviously, all the kinks and quirks of American dysfunction were the fault of mothers who'd been too withholding, or too dominating – mothers who'd denied a breast, or exposed it, who'd enforced potty-training too early, or ignored it too long, who picked up squalling babies too quickly, or let them scream incessantly, who'd permitted too much, or not enough, of just about anything in their secretive and exclusive control of their children. Fathers in the 1940s weren't around enough to be much of an influence on anything.

Perfect physical specimens like my parents were obviously able to conceive – why couldn't *she* carry them to term? My father had been a Golden Gloves champion in two countries; my mother was an avid ice-skater and field hockey player. My father had the barrel chest, arms, and shoulders of a heavyweight, in a short-legged lightweight's frame. Even into her mid-fifties my mother could kick her legs far over her head. She could thrum her fingers on a tabletop with the force of small hammers. What was wrong with them together, or with her?

Maybe she *really* didn't want children. Perhaps *unconsciously* (that sophisticated, all-explaining, European word) she'd been fighting against the role, or definition, of motherhood. She was educated, she'd had a European life, she was an artist, she felt superior to her husband and everyone in his furniture-salesman's life; *unconsciously*, she must have felt she'd made a terrible mistake. During her first pregnancy she'd taken all the proper steps, as they were understood in 1940. She still smoked, but she'd given up driving. My birth was uneventful. She took me up to Winnipeg a few months later to be assured by her father, a doctor. "Don't worry, Annie, he'll never be a boxer," he'd said. (I was never a fighter although over my childhood and high-school years, I served as the classic schoolyard punching bag. If there had been today's high-school culture of lethal vengeance, I might have made history.)

At about nine months, I fell into a mysterious decline: my eyes grew dull, my body toneless, I flopped in my high chair as though I had no bones or spine. One morning my mother found me with both legs around my neck, paddling with my hands like a self-propelled beach ball. I stayed physically and mentally undefined until I was three and a half years old. By then, we had moved to Cincinnati, the second of thirty towns and cities, north and south, Canadian and American, before my parents' inevitable divorce fifteen years later. My condition was diagnosed as *amytonia congenita*, a form of muscular dystrophy that was considered fatal. My mother didn't give up. She read to me, even though I didn't respond. She took me to doctors, finally finding one who prescribed a new wartime thyroid extract. At about the age of four, the pills, or something, kicked in; I sat up, I talked, and I walked.

Fifteen years later, in Pittsburgh, during the time of my parents' divorce, I asked our family doctor what was wrong with me: pudgy, slow, and uncoordinated. Soft. I have never been able to do a push-up. I don't know what it's like to launch a one-handed jump shot. In high school, I weighed a corky two hundred and thirty pounds: a football lineman's weight. Where would it end? I could see a limitless, freak-show trajectory.

Was there a name for it, when people asked? "A kind of dystrophy," the doctor remarked. It kept me out of high-school and college gym. Nothing more was said; given my fascination with sports, it was my own quiet form of disappointment.

Seven years after that, between college and graduate school, just before entering the Writers' Workshop in Iowa City, I was called up for my army physical. I stood at attention in a line of nude young farm boys, while someone tried to pass a single sheet of paper between my knees. My legs form a kind of geometry, like two letters "K" placed back-to-back. The sheet of paper tore. I would be unable to stand at attention without passing out. Knock-kneed: it offered a respectable deferment.

A year later, I was married. Our first son was born while my wife and I were still in the Workshop. He was a beautiful, lusty, active baby, out of his crib at seven months, dark-haired and light-eyed with a peachy complexion born of my wife's genetic contribution. She is Calcutta-born. Hybridization actually works, I thought.

My mother was one of those supremely rationalistic women of the 1920s, a Canadian version of Evelyn Waugh's "Bright Young Things," a Winnipeg college graduate in "Arts" who'd left her father's stern Methodism and drifted far from her prairie origins into Eastern wisdom, theosophy and atheism. She could stand in for any number of Alice Munro or Carol Shields heroines. She aspired to a career in design, against her father's inflexible will. So she taught for three years in rural Saskatchewan and Manitoba schools, saved her wages, and, in the summer of 1929, took off for Europe. She worked first in London, then, dissatisfied by the stodgy standards of local design, removed herself to the centre of modernism, Germany. She enrolled in an art school in Dresden, and took classes in Dessau, at the Bauhaus. With the closing of the schools in 1933, she escaped to Prague, using her German, and stayed there till 1935 when friends suggested she leave. With a Canadian passport, she'd found herself suddenly desirable in the eyes of many older, interesting, accomplished men. But she returned to London for a year, then back to Canada.

There was something else, she would tell me later, about her London years. She felt herself growing "strange." Perhaps because she was Canadian, her British girl friends thought of her as a free spirit, without the Americans' wealth and vulgarity or the Britishers' snobbish reserve. When she said "strange," she meant that her readings were in occult subjects, and at parties while some women played the piano or sang, she offered to read tea leaves. It started out as a light diversion, but she soon grew very good at it. Annie's little corner of the parlour drew a crowd. She could see patterns through the tea leaves. She could sniff out darker outlines. And then people started shunning her, asking her, please, not to read. They were disturbed, and my mother was having nightmares. She returned to Canada, to the only city she could tolerate by then, Montreal, in 1937.

By that time, my father, the second-youngest of nineteen children (fourteen of whom had died in childhood), born in a village in southeastern Québec, had walked out of the monastery where he'd been stashed as a *donné*, a priest in the making, then moved on as a child labourer to Lewiston, Maine, and next to Manchester, New Hampshire, where he brawled and married and beat his first wife into suing for divorce. Some fifteen years ago, when I was researching a book on my father, a Manchester policeman with a French name looked up my father's police records for me. He said, "Yer fatha musta bin a real bastid. Those old French guys beat on their wives all the time but they never got divorced!"

A late cousin of mine who remembered him from her childhood told me, "My mother said not to hang around Uncle Léo too much."

"Why?" I asked.

She was then in her seventies, I in my fifties, and she said, "A boy shouldn't know bad things about his father."

Around 1925, he put away his boxing gloves and went back to Canada to sell cars, to sing in a restaurant, and eventually, thanks to Prohibition, to ride shotgun, literally, on the nightly liquor trucks from Montreal through Adirondack backroads down to Troy. He did his job, went to jail, added an "e" to his last name to make it look more "French" (meaning "Parisian"), and then, in 1937, took a job selling furniture at Eaton's big store in Montreal.

(What a satisfying vengeance on Protestant rectitude! Jews in Montreal distilled the liquor, French Canadians drove it in, the Irish in Albany unloaded it and sent it on to the Italians in New York for national distribution. Not only did Prohibition spread the wealth to America's East-Coast outcasts, it created a literary shuffle: Richler-to-Blaise-to-Kennedy-to-Puzo.)

And so, my parents met in Montreal in 1937. My mother was older, taller, heavier, educated, and also his boss; he was handsome, raw, ambitious, violent, and effectively illiterate. My mother's socialism brought them together. As a French Canadian, Léo Blais (or his Gatsbyan counterpart, Lee Blaise) was not allowed to collect a commission on sales to an "English" customer. He threatened to assault an "English" salesman. She saw the injustice, and addressed the unofficial policy.

My jolly grandmother Orienne Blais, four feet ten inches tall, undertaker to fourteen, lived with my parents for her final two years. She once asked my mother, "Why did a good woman like you marry a boy like Léo?" In the fateful month of September 1939, with my mother pregnant with me, her mother-in-law died. Her death was the release my father had been waiting for. My parents left for Winnipeg and then North Dakota, and at that point the story gets interesting.

Over the years I have taken great comfort from my French-Canadian half-identity derived from my father. Montreal is the "hometown" (out of thirty) that I claim. French-Canadian is the identity I answer to. The happiest years of my life were spent in Montreal. Our younger son was born in Montreal; my wife and I taught there for a dozen years. The life and language of Québec still delight me. The tenacity of that small, threatened culture is heroic. These qualities, along with the suffering and poverty, the harsh conditions, the low esteem, the tight little gene pool in which, after four hundred years, everyone is related, have always told me everything I needed to know about myself. I might have been an only child, but I have six million cousins.

After my parents' divorce, my father married two more times and suffered mightily for what he knew to be his sins. The wife he left my mother for tried to kill him. The next one succeeded. He bled to death, the result of a malicious error in dosage for clotting medication. He was seventy-two, and is buried in "*le petit coin du Canada,*" in the old French-Canadian ghetto of now-gentrifying Manchester. By then, my mother, who lived ten more years, did not recognize his name, or mine. She died of Alzheimer's Disease at eighty-four, where she started, in Winnipeg.

In my growing up, the stories my mother told me of my various potential fathers fired me with nostalgia for a life I couldn't live. This is partial compensation for having an "old" mother, especially in the rural South of my childhood when toothless grandmothers often were thirty or younger. My mother was in her mid-forties by the time I started school. For me, in Pittsburgh or deep in Florida and Georgia, or back in Winnipeg, physical and economic life would always be a struggle. We'd always be renting back rooms in other people's houses, or duplexes, and there would always be new schools twice a year with new bullies, each town worse than the one before. The few stories she told me about earlier boyfriends – *beaux*, she called them – made them seem like parachuters, dozens of father-insurrectionists landing behind family lines.

"Of course, you wouldn't be you," she'd say, easily detecting the calculations I was making. That was okay with me; I didn't much like the fate I'd been dealt. We wouldn't be in Florida or Georgia or Alabama. We wouldn't be American. I would be Canadian, or European. I'd be cultured. I'd be lean, hard, and athletic. I would be English or German or Czech or Hungarian. I went to the atlas and looked up those countries. They were, by the faintest thread of imagination, mine. I'd be Jewish, an artist or intellectual, or some kind of deposed aristocrat. If my father had been the Toronto architect who figured prominently in many of my mother's London stories, whose old letters she sometimes took out and read, whose accomplishments she was able to trace through the Canadian magazines that followed us in her American exile, what might that have meant for me?

My father was the reason, obviously, that I wasn't taller or smarter or richer. I would have settled for some of his good looks and bullish strength, but he didn't pass them on, the selfish bastard. He was the reason we lived among violent people who spoke darkly of "traits." He was the one who lied about his origins, or covered them up, lived a secret life with other women, all known to my mother. He was the one terrified of being "discovered," who caused us to flee landlords and processors deep in the night. Without him, life wouldn't be so endlessly unfair, such an unwinnable struggle.

"Your father should be respected. He's had a lot to overcome," she'd say. "You have to admire what he's made of himself."

All of that was true. Many of my father's traits were admirable. He worked harder than any two men. He had to. He could read the baseball box scores, but little more. Keeping up with Boudreau and Durocher. He wrote numbers, not letters. Pencils and ballpoint pens snapped in his hands; their points ripped through the pages. His life, his constructed "French" life, with a Paris education, with vineyards in the countryside, was an embarrassing lie and if we'd moved in sophisticated circles, he would have been easily exposed. He'd been born poor, Catholic, and French in a time and place that sent boys off to work, or the priesthood, as soon as they could toddle. To have transcended all of that was heroism enough, though he, and I, didn't honour it at the time.

"Architects make a lot of money, don't they?" I'd ask. They designed things, and I was busy filling up writing tablets with plans for future cars, planes, trains, and buildings. That famous Canadian architect who figured in my mother's Manitoba-girl-against-the-world London and Dresden and Montreal stories was still living in Toronto. Toronto was not an architectural triumph sixty or more years ago, but that hardly mattered. ("Toronto architect" still carries an oxymoronic ring to me, unfairly, even now.) Of course he was married, but he'd been married then, too, and studying in London. That didn't matter. My mother wasn't shy about the implications. "Gordon" was the love of her life, and she'd met my father on the rebound. My father hid his string of mistresses; my mother's lovers were all embedded in history.

Many years after she was gone, I learned to appreciate the fact that a first-time, forty-year-old mother had had a full life, she had done her living and growing before I was born. She was always a fully-formed individual; she seemed to me infallible. But "older mothers" are another oxymoron; our years together were numbered. Alzheimer's began claiming her by her middle sixties – my age now. We could never be adults together. Her full life is one I'll never know, and the absence fills me with wonder and regret. What she gave me is the gift and the right to imagine alternate selves, what she, and I, might have been, and to frame her life as a rather dazzling young woman, free of cares, free of me. It's the countries and cities, especially Montreal, she talked of that became mine.

What she wanted from me was someone to listen to her, to understand her hard and embittering choices and to take from them a certain caution, not to be so trusting. Her life had started on the Canadian frontier, it had leaped to pre-War Europe and to Montreal: she'd enjoyed as full a life as any available in that time and place. Then she'd failed her promise, she'd panicked (today we'd talk of the "biological clock"). I became her only consolation. The brutal years in the rural South, the empty years in northern cities, then back to a 1960s and 1970s Montreal more French and unforgiving than the English and European Montreal she'd known, before ending where she'd started, in Winnipeg. A shelf of history vanished with her memory; no Canadian woman had lived a life like hers. She gave me life, she saved my life, she gave me a profession, and in her last years of clarity, she was able to pass those same stories, with the same passion, on to our children.

It has taken many years for the mystery of my mother's poisoned womb to resolve itself. In the past few years, what is now called *amytonia congenita*, Myotonic Dystrophy, has reappeared. As modern medicine has discovered, each of my children has a 50-50 chance of inheriting the trait. Half of our genetic makeup comes from each parent. I have a "good" allele (the possible mutational form of a gene) from my mother, and a "bad" one from my father. (My mere survival indicates that my father, not my mother, is the source of my dystrophy.) I have to assume that many of my mother's pregnancies spontaneously aborted because of myotonia. It is the mysterious "antibody," the poisoned womb.

In my marriage, my wife contributed two sturdy, Bengali alleles. If a child inherits one of my mother's two "good" alleles and either of my wife's, he or she is entirely free of the problem. But if the "bad" one of my father's alleles shows up, it will dominate, causing huge numbers of genetic copies (in a kind of stutter), like zebra mollusks clogging an intake pipe. The muscles are literally starved of sugar. We have two sons, one free of the problem, the other not.

Myotonic Dystrophy is almost the reverse phenomenon from, say, what afflicts Jerry Lewis's Duchenne's sufferers. It presents later in life, at about the time Duchenne's claims its victim. It starts in the limbs, not the trunk. Myotonic sufferers cannot relax their clenched muscles. They're subject to cardiac arrhythmia. One by one, the muscles die, the little muscles of the ear, leading to deafness, the little muscles of the eye, and eyelids, bringing on blindness. One of our sons noticed in high school – even as he ran high hurdles – that if he balled up his fist, he had to unfurl it, finger by finger, with the other hand. We never knew; and he thought nothing of it, not that anything could have been done. A couple of years ago, the effects became increasingly apparent; we did the modern thing and took DNA samples. I am "mild" with sixty genetic replications. Sixty stutters. My older boy, the active little beauty in our family, is "classic," with three times as many.

It is strangely comforting to finally have a name for everything that can possibly go wrong, a new identity to go with all the others, a certain fate. I wish only that I could go it alone.

Fortunately, says the literature, the "genetic drift" that causes the condition is limited largely to isolated pockets, those small-population gene pools grown scummy from long inbreeding. A much-studied outcropping is found in the Lac St-Jean region of Québec. Probably my father had no more than twenty replications, not enough to register a single complication on his magnificent physique. But it is the nature of this condition to increase the stutter, generation by generation, and for our dark, secret trait to grow more devastating, until nothing remains.

I still cherish my millions of cousins and the living fact that in Québec we are all linked by less than six degrees of separation. On each new visit to Montreal I take new pride in my people's self-reinvention, even as I see them in my dreams, robed and hooded, chanting prayers I can't comprehend, against an enemy I know too well.

This page intentionally left blank

Autobiographical Annex: 1985–2006

I DISCOVERED MY Americanness in Canada, and my Canadian-ness after I returned to the United States. Libraries classify my books as "Canadian" although I was born, and have lived most of my life, in the United States, as an American. Yet I cannot deny that I am psychologically a child of my parents' Canada, French and English.

It is the self-defeating paradox of my writing life that I was never more an "American" writer than when I lived in Canada (1966–1980) and wrote the stories that made up *A North American Education* and *Tribal Justice*, and the novels *Lunar Attractions* (written in New Delhi while on leave from teaching in Montreal) and *Lusts* (begun in Toronto, completed in Iowa City), and never more the "Canadian" writer than in my subsequent American-written books, in particular, *The Sorrow and the Terror* (co-authored with Bharati Mukherjee), *Resident Alien*, *I Had a Father*, *Man and His World*, and, most notably, the biography-cum-intellectual-history *Time Lord*. The four volumes of my *Selected Stories* (*Southern Stories, Pittsburgh Stories, Montreal Stories*, and *World Body*) have appeared (2000–2006) only in Canada with my long-term Canadian publisher, The Porcupine's Quill, while I've been living in California and New York. My most "American" book (in that it doesn't mention Canada at all) is the Asia- and Europe-set counter-picaresque *If I Were Me*; it too has appeared only in Canada, although its protagonist is a Brooklyn-born Jewish sociolinguist.

It is the nature of the border-crosser to be the wrong person in the wrong place at the wrong time. Re-establishing myself in 1980 as a forty-year-old immigrant to the United States and having to go through naturalization into the country of my birth and upbringing is, I suppose, a predictable complication for someone who has lived on both sides of a border, who has claims on both sides, and who wishes, profoundly, to continue living inside the shadows they cast, claiming both identities. Border-dwellers are like the shy and furtive rabbits hiding inside Frost's "Mending Wall" ("'Good fences make good neighbors'"), flushed only by storms, and hunters.

For our first job in the new/old country, Bharati and I split a single professorship at Skidmore College in Saratoga Springs, New York. The Degas-evoking racetrack-and-ballet resort town had fallen on hard times throughout the sixties and seventies; we came from go-go Toronto with just enough house-sale money to buy one of Saratoga's glorious twenty-room relics with a five-room carriage house behind. It was in Saratoga that I began jogging; and for the next fifteen years, in twenty-five states, eight provinces, and fourteen countries, until my knees gave out, I put in my daily four miles and knew the only period of off-the-rack body shape that I've ever enjoyed.

We soon discovered, however, that one salary could not maintain us and our two sons; therefore, while one of us taught at Skidmore, the other accepted a job wherever it opened. Bharati went to the Writers' Workshop at Iowa for a year, then she returned to Saratoga and I went off to Iowa. I took the boys with me – it would be Bart's senior year, and Bernard was in the eighth grade. After their first day in Iowa City schools they held me to a promise: we will stay here till Bernard graduates. They had gone to five different schools in two languages and four countries in the past five years. They were fed up, and Saratoga's school was unbearable. I was doing to them on a grander scale what my parents had done to me (I'd only gone to thirty schools in my first eight years). And so, in 1984 we resigned from Skidmore and moved to Iowa City without a job, and bought a house with our Saratoga proceeds. It turned out to be the house where John Irving had lived while writing *Garp*, complete with the infamous damaged garage-pillar.

The eighties were our decade of testing. We'd given up a country because of racial violence against Indian immigrants ("Keep Canada Green – Paint a Paki" read a favourite bumper sticker of the time), surrendered two extraordinary jobs in an exciting city (we've never been able to hold comparable jobs in the same city since leaving Montreal), and taken on a new country and literary culture that took no notice of two middle-aged Canadians. We had to bridge four years as freelancers and part-timers while Bernard breezed through a very happy high-school experience. In the summer of 1983, I taught in Saskatchewan on a reserve, carrying a small fence post with me on my morning jogs when the half-wild dogs took too great an interest. That fall, I taught in Nelson, British Columbia – my first time in the mountains, in the West, keeping an eye on fermented-apple-drinking bears sleeping it off in the apple trees, living in a motel, and sending my measly Canadian salary back to Iowa City. One of us was always able to stay there to provide a home life (by then, Bart was enrolled at the University of Iowa).

I wrote an espionage novel, *Embassy*, based on the years we'd spent in India; it failed and was not published – too much Graham Greene, and not enough Robert Ludlum, according to the only person who read it, my friend David Morrell. I did baseball journalism for *Sport*, more sports commentary for *TV Guide* (Canada), book reviews, travel pieces, stories. And as a result of memories that came flooding back to me while teaching again in Canada, I began to write the stories and the autobiographical pieces that would form *Resident Alien*. My mantra, through good times and bad, has always been: trust to the writing. Blind trust, a faith in writing, has often been my only ally.

In the lowest time of our life, particularly in Bharati's, one winter morning in 1984 when money was tightest and prospects non-existent, she received a providential (and, as it turned out, a resurrectional) phone call from Emory University in Atlanta, inviting her to teach a semester. She hadn't published a book since our joint *Days and Nights in Calcutta* (1977), and had begun to doubt that she would write again. Bharati's agent even told her there was no market in writing about Indian immigrants. How did the offer happen? Our old Iowa classmate, the poet James Tate, on a brief stay at Emory, had suggested her name. We hadn't seen Jim in fifteen years. He wasn't exactly a stranger, but his kindness saved a life and re-ignited a career.

Three months after arriving in Atlanta Bharati had written an entire story collection, *Darkness*, about Indian immigrants in Canada, Germany, and the United States. It was published a few months later in 1985 by Penguin Canada. I was invited to Emory the following semester, and then asked to run their summer writers' festival, which I did for the next few summers. Except for a couple of months in the middle of my undergraduate work, it was my first return to the South since 1950, when I left Florida. The next year, 1986-87, I was invited back to my old university in Montreal as visiting writer, flying up two days a week.

I'd always thought of our marriage as heroic, larger than life; we were a legendary writing couple who'd taken big risks for the hope of big payoffs. By the mid-eighties I was asking, "Where had it gone? What heroism, what legend, what success?" When we married in 1963, there were very few intercultural marriages like ours. We were parents by twenty-four. I thought nothing of pursuing my lifelong identity crisis by taking on Canada, pulling a reluctant wife with me; we wrote early and often, won prizes and got attention, and then the early fame, the confidence, all began to slip away. In Toronto in 1979, our younger son developed diabetes, and our older son kept an even more dangerous medical secret from us and himself. Canada, particularly Toronto, turned racist, and we left it. Bharati couldn't write; I wrote, but my fifth book for Doubleday, the novel *Lusts*, received no in-house support and very few reviews. I had stumbled onto the new publishing reality: *Lusts* was expected to build on the reputation I'd won with *Lunar Attractions*, and its opening pages had earned me a National Endowment grant, but the finished book failed to earn back its advance. Our good luck and boldness had deserted us. What we had were two stalled writing careers, itinerant teaching gigs, and an inability to put milk and orange juice on the same table.

A tragic event occurred in Canada on June 23, 1985. An Air India 747 bound for London and Bombay from Toronto and Montreal exploded in midair about 110 miles off the southwest coast of Ireland, killing all 329 aboard. At nearly the same time, a suitcase from a second Air India 747 exploded in the Narita baggage-handling shed, killing two workers. One plane had arrived early, the other was late; it was forensically established that bombs were intended to bring both planes down and they had been timed to explode simultaneously on opposite sides of the world and kill over seven hundred. Until 9/11, the 331 deaths were the bloodiest air-terrorist incident in history. A Calcutta classmate of Bharati's had been aboard. I think every Indian in Canada knew someone who had perished. As it was a late-June flight, the first flight after schools closed, the majority of victims were women and children; the husbands had stayed back. Everyone suspected terrorism. Everyone suspected "Sikh terrorism," a payback for the Indian Army's invasion of the Golden Temple in Amritsar the year before. Japanese forensic experts extracted bits of embedded plastic from the body of a baggage handler: the plastic had come from a radio-tuner, the registration number was lifted, and the purchase traced to a ship's electrician in a small town on Vancouver Island. His name was important: Inderjit Singh Reyat. Sikh, yes, but more importantly, a fundamentalist, baptized Khalsa ("the pure"), part of a network of temples (*gurdwaras*) on the West Coast whose priests openly called for war against India, independence for Punjab, and who intimidated less militant Sikhs, even to the point of assaults and threatened murder. No one had expected that the Khalistani call for vengeance would be played out in open, liberal, uninvolved Canada. The victims' families in Canada were demanding a formal parliamentary investigation. If such a tragedy had happened to "white" families, if an Alitalia plane had gone down, would the government have been so dilatory?

As the one-year anniversary approached and the Canadian government had shown insufficient urgency in pursuing the killers, victim-families were going on record, accusing the government of racist indifference. (A standard Canadian defence: "This is a peaceful country. Why don't you people keep your messy problems on your side of the world?") The outraged cries of Indians in Canada, their sense of alienation, were all too familiar to Bharati. That semester I was in Atlanta, she in Iowa. "We should write the book," she declared. At that time, following the success of *Darkness*, she felt more empowered than I. And so began our second India-centred collaboration, the project that was to become *The Sorrow and the Terror: The Haunting Legacy of the Air India Tragedy*. Bharati's *Darkness* publisher, Penguin Canada, bought the proposal immediately. The United States was not interested in terrorism, especially in a Canadian event with complicated names and an Asian provenance, even though, as we were able to demonstrate, many of the Khalistani cells had American collaborators, and many anti-Indian plots were hatched in the United States, not Canada. (The same complacency that drove the Canadian tragedy clearly explains the U.S. failure to react to intelligence pointing to the 9/11 bombings.) Since I was the more mobile partner, I took weekly trips to Toronto and Montreal to interview victims' families, and to meet in odd corners of shopping malls with shadowy members of India's vast overseas counter-intelligence network, often shaved, unturbaned Sikhs themselves. There were Canadian police, politicians, RCMP, and informed members of the Indian community from all sides of the issue; there were trial documents to read and ongoing trials to attend. I spent three days a week in the Toronto Research Library Xeroxing old newspaper files (no Internet in 1986), and three days back at Emory. For several months in 1986-87 we lived the lives of investigative reporters; it was a time of large emotions: rage, sorrow, and cynicism. There were death-threats against us, and RCMP protection. In the summer, we went out to Vancouver and since by then we had learned the still-unpublished names of the chief suspects, we simply called them up, posing as financial journalists, and talked to them as well. (Those suspects, in 2003-04, were finally named and brought to trial.)

In 1985, I received a Guggenheim grant for the opening pages of a new project, a combination of fiction and autobiography, called *Resident Alien*. Penguin Canada published it the next year in the same short-story series as *Darkness*: four related Canadian/American stories about a French-Canadian family, starting out in Florida and Pittsburgh as the Porters, ending in Montreal as the Carriers, the fiction surrounded by two long autobiographical essays. The intent: a picture of the fiction-writing mind, building story from fact, growing increasingly invented, less tethered to autobiography, until the fictional voice takes over. The model was V.S. Naipaul's *In a Free State*.

Resident Alien was my resurrection: in it, I remembered my Winnipeg, Anglo-Canadian childhood, an experience I had always avoided. I took on a first-person French-Canadian consciousness from a world and time I had never lived through. The last two stories, "North" and the novella-length "Translation," were my first wholly invented stories. A few copies were imported into the United States – enough to earn a long and poisonous *New York Times Book Review* half-pager by the distinguished novelist Paul West, which effectively killed it. (In 1988, when I was inducted as a "Literary Lion" by the New York Public Library, the group photo has me standing next to West.)

When our younger son, Bernard, was accepted to Reed College in Oregon in 1986, we sold the Iowa house and moved to New York. Bharati secured a professorship at Monclair State in New Jersey. I got a series of adjunct professorships at Columbia and NYU; we rented in Upper Montclair, Long Island City, and as subletters in Manhattan. After a year, she was offered a professorship at CUNY-Queens. We were now paying for a child in college; we both taught evenings at Columbia and NYU and I even added Sarah Lawrence twice a week. The necklace of part-time jobs – five

thousand dollars each with no benefits – plus Bharati's professorship at New Jersey, and then at CUNY-Queens, kept us in Manhattan at a subsistence level. Still, Bharati wrote her second story-
collection, *The Middleman and Other Stories*, which won the 1988
National Book Critics Circle Award, and the follow-up novel *Jasmine*, a *New York Times* front-page-review book, much of which
detailed the Iowa life we'd just lived through, seen through the
eyes of a plucky, young, widowed illegal immigrant. Following a
long decline into Alzheimer's disease, my mother died in a Winnipeg nursing home in 1987. The money I inherited, twenty thousand dollars, was the untouched amount she'd been left in her
divorce twenty-six years earlier. With it, we were able to buy the
cheapest co-op listed in *The Village Voice*: the windows rattled, the
mice and rats ran free, nothing worked, the lead-drenched plaster
crumbled, the light sockets sizzled and snapped.

In 1986, I was driving from New York City north to Saratoga
when the car radio announced the news that an American author
had died. It got my attention, of course, and I waited to hear the
name, my mind riffling through the Rolodex of possibilities. The
only name I would never connect with death was that of my
friend, mentor, and father figure, Bernard Malamud. He had died
in the kitchen of his New York apartment while preparing a little
lunch, on a break from his morning writing. Writers don't die in
the middle of projects – they can't, there's some sort of divine
energy that props them up. So many times I'd had lunch or dinner
with Bern and his wife Ann in New York, or in Bennington: there
was always some cold meat, good bread, a shared beer, a walk and
a talk.

I have known two great men in my life: the Bengali filmmaker
Satyajit Ray, and Bernard Malamud. Their every word and gesture,
and of course their films and books, celebrate a confident and
unshakeable vision of the world, and of humanity. Passion and
clarity, nothing showy, nothing extraneous; if the material is there,
it will speak for itself, in its proper manner. I've come to realize,
over the years, that I was writing for Bern, and probably still am.

He called fiction "the dramatization of the multifarious adventures of the human heart" (unflinchingly, in the ambitious, form-stretching sixties). "Dramatize, dramatize," he urged, far more the Jamesian than most casual readers would have thought.

In the late eighties I was invited back for a year to the Writers' Workshop at Iowa, and Bharati was offered a major position at the University of California-Berkeley. We took a trip out to San Francisco in January 1989, to walk through the campus eucalyptus grove in just the lightest jackets, to see the alternate life, perhaps a reward for the decade we'd managed to survive. She was a hot ticket, perhaps the hottest in academe that year. To put it mildly, I was not. The sobering disparity sent me back to Iowa where a new position was opening up, that of Director of the International Writing Program.

The IWP is a residency program, started by Paul Engle and his wife, for thirty-five authors from all parts of the world. The writers come to Iowa for three months in the fall of every year – their passage and residency paid for, largely, by the U.S. State Department – to associate informally with writers in the Writers' Workshop, give talks and readings in Iowa and around the country. Iowa is America's most genial face; there's little doubt that when the program was started in 1965 it had a soft propaganda aim. It's true as well that over the first twenty-five years of its existence, the original impulse had diffused. The writers had little contact with the University; they were seen as amiable but disconnected presences. I was selected to heal the breach, and became the IWP's second full-time Director.

The University, however, had new expectations. The writers were to be younger, more fluent in English, and I would not be inheriting access to the Engles' extensive fundraising network. And so, for the 1990s, I became a fundraiser and world traveller, the wineglass tapper at the end of banquets, the visitor to a dozen different arts organizations on every continent but Africa (there we still counted on the State Department to find and bring the writers). For nine years, I was a faithful annual visitor to any country capable of sending us a writer, and when the writers were there, I did the television and radio interviews, introduced them at readings, and accompanied many of them on their national tours. In the second semester, the fundraising half of the year, I was able to spend weeks in San Francisco with Bharati, and to write the stories and draft new books.

Thanks to some autobiographical proddings, and perhaps an increased use of French in my Iowa job, I went back to my father's Québec, researching what I could of his family tree, his birth, and the early years he never talked about. The book *I Had a Father: A Post-Modern Autobiography* was published in the United States and Canada to some slight attention, but general confusion. Was it my autobiography seen through the lens of my father's Québec identity – or his sketchy biography, clouded by my own eager interventions? Both are true (hence the subtitle), and it has pleased me, over the past decade, to have been included in a number of Québec and Franco-American events, an assertion of a legitimate strand of my complicated identity and a demonstration of how removed from it I truly am.

In 1993, I established a connection with The Porcupine's Quill, a small, arts publisher in Erin, Ontario. Perhaps I should say they came to me in the person of John Metcalf, one of the original "Montreal Story Tellers" from those early-seventies years when five of us drove around Montreal and environs, reading our stories to high-school students. John, who has become the major anthologizer and editor of short stories in Canada, is the Quill's senior editor and in that capacity has taken on the preservation of my work in a series of beautifully presented volumes of stories. A collection of new work, *Man and His World* appeared in 1993 (stories now totally invented – I've exhausted the usable autobiographical elements in my life); 1997 saw the novella-as-stories *If I Were Me*, in which I luxuriated in my Iowa-based travel experiences, sending my character, Gerald Lander, to Japan, India, Israel, Estonia, and Poland as well as New York, Chicago, and

Boston. The remaining project, perhaps a twilight experience, has been to bring the earlier, long-out-of-print stories back for new readers. In 2000 came *Southern Stories* (incorporating the Florida-based stories of my first two books, plus two previously unpublished stories from my undergraduate, Denison writing); in 2002 *Pittsburgh Stories* (continuing to piece together an adolescent narrative from *Tribal Justice, Lusts, Resident Alien*, and *Man and His World*, plus two new stories); in 2003 *The Montreal Stories* (including two new ones); and finally, in 2006, the stories of the broader world, called *World Body*, largely the sum of my fiction-writing in the 1990s.

That catches us up, except for the biggest development in my writing life. In 1997, in Iowa, I was writing a sequel to the book on my father – my mother's Saskatchewan and Manitoba childhood, her European art education and pre-War Montreal return – when a word I'd used, "time-zone," suddenly caught my eye. It seemed, that night, a strange word. I had meant only to say "our lives are like time-zones," meaning that one life can contain so many multitudes, just as a time-zone passes over cities and oceans, swamps and tundra, languages, races, and religions, so I went to the encyclopedia, just to inform myself of its origins. And there, spilling out before me, came my next book. Time-zones originated in the Prime Meridian Conference of 1884, convened by a Scottish-born Canadian engineer, Sandford Fleming. He and I were both fifty-seven years of age. The more I read, the more fascinated I became; I could see the outlines of my mother and my maternal grandfather in the stolid, inventive, persistent figure of Fleming. I felt that I knew him, and his world, far better than I knew my father's or even my own. I looked him up online, accessed a museum in his name, secured some of his scientific papers, wrote a thirty-nine-page proposal for *Time Lord: Sir Sandford Fleming and the Creation of Standard Time*.

Pantheon and Knopf Canada immediately bought it with a generous (for me) advance, large enough to pose a certain dilemma. Then six foreign publishers bought it, reinforcing the dilemma. Quit the teaching, I resolved, devote yourself to this book. The University unconsciously helped with the decision; it cut its subsidies to the IWP, and a new administration (my third dean and third president in nine years) seemed determined to run the program into the ground. (After a year of drama, and a new president, the University came around and acknowledged the unique importance of the IWP and has reconstituted it with more money and an energetic administration.) And so, in June of 1998, I sold my house in Iowa and moved permanently, I thought, to be with Bharati in the Bay area. The separations and hard times seemed to be over. I even taught happily at Berkeley on an adjunct basis.

Our lives can never be planned so exactly. The long-buried medical problems of our older son began to manifest themselves; it is a form of muscular dystrophy. It is my genetic contribution, just as it was my father's, the French-Canadian component, one might say, the genetic contribution of a confined gene pool. My father, a prizefighter, showed no signs of any complication (except perhaps an exaggerated musculature; his muscles might have remained flexed even in repose); I am "light" myotonic, with sixty replications of my genetic makeup; our son has three times as many, with obvious implications. And so, when an opportunity arose in 2002 to take a job in eastern Long Island at Southampton College, I took it, and for the past three years have been living again separated from Bharati except for summers and sabbaticals, but keeping a weekend home available for our boy, his wife, and adopted grand-daughters who live in our now-renovated upper west side apartment.

For now, we have three dwellings: Manhattan, Southampton, and San Francisco, where Bharati continues to teach at Berkeley. Her later novels – *The Holder of the World, Leave It to Me, Desirable Daughters*, and *The Tree Bride* – command serious attention and decent sales, but not the frenzy of *Jasmine* and *The Middleman and Other Stories*. My *Selected Stories* have been preserved in four handsome volumes; a collection of my essays will come out soon. *Time Lord* is still in print, as is *Lunar Attractions*. I have added a couple of chapters to *I Had a Father*, though it still requires a publisher to rescue it from oblivion. Meanwhile, I am retired, free to write full-time. Southampton College has been reabsorbed by its main campus, Long Island University, in Brooklyn. I will not be making the commute. The house we bought in Southampton – my first swimming pool! – will be sold, and perhaps we'll find a smaller place in New York to be close to the next generation. By then, I hope, I'll add a novel or two, now that the travelling itch has been scratched and time, one of my few areas of expertise, again seems to have fallen in my lap.

This page intentionally left blank

THE WORLD OF CLARK BLAISE:

A BIBLIOGRAPHY

of His 'Occasional' Critical Writing,

Autobiographical Writing, and Nonfiction Writing

BY J.R. (TIM) STRUTHERS

with Andrew C. McKague and with Marlys Chevrefils

This page intentionally left blank

Contents

This page intentionally left blank

A Preface

to "The World of Clark Blaise: A Bibliography . . ."

THIS BIBLIOGRAPHY takes as its starting point what for Clark Blaise was the autobiographically crucial and creatively inspiring time of his arrival at the beginning of the summer of 1966 from the United States (where twenty-six years earlier he had been born to an English-Canadian mother and a French-Canadian father) to take up residence, for what proved to be a twelve-year period, in Montreal, Quebec, just six months before Canada launched the centennial celebrations marked most impressively by Montreal's hosting of the magnificent World's Fair "Expo 67." To make this bibliography as scrupulously detailed, as creatively organized, as richly suggestive as scholarly skill and imaginative ability, research tools and library holdings, would allow has involved sustained personal and intellectual concentration on the part of the primary bibliographer and the equally important personal and intellectual generosity of key collaborators and numerous correspondents. Clearly the present bibliography does not aim to document Blaise's very substantial achievement as a fiction writer but instead chooses to focus – for the first time – on the other half of his *oeuvre*: Blaise's 'occasional' (but hardly infrequent!) critical writing and autobiographical writing and nonfiction writing. And because this bibliography starts with the summer of 1966, it does not, therefore, include assorted (in many instances irretrievable) publications from the time beginning with Blaise's undergraduate days at Denison University in Granville, Ohio, and continuing on through his MFA days in the Writers' Workshop at the University of Iowa to his first two years of teaching and writing, marriage and parenting, immediately before he came to Canada. Nor does this bibliography cite absolutely all of the (in some cases irretrievable) critical writing and autobiographical writing and nonfiction writing published by Blaise since that life-changing summer of 1966. Of course there are further items about which I possess only glimmerings of knowledge at this time and for which I need to continue searching; but that's another story.

What this bibliography concentrates on – and seeks to direct readers' attention to – is the twin half if you will (to the fiction) of Blaise's *oeuvre*: the three seemingly different, certainly important, in fact often merging kinds of work that Clark Blaise has undertaken with great passion and great frequency and extremely impressive results for more than forty years: (i) critical writing (broadly defined as is suggested by the heading of the first of the thirteen categories in which I have sought to design this bibliography, "1. Critical Writing on Time, Place, History, Geography, Borders, Cultures, Literatures"); (ii) autobiographical writing; and (iii) nonfiction writing. For although a milestone bibliographical work such as *The Clark Blaise Papers* (1991), compiled by Marlys Chevrefils, and a milestone critical work such as *An Other I: The Fictions of Clark Blaise* (1988), by Robert Lecker, were exemplary in their own ways, both were significantly, if to a large degree necessarily, limited. Not only confined to examining essentially the first twenty to perhaps twenty-five years of Blaise's achievement, up to the publication of *Resident Alien* (1986) – his seventh book out of a total, now, of eighteen books – but also confined by the focus or the method of each study. *The Clark Blaise Papers*, though oriented towards documenting all the different forms and types of work by Blaise up to 1986, limited to materials supplied to The University of Calgary by the author. *An Other I*, restricted to studying Blaise's books of fiction, of autobiography and fiction, of autobiography, up to 1986, omitting any discussion of the substantial amount, even at that time, of his 'occasional' critical writing and autobiographical writing and nonfiction writing (except for a brief analysis of the 1972 piece "To Begin, To Begin") other than to use a few selections as a way of illuminating Blaise's fiction and overall aesthetic.

Typically, even a very fine critical essay on Blaise's fiction such as Robert M. Luscher's "In Search of Lost Time: Clark Blaise's *Pittsburgh Stories* as a Short Story Sequence" in *Clark Blaise, Proprietor*, ed. J.R. (Tim) Struthers [*Short Story* (Fall 2007)] would likely, and by and large appropriately, cite at most a few pieces of Blaise's critical writing or autobiographical writing or nonfiction writing. The "Works Cited" of the one full-length critical study to date, Robert Lecker's admittedly twenty-year-old *An Other I: The Fictions of Clark Blaise*, lists only 10 essays by Blaise. By contrast, however, and the contrast is, I feel, dumbfounding, "The World of Clark Blaise: A Bibliography . . ." includes more than 150 'occasional' pieces – let me repeat that, as Clark Blaise's and my dear friend the late Hugh Hood would say of particular phrases during a reading, let me repeat that – more than 150 'occasional' pieces of critical writing and autobiographical writing and nonfiction writing, Altogether, this represents a very rich body of writing by Clark Blaise since that moment at age 26 when he crossed another border – via Windsor, Ontario – to begin to claim the heritage he imagined for himself in Canada and to continue to forge the writing career he imagined for himself in the world.

Prior to the thorough bibliographical research and the preliminary critical reflections offered by the present work, the very substantial, now more than forty year, expanse of Clark Blaise's critical writing and autobiographical writing and nonfiction writing was to a large extent undocumented and unexamined – bibliographically and, especially, critically. "The World of Clark Blaise: A Bibliography . . ." has, therefore, two main purposes. The first is to find and to foreground a wealth of hitherto unearthed bibliographical details crucial to understanding the amplitude of Clark Blaise's thought and achievement and crucial to developing state-of-the-art studies of his writing. The second is to suggest and to stimulate new ways of approaching, in whole or in part, the entire *oeuvre* of Clark Blaise – both the fiction and the twin to that presented here – by means of a reconfigured method of research and reading and interpretation that, I would argue, the design invented for this bibliography serves to model and to advocate. "The World of Clark Blaise: A Bibliography . . ." is divided into thirteen sections; with a nod to Wallace Stevens I might have called it "Thirteen Ways of Looking at Clark Blaise." But as those who know my fondness for complex numerologies might expect, this bibliography is also grouped into three sets of sections: the first, consisting of five parts finishing with "5. On Fiction and Interpretation"; the second, five more parts finishing with "10. On Autobiography and Interpretation"; the third, three parts ending with "13. On Nonfiction and Interpretation." In addition, the three sections just named form a theoretically oriented and implicitly self-reflexive triptych. Back up one section from these three and you find – or create – an equally interesting analytically oriented and explicitly self-reflexive triptych: "4. On His Own Fiction," "9. On His Own Autobiographical Writing," "12. On His Own Nonfiction."

Entire groupings in this bibliography, or parts of them, can of course be read in uninterrupted sequences. Readers wanting an impression of the subjects Blaise has chosen for his own memoir writing, of his thoughts on other memoirists and autobiographers, of the great extent of his own autobiographical writing, of instances where he has commented on it, of his ideas about writing and interpreting autobiography, can review the contents of "6. On Some Artists, Fellow Writers, Mentors," "7. On Some Writers of Autobiography, Memoir, Personal Nonfiction," "8. Autobiographical Writing," "9. On His Own Autobiographical Writing," "10. On Autobiography and Interpretation." Alternatively, readers wanting to learn about the range, and the specifics, of Blaise's reflections on the art of fiction can review the contents of sections 1. to 5., including thirty-two different pieces in "2. On Some Novelists" and eleven more pieces in "3. On Some Short Story Writers." Or particular sections can be read singly – though, as my decision to list certain items in more than one section of this bibliography implies, none of the thirteen sections here stands alone. Indeed, it is my intention to stress the degree to which the

contents of ostensibly separate sections of this bibliography con-
verge, overlap, enter into new dynamics, to stress the degree to
which new understandings are made possible by multiple-listing.
Those readers interested in an overview of the kinds of writing
represented here might choose to consider the three sections – "1.
Critical Writing on Time, Place, History, Geography, Borders,
Cultures, Literatures," "6. On Some Artists, Fellow Writers, Mentors," "11. Nonfiction" – that lead off the three larger groupings
into which this bibliography is divided. Other readers might
choose, as I have already suggested, to consider the three sections about fiction or autobiography or nonfiction and interpretation that conclude the three larger groupings. And then circle
back to the beginning of this bibliography and give careful
thought to the impressive array of forty essays in the opening
section. And then get on with the true task before us: READING
CLARK BLAISE.

     Seeking to establish such bibliographical details for even a sin-
gle entry gives rise to a host of questions, involves intense research
and vast correspondence – especially in the case of such a widely
respected and widely travelled figure as Clark Blaise, founder and
director for much of the 1970s of the MFA in Creative Writing at
Concordia University in Montreal, guest instructor and guest lecturer at many universities and writing programs and literary
events in Canada and the United States and around the world,
director from 1990 to 1998 of the highly prestigious International
Writing Program at the University of Iowa, author now, as I say, of
eighteen books. Occasionally the bibliographer may have the sudden sensation of beholding cavernous depths – no more dramatically than when Clark Blaise stated in response to one of my cease-
less queries, "I know I wrote a piece about it, but have no idea
where it might be (probably in the bottom of one of the 500 boxes
of my manuscripts rotting in an Iowa storage locker)." Almost
invariably, however, the combined labours of assorted individuals
prevailed, producing a definitive and gratifying result. Upon
learning about one of the myriad pieces recovered from long ago

or far away, Clark Blaise exclaimed: "amazing! As I always say, nothing in the universe is ever lost." Gradually, cumulatively, and finally overwhelmingly, answers replaced questions, solutions replaced mysteries – and I found myself thinking of my correspondents, as I observed in an e-mail to Ilkka Välimäki, Researcher, The Literary Archives, The Finnish Literature Society, Helsinki, Finland, "You are a bibliographer's dream come true!"

For their magnanimous and judicious assistance with this bibliography, I wish to express particular gratitude to Andrew C. McKague and Marlys Chevrefils and especially Clark Blaise. And as well as acknowledging the gracious and helpful members of library staffs at the University of Guelph and other institutions, I wish to thank numerous individual correspondents for the kindliness and the acumen with which they responded to my inquiries. Geographer Dean Louder, when asked about a paper delivered by Clark Blaise in 1990 at Laval, provided me not only with very helpful bibliographical information but also with a vivid personal reminiscence. Of the occasion at *le Petit Séminaire* in the old part of Quebec City when Clark Blaise gave his paper "Latin Americans of the North," Dean Louder remarks: "I can still see Clark there, eighteen years later, telling his story." And so can we experience Clark Blaise telling his own, his family's, Canada's and the United States's, North America's, the world's story – as we read for the first time, or revisit, any one of the more than 150 forcefully argued, always memorable 'occasional' pieces by Clark Blaise listed in this bibliography. Furthermore, attention to even a single item cited here can open up opportunities for highly revealing literary analysis. In the instance of a work listed in "8. Autobiographical Writing" – the opening section, called "The Voice of Unhousement," of Blaise's volume *Resident Alien* (1986) – the details given in my annotation for that entry direct the reader to find five earlier pieces by Blaise which he used in constructing "The Voice of Unhousement" and thus invite the reader to appreciate much more fully its unique emphasis, artifice, phrasing, development, and effect.

Only in the last few days while finishing this bibliography did I recall, and realize the significance of, a particular series of comments by Clark from our extensive e-mail conversation where, describing the basis for his early undergraduate fascination with Thomas Mann, Clark refers to a now fifty-year-old personal dream: "As a young aspirant to a writing career (although wrapped up in a Geology major), and as the son of an immigrant shop-owner in a provincial city, I caught a whiff of brotherliness with Mann (especially with my mother's long-term residence in Weimar). I started reading the novels right after the stories, and was always impressed by those Knopf Borzoi imprints, with the pages at the end dedicated to Mann's long bibliography. I wanted that for myself." It delights me to have helped make this long-held dream a reality. Bibliographical work is serious, of enduring significance – but it is also fun. Readers of this preface who like baseball as much as Clark Blaise does and who like numerologies as much as I do will be amused to count the number of paragraphs I've written; that's part of the fun, too.

As I have sought to emphasize, bibliographical work is by definition collaborative work: it builds on the efforts of people in the past, depends profoundly on the assistance of others in the present, will involve the efforts of many in the future. And, as I first stressed in 1981 in "Some Highly Subversive Activities: A Brief Polemic and a Checklist of Works on Alice Munro," credit needs to be given where credit is due. For their support, then, of my own bibliographical, editorial, and critical work over a period of more than thirty years, I would like to acknowledge the late literary historian Carl F. Klinck at Western for having encouraged the pioneering research on Alice Munro that I began publishing in 1975; Jack David and Robert Lecker for inviting me to do the work on Hugh Hood included in ECW Press's and my own first book, *Before the Flood*, ed. J.R. (Tim) Struthers (ECW Press, 1979) and in much-expanded form in *The Annotated Bibliography of Canada's Major Authors*, ed. Jack David and Robert Lecker, Vol. 5 (ECW Press, 1984); Michael Taylor for publishing my "Some

Highly Subversive Activities: A Brief Polemic and a Checklist of Works on Alice Munro" in *Studies in Canadian Literature* 6.1 (1981); Geoff Hancock for publishing my "A Preliminary Bibliography of Works by Leon Rooke" in *Canadian Fiction Magazine* 38 (1981); Stan Dragland at Western for supervising my Ph.D. dissertation, "Intersecting Orbits: A Study of Selected Story Cycles by Hugh Hood, Jack Hodgins, Clark Blaise, and Alice Munro in Their Literary Contexts" (1982); Simon Dardick for publishing my "A Checklist of Works by The Montreal Story Tellers" in *The Montreal Story Tellers*, ed. J.R. (Tim) Struthers (Véhicule Press, 1985); all those who for going on twenty-five years have believed in Red Kite Press, which issued my "John Metcalf at Fifty" in *What Is A Canadian Literature?*, by John Metcalf (Red Kite Press, 1988); Ron Smith and Rhonda Bailey for publishing my "A Checklist of Works by Jack Hodgins" in *On Coasts of Eternity*, ed. J.R. (Tim) Struthers (Oolichan Books, 1996); Don LePan for publishing my "Once More to the Lake: Towards a Poetics of Receptivity" in *New Contexts of Canadian Criticism*, ed. Ajay Heble, Donna Palmateer Pennee, and J.R. (Tim) Struthers (Broadview Press, 1997); John Metcalf for inviting me to undertake "The World of Clark Blaise: A Bibliography . . . , " and Dan Wells for publishing it, as part of *Selected Essays*, by Clark Blaise (Biblioasis, 2008). Nor will I ever forget the generous and sustaining courtesy, indeed the indulgence, of the subjects of my bibliographical work while I have persisted with my visions.

1. Critical Writing on Time, Place, History, Geography, Borders, Cultures, Literatures

"Neo-Fascism and the Kennedy Assassins." *Canadian Dimension* Sept.-Oct. 1967: 26-27.

Data in part gathered from *The Clark Blaise Papers* (1991), comp. Marlys Chevrefils. The title cited here is what appears at the start of the actual piece. Another title, "New Evidence Supports Garrison," is given in the list of contents.

"The Big Lie, American Style." *Saturday Night* Oct. 1967: 37-40.

Data in part gathered from *The Clark Blaise Papers* (1991), comp. Marlys Chevrefils. Signed "J.M. LaBrune."

"Writing Canadian Fiction." Canada Week. St. Lawrence U, Canton, NY. 16 Apr. 1975. Address. *Fiction International* 6-7 (1976): 5-11. Print.

Data in part gathered from *The Clark Blaise Papers* (1991), comp. Marlys Chevrefils, and with further help from Joe David Bellamy and Marlys Chevrefils.

"[Canadian Convocation]." St. George's School, Montreal, QC. 30 May 1975. Address. "Canadian Convocation: Graduation Address – St. George's School." *Anthol* 4 (Winter 1975): 28-38. Print.

Data in part gathered from *The Clark Blaise Papers* (1991), comp. Marlys Chevrefils, and with further help from Marlys Chevrefils. Title for original address devised by J.R. (Tim) Struthers and approved by Clark Blaise via e-mail between them on 25 Sept. 2008. Listed in 1., 4., 8.

"Visions and Revisions: The Commonwealth Writer and His Material." Fourth Triennial Conf. of The Assn. for Commonwealth Lit. and Lang. Studies. Jawaharlal Nehru U, New Delhi. 3 Jan. 1977. Address. Abbr. as "The Common-wealth Writer and His Material." *Awakened Conscience: Studies in Commonwealth Literature.* Ed. C.D. Narasimhaiah. New Delhi: Sterling; Atlantic Highlands, NJ: Humanities, 1978. 118-26. Print.

Data in part gathered from *The Clark Blaise Papers* (1991), comp. Marlys Chevrefils, and with further help from Clark Blaise. Version published in

Awakened Conscience: Studies in Commonwealth Literature deletes four paragraphs from the end of TS of original address.

Blaise, Clark, and Bharati Mukherjee. "How It All Turned Out . . . ." *Days and Nights in Calcutta*. By Clark Blaise and Bharati Mukherjee. Markham, ON: Penguin, 1986. 301, 303-14.
   Listed in 1., 9.

Blaise, Clark, and Bharati Mukherjee. "A Shattered Dream." *Maclean's* 25 May 1987: 42-45.
   Abbr. from Part Three, Chapter 6 of *The Sorrow and the Terror: The Haunting Legacy of the Air India Tragedy*. By Clark Blaise and Bharati Mukherjee. Markham, ON: Viking/Penguin, 1987.
   Data gathered with the help of Andrew C. McKague.

Blaise, Clark, and Bharati Mukherjee. Introduction. *The Sorrow and the Terror: The Haunting Legacy of the Air India Tragedy*. By Clark Blaise and Bharati Mukherjee. Markham, ON: Penguin, 1988. ix-xxii.
   This 1988 paperback edition offers a much-expanded version of the Introduction found in the original 1987 hardcover edition, including fuller comments on the authors' research methods. Listed in 1., 12.

"Southern Discomfort: V.S. Naipaul, Acerbic Observer of the Third World, Announces His Admiration for American Rednecks." Rev. of *A Turn in the South*, by V.S. Naipaul. *Saturday Night* June 1989: 61-63.
   Data gathered with the help of Andrew C. McKague. Listed in 1., 7.

"The Border as Fiction." *The Border as Fiction [and] Borderlines and Borderlands in English Canada: The Written Line*. By Clark Blaise and by Russell Brown. Borderlands Monograph Ser. 4. Orono, ME: Borderlands Project, The Canadian-American Center, U of Maine, 1990. 1-12. Rpt. (trans.) as "La frontière comme fiction." *Une frontière dans la tête: Culture, institutions et imaginaire canadiens*. By Lauren McKinsey and Victor Konrad, Roger Gibbins, et al. Pref. Albert Desbiens. Trans. Marie-José Daoust, Jean Papineau, and Laurent-Michel Vacher. Montreal: Liber, 1991. 133-50. Rpt. (abbr. and rev.) in Chapter Six of *I Had a Father: A Post-Modern Autobiography*. By Clark Blaise. Reading, MA: Addison-Wesley, 1993. Toronto: HarperCollins, 1993. Rpt. (rev.) in *Selected Essays*. By Clark Blaise. Ed. John Metcalf and J.R. (Tim) Struthers. Emeryville, ON: Biblioasis, 2008.
   Data gathered with the help of Clark Blaise, Rhea J. Côté Robbins, Jim Bishop, Russell Brown, Robert Lecker, and Victor Konrad. Listed in 1., 8.

Blaise, Clark, and Bharati Mukherjee. "After the Fatwa." *Mother Jones* Apr.-May 1990: 28-31, 61-65.
Data gathered with the help of Clark Blaise and Andrew C. McKague.

"Latin Americans of the North." First annual colloquium of la Chaire pour le développement de la recherche sur la culture d'expression française en Amérique du Nord (CEFAN), l'université Laval. Petit Séminaire de Québec, Faculté d'architecture, l'université Laval, Sainte-Foy, QC. 16 June 1990. Address. *Le Québec et les francophones de la Nouvelle-Angleterre.* Ed. Dean Louder. Sainte-Foy, QC: Presses de l'université Laval, 1991. 227-37. Print. Rpt. (rev.) in Chapter Seven to Chapter Thirteen of *I Had a Father: A Post-Modern Autobiography.* By Clark Blaise. Reading, MA: Addison-Wesley, 1993. Toronto: Harper-Collins, 1993.
Data gathered with the help of Clark Blaise, Jim Bishop, Dean Louder, Jeanne Valois, Guy Dinel, and James Lambert. Listed in 1., 8., 9.

"*The Thing*: The Real Thing." *The Movie That Changed My Life.* Ed. David Rosenberg. New York: Viking/Penguin, 1991. 50-59.
Data gathered with the help of Clark Blaise. Listed in 1., 8.

"[Memory, Europe, and the East-West Dialogue]." Lahti Intl. Writers' Reunion. Mukkula Manor Hotel, Mukkula, Fin. 18 June 1991. Address. TS and reel-to-reel tape (now digitized). Kirjallisuusarkisto, Suomalaisen Kirjallisuuden Seura [The Literary Archives, The Finnish Literature Society], Helsinki, Fin.
Data gathered with the help of Clark Blaise, Mirja Halonen, and Ilkka Välimäki. Title given by Clark Blaise in the Epilogue to *I Had a Father: A Post-Modern Autobiography.* By Clark Blaise. Reading, MA: Addison-Wesley, 1993. Toronto: HarperCollins, 1993. Title confirmed by Clark Blaise via e-mail with J.R. (Tim) Struthers on 19 Sept. 2008. TS is 5 pp. long. Listed in 1., 8.

"I Had a Father: A Post-Modern Autobiography." Magnum Readings. Magnum Book Store, Ottawa, ON. 27 Sept. 1992. Address. *I Had a Father: A Post-Modern Autobiography.* Magnum Readings 15. Ottawa, ON: Magnum Book Store, 1992. Print. Rpt. (rev.) in Introduction and Chapter One to Chapter Three of *I Had a Father: A Post-Modern Autobiography.* By Clark Blaise. Reading, MA: Addison-Wesley, 1993. Toronto: HarperCollins, 1993.
Data gathered with the help of John Metcalf. The Magnum Readings material consists of thirty-six pages of subsequently revised TS "Here first published in an edition of thirty copies of which four are *hors de commerce* and twenty-six are numbered and signed." Listed in 1., 8.

"Culture Wars in Lake County." 1994. TS. Collection of the author, Clark Blaise, San Francisco, CA.
    Data gathered with the help of Clark Blaise. TS is 22 pp. long. Listed in 1., 8.

"Eating in Tokyo." 1994. TS. Collection of the author, Clark Blaise, San Francisco, CA.
    Data gathered with the help of Clark Blaise. TS is 20 pp. long, including almost 11 pp. of text proper and more than 9 pp. of "notes for sidebars." Listed in 1., 8.

"Essay." *Censorship, Silence, and Shadowplay: Freedom of Expression in Indonesia, 1994.* A PEN American Center Freedom-To-Write Committee Report. By Siobhan Dowd. Ed. Faith Sale. Pref. Bharati Mukherjee. Essay by Clark Blaise. New York: PEN American Center, 1994. 46-50.
    Data gathered with the help of Andrew C. McKague.

"American Fiction." Meiji U Intl. Exchange Programs. Center for Intl. Programs, Meiji U, Tokyo. 7 May 1994. Address. *Here, There and Everywhere.* By Clark Blaise. Meiji U Intl. Exchange Programs Guest Lecture Ser. 1. Tokyo: Center for Intl. Programs, Meiji U, 1994. 7-31, 71-72. Print. Rpt. (rev.) in *Selected Essays.* By Clark Blaise. Ed. John Metcalf and J.R. (Tim) Struthers. Emeryville, ON: Biblioasis, 2008.
    Data gathered with the help of Clark Blaise and Rick Visentin.

"Some Thoughts on Canadian and Australian Fiction." Meiji U Intl. Exchange Programs. Center for Intl. Programs, Meiji U, Tokyo. 9 May 1994. Address. *Here, There and Everywhere.* By Clark Blaise. Meiji U Intl. Exchange Programs Guest Lecture Ser. 1. Tokyo: Center for Intl. Programs, Meiji U, 1994. 32-52, 72. Print. Rpt. (rev.) in *Selected Essays.* By Clark Blaise. Ed. John Metcalf and J.R. (Tim) Struthers. Emeryville, ON: Biblioasis, 2008.
    Data gathered with the help of Clark Blaise and Rick Visentin. Listed in 1., 8.

"Beyond the Bridge and Tunnel: The Queens Indians." *Patchwork of Dreams: Voices from the Heart of the New America.* Ed. Morty Sklar and Joseph Barbato. New York: The Spirit That Moves Us, 1996. 137-47.
    Data gathered with the help of Clark Blaise.

"Ruth." *Communion: Contemporary Writers Reveal the Bible in Their Lives.* Ed. David Rosenberg. New York: Anchor/Doubleday, 1996. 103-13.
    Data gathered with the help of Clark Blaise. Listed in 1., 8.

"Quebec's Soul City." *The Wilson Quarterly* 20.1 (Winter 1996): 68-75.
Data gathered with the help of Clark Blaise and Andrew C. McKague.
Listed in 1., 8.

"From Village to Millage: A Manchester Novel; Notes Toward a Franco-
American Saga." Cultural Identity in French America: Legacy, Evolution, and
the Challenges of Renewal / Identité culturelle en Amérique française:
héritage, évolution, et défis au renouvellement. U of Maine and U d'Angers.
Atlantic Oakes Hotel and Convention Center, Bar Harbor, ME. 23 May 1996.
Address. TS. Collection of the author, Clark Blaise, San Francisco, CA. Trans. as
"Création d'une conscience: notes pour une saga franco-américaine." Trans.
Viateur Boutot. *Vision et visages de la Franco-Amérique*. Ed. Dean Louder, Jean
Morisset, and Eric Waddell. Sillery, QC: Septentrion, 2001. 21-29, 323. Print.
Data gathered with the help of Clark Blaise, Rhea J. Côté Robbins, Jim
Bishop, Dean Louder, and Viateur Boutot. TS is 11 pp. long. Listed in 1., 4.

"The International Novel." The Loft Literary Center, Minneapolis, MN. 7 Sept.
1996. Address. *Selected Essays*. By Clark Blaise. Ed. John Metcalf and J.R. (Tim)
Struthers. Emeryville, ON: Biblioasis, 2008. Print.
Data gathered with the help of Clark Blaise, Dara Syrkin, and Jerod Santek.
Listed in 1., 8.

"Looking at India: An Iowa Perspective." Narratives of Displacement in South
Asian Experience, Movement and Memory Workshop, U of Iowa South Asian
Studies Program. Pappajohn Business Building, U of Iowa, Iowa City, IA. 26
Sept. 1996. Address. Audiocassette. Collection of Paul R. Greenough, Iowa
City, Iowa. TS. Collection of the author, Clark Blaise, San Francisco, CA.
Data gathered with the help of Clark Blaise, Susan K. Lohafer, Jo Dickens,
Jonathan Wilcox, Peter Nazareth, Mary Nazareth, Nancy L. Baker, David F.
McCartney, Philip A. Lutgendorf, Frederick M. Smith, and Paul R. Greenough.
TS is 9 pp. long. Listed in 1., 8.

"Kerouac in Black and White." *Ishmael Reed's Konch Magazine* 9 (Fall
1996-Spring 1997): 12-15. Reissued on Web. <http://www.ishmaelreed.com/
articles/blaise1.html>. Rpt. (rev.) in *Selected Essays*. By Clark Blaise. Ed. John
Metcalf and J.R. (Tim) Struthers. Emeryville, ON: Biblioasis, 2008.
Data gathered with the help of Clark Blaise and Robin Philpot. This
printed piece (later posted online) was followed, after the journal switched to
publishing online in 1998, by Robin Philpot's online piece "Kerouac, Blaise,
Quebec: In Black and White" (cf. <http://www. ishmaelreed.com/articles/
Philpot.html>) in *Ishmael Reed's Konch Magazine* ([Fall 1998]). An earlier printed

piece by Robin Philpot, "Quebec: Bucking the Monoculturalists' Current," had appeared – without Blaise knowing it, he states in an e-mail to J.R. (Tim) Struthers on 13 Sept. 2008 – in *Ishmael Reed's Konch Magazine* 8 (Fall 1995): 18-20. Blaise and Philpot subsequently published two more items in the same journal, as noted later in this section. Listed in 1., 8.

"[On the Multiculturalism Debate]." U.S./Canadian Writers' Perspectives on the Multiculturalism Debate: A Round Table Discussion and Reading at Harvard U. Moderated by Graham Huggan and Winfried Siemerling; with panelists Clark Blaise, Dionne Brand, Nicole Brossard, George Elliott Clarke, Bharati Mukherjee, Paul Yee. Harvard Hall, Harvard U, Cambridge, MA. 10 May 1997. Address. In "U.S./ Canadian Writers' Perspectives on the Multiculturalism Debate: A Round-Table Discussion at Harvard University." By Graham Huggan, Winfried Siemerling, et al. *Canadian Literature* 164 (2000): 87-93. Print.

Data gathered with the help of Winfried Siemerling. Title devised by J.R. (Tim) Struthers and approved by Clark Blaise via e-mail between them on 11 July 2008. Listed in 1., 8.

"Sci-Fi & I." Scholars Convocation. Grinnell Coll., Grinnell, IA. 19 Feb. 1998. Address. Grinnell Coll. Archives, Burling Lib., Grinnell Coll. Libs., Grinnell Coll., Grinnell, IA. Videotape. TS. Collection of the author, Clark Blaise, San Francisco, CA.

Data gathered with the help of Clark Blaise, Paula Smith, and Cheryl Neubert. TS is 9 pp. long. Listed in 1., 8.

"Racism in Québec: A Response to Robin Philpot." *Ishmael Reed's Konch Magazine* ([Fall 1999]). Web. <http://www.ishmaelreed.com/articles/Blaise2. html>.

Data gathered with the help of Clark Blaise and Robin Philpot. This online response to Robin Philpot's online piece "Kerouac, Blaise, Quebec: In Black and White" (cf. <http://www.ishmaelreed.com/articles/Philpot.html>) published a year earlier in *Ishmael Reed's Konch Magazine* ([Fall 1998]) was posted with Robin Philpot's follow-up online response to it "Reply to Clark Blaise" (cf. <http://www.ishmaelreed.com/articles/philpot1.html>) in *Ishmael Reed's Konch Magazine* ([Fall 1999]). Listed in 1., 8.

Blaise, Clark, and Bharati Mukherjee. "Celebration: Hawaii." Photographs by Len Jenshel and Diane Cook. *The New York Times Magazine* 18 Nov. 2001, sec. The Sophisticated Traveler: 59-65.

Data gathered with the help of Clark Blaise and Andrew C. McKague.

"Exile and Memory." Cultural Section U.S. Consulate General Monterrey. Monterrey, Mex. 24 Sept. 2003. Address. *Selected Essays*. By Clark Blaise. Ed. John Metcalf and J.R. (Tim) Struthers. Emeryville, ON: Biblioasis, 2008. Print.
    Data gathered with the help of Clark Blaise. Listed in 1., 8.

"1884: A Brief History of Standard Time." *1884*. Geneva: Andersen Genève, 2004. 10-21.
    Data gathered with the help of Clark Blaise. The sixty-three-page booklet *1884*, Blaise explains in a pair of e-mails to J.R. (Tim) Struthers on 27 Mar. 2007, was produced to accompany a limited-edition timepiece (120 numbered watches) produced by Andersen Genève in honour of Sir Sandford Fleming and the 120th anniversary of standard time. The first nine pages of the booklet contain photographs of the watch, a portrait of Fleming, a picture of the Greenwich prime meridian, instructions on how to 'set' the watch depending on the time-zone in which the user is living; these are followed by Blaise's essay then French and German and Spanish translations of it. The essay is divided into four sections: "Sandford Fleming," "The Prime Meridian Conference," "Cosmic Time," and "Cosmic Time Today."

"Border-Crossing." Crossing Borders: The Immigrant Voice in American Lit. Key West Literary Seminar. San Carlos Institute, Key West, FL. 9 Jan. 2004. Address. Rev. as "The Smuggler's Son Grows Older." *Clark Blaise, Proprietor*. Ed. J.R. (Tim) Struthers. *Short Story* 15.2 (Fall 2007): 57-64. Print. Rpt. (rev.) in *Selected Essays*. By Clark Blaise. Ed. John Metcalf and J.R. (Tim) Struthers. Emeryville, ON: Biblioasis, 2008.
    Data, gathered with the help of Clark Blaise. Listed in 1., 8.

"Minding the Gap." Arts and Religious Studies Convocation. McGill U, Montreal, QC. 2 June 2004. Address. Rev. as "The Subtle Contingencies of History." *Canadian Notes & Queries* 67 (Spring-Summer 2005): 4-6. Print.
    Data gathered with the help of Clark Blaise. Address delivered on the occasion of Clark Blaise's receiving an honorary doctorate from McGill U. Listed in 1., 8., 12.

"Water." Freshman Global Lecture Ser. Southampton Coll. of Long Island U, Southampton, NY. 13 Sept. 2004. Address. TS. Collection of the author, Clark Blaise, San Francisco, CA.
    Data gathered with the help of Clark Blaise and Anne Algieri. TS. is 18 pp. long. Listed in 1., 8.

"[Resolving the Nightmare of Time]." Time Contemplates and Celebrates the Windy City. Chicago Humanities Festival. Julius Lewis Auditorium, Alliance Française de Chicago, Chicago, IL. 13 Nov. 2004. Address. TS. Collection of the author, Clark Blaise, San Francisco, CA.

Data gathered with the help of Clark Blaise and Amanda Burr. Title given by Clark Blaise in an e-mail to J.R. (Tim) Struthers on 4 Mar. 2007. TS is 18 pp. long. Listed in 1, 12.

"[The Orchestrating of Standard Time]." Space and Time. SBC Honors Program and the Coll. Lectures and Events Committee. Cochran Lib. Browsing Room, Sweet Briar Coll., Sweet Briar, VA. 21 Feb. 2006. Address. TS. Collection of the author, Clark Blaise, San Francisco, CA.

Data gathered with the help of Clark Blaise. Title chosen by Clark Blaise from suggestions offered by J.R. (Tim) Struthers via e-mail between them on 13 July 2008. TS is 12 pp. long.

"The Possibility of Cultural Transformation in a Time of Cultural Extremism]." Open Inquiry in the Face of Cultural Extremism. NAFSA: Assoc. of Intl. Educators. Queen Elizabeth Hotel, Montreal, QC. 22 May 2006. Address. TS. Collection of the author, Clark Blaise, San Francisco, CA.

Data gathered with the help of Clark Blaise and Andrew C. McKague. Title devised by J.R. (Tim) Struthers and approved by Clark Blaise via e-mail between them on 13 July 2008. TS is 15 pp. long. Listed in 1., 12.

"The 'Wickedness' of Herman Melville." 2007. TS. Collection of the author, Clark Blaise, San Francisco, CA.

Data gathered with the help of Clark Blaise. TS is 11 pp. long. Listed in 1., 8.

2. On Some Novelists

"A 'Respectable' Melodrama." Rev. of *The Hostages*, by Charles E. Israel. *The Montreal Star* 20 Aug. 1966, sec. Entertainments: 7.

"To the Palace of Wisdom." Rev. of *The Words of My Roaring*, by Robert Kroetsch. *The Montreal Star* 17 Sept. 1966, sec. Entertainments: 8.

"Balchin's Glossy 'Meller'." Rev. of *In the Absence of Mrs. Petersen*, by Nigel Balchin. *The Montreal Star* 29 Oct. 1966, sec. Entertainments: 9.

"The Words of Iris Murdoch." Rev. of *The Time of the Angels*, by Iris Murdoch. *The Montreal Star* 12 Nov. 1966, sec. Entertainments: 6.

"Conrad Richter Trilogy." Rev. of *The Awakening Land: I. The Trees; II. The Fields; III. The Town*, by Conrad Richter. *The Montreal Star* 3 Dec. 1966, sec. Entertainments: 16.

"An Informal Account of a Writer's Life." Rev. of *It Has Its Charms*, by Charles W. Morton, and *Westward Lies Heaven*, by Petru Dumitriu. *The Montreal Star* 10 Dec. 1966, sec. Entertainments: 11.
   Listed in 2., 7.

"Norman the Conqueror: Myth and Memoir." Rev. of *Making It*, by Norman Podhoretz. *Canadian Dimension* Feb. 1969: 48-49.
   Data in part gathered from *The Clark Blaise Papers* (1991), comp. Marlys Chevrefils.

"Notes: On Hawkes." *The Supplement* [*The Georgian*] [Sir George Williams U, Montreal, QC] 16 Oct. 1970: [p. unknown].
   Data in part gathered from *The Clark Blaise Papers* (1991), comp. Marlys Chevrefils, and with further help from Marlys Chevrefils. This particular instalment of *The Georgian* is not included in the microfilm version of the newspaper. However, an original clipping of Blaise's piece is on deposit in The Clark Blaise Papers, Archives and Special Collections, U of Calgary Libraries and Cultural Resources, U of Calgary, Calgary, AB.

"'Rich and Funny, It's Richler's Best Book Yet'." Rev. of *St. Urbain's Horseman*, by Mordecai Richler. *The Gazette* [Montreal] 22 May 1971: 44.

Data in part gathered from "Mordecai Richler: An Annotated Bibliography," by Michael Darling, *The Annotated Bibliography of Canada's Major Authors*, ed. Jack David and Robert Lecker, Vol. 1 (1979), and with further help from Andrew C. McKague.

"Stud Errant: Kosinski Defends the Landscape of Desire with Airbrushed Prose." Rev. of *Passion Play*, by Jerzy Kosinski. *The Gazette* [Montreal] 13 Oct. 1979: 75.

Data in part gathered from *The Clark Blaise Papers* (1991), comp. Marlys Chevrefils, and with further help from Andrew C. McKague.

"V.S. Naipaul." *The Globe and Mail* 27 Oct. 1979: 7.

Data gathered with the help of Andrew C. McKague. Published in "Letters to the Editor" section.

"Oates Uproots the Groves of Academe." Rev. of *Unholy Loves*, by Joyce Carol Oates. *The Gazette* [Montreal] 23 Feb. 1980: 97.

Data in part gathered from *The Clark Blaise Papers* (1991), comp. Marlys Chevrefils, and with further help from Andrew C. McKague.

"Vanishing Totems." Rev. of *The Charcoal Burners*, by Susan Musgrave. *Saturday Night* Nov. 1980: 72-73.

Data in part gathered from *The Clark Blaise Papers* (1991), comp. Marlys Chevrefils, and with further help from Andrew C. McKague.

"A Novel of India's Coming of Age." Rev. of *Midnight's Children*, by Salman Rushdie. *The New York Times Book Review* 19 Apr. 1981: 1, 18-19. Rpt. (rev.) in "Rushdie as Novelist, Rushdie as Critic." *Selected Essays*. By Clark Blaise. Ed. John Metcalf and J.R. (Tim) Struthers. Emeryville, ON: Biblioasis, 2008.

"Relearning Freedom." Rev. of *Alex Driving South*, by Keith Maillard. *Canadian Literature* 89 (Summer 1981): 131-33.

"Ideas Suggested by Nerves." The British Image in World Lit. MLA Annual Convention. New York. 29 Dec. 1981. Address. *Selected Essays*. By Clark Blaise. Ed. John Metcalf and J.R. (Tim) Struthers. Emeryville, ON: Biblioasis, 2008. Print.

Data in part gathered from *The Clark Blaise Papers* (1991), comp. Marlys Chevrefils, and with further help from Marlys Chevrefils.

"Murderous Mormons, Ghosts, UFOs, Cancerous Cats and Dusty Philosophers. Which of Three Grotesque Novels Is John Gardner Really Trying To Write?" Rev. of *Mickelsson's Ghosts*, by John Gardner. *The Globe and Mail* 3 July 1982, sec. Entertainment: 12.
    Data gathered with the help of Andrew C. McKague.

"Tale of Two Colonies." Rev. of *Bodily Harm*, by Margaret Atwood. *Canadian Literature* 95 (Winter 1982): 110-12.

"Mailer's Excesses Not Without Merit." Rev. of *Ancient Evenings*, by Norman Mailer. *The Globe and Mail* 23 Apr. 1983, sec. Entertainment: 15.
    Data gathered with the help of Andrew C. McKague.

"Mother, Armed." Rev. of *The Upper Room*, by Mary Monroe. *The New York Times Book Review* 3 Mar. 1985: 31.
    Data gathered with the help of Andrew C. McKague.

"Atwood Fires Poisoned Valentine at U.S. Males: High Priestess of CanLit Creates Anti-Utopia Where Women Are Powerless, Pregnant, Poor." Rev. of *The Handmaid's Tale*, by Margaret Atwood. *The Gazette* [Montreal] 5 Oct. 1985: B-7.
    Data in part gathered from *The Clark Blaise Papers* (1991), comp. Marlys Chevrefils, and with further help from Andrew C. McKague.

"Clark Blaise on Arun Joshi's *The Strange Case of Billy Biswas.*" *Rediscoveries II: Important Writers Select Their Favorite Works of Neglected Fiction.* Ed. David Madden and Peggy Bach. New York: Carroll & Graf, 1988. 30-33.
    Data gathered with the help of Clark Blaise.

"Don't Give In to the Baggy Grown-Ups." Rev. of *The Beautiful Room Is Empty*, by Edmund White. *The New York Times Book Review* 20 Mar. 1988: 7.
    Data gathered with the help of Andrew C. McKague.

"Versions of the Self: Alison Lurie's Romantic Irony." Rev. of *The Truth about Lorin Jones*, by Alison Lurie. *The Washington Post* 4 Sept. 1988, sec. Book World: 3, 9.
    Data gathered with the help of Clark Blaise and Andrew C. McKague.

"A Guru by Night." Rev. of *The Buddha of Suburbia*, by Hanif Kureishi. *The New York Times Book Review* 6 May 1990: 20.
    Data gathered with the help of Andrew C. McKague.

"Voyages of Discovery." Rev. of *Such a Long Journey*, by Rohinton Mistry, and *No New Land*, by M.G. Vassanji. *The Globe and Mail* 4 May 1991: E1.
    Data gathered with the help of Andrew C. McKague.

"Passages from India: Tharoor Leads a Wave of New Indian Writers Who Are Making Indian History the World's Business." Rev. of *The Great Indian Novel*, by Shashi Tharoor. *The World & I* July 1991: 343-49. Reissued on Web. <http://www.worldandi.com/>, article # 19189.
    Data gathered with the help of Clark Blaise, Andrew C. McKague, and Kaci Gaskill.

"Introduction to *Shoeless Joe*." 1992. TS. Quarry Press Fonds, Queen's U Archives, Kathleen Ryan Hall, Queen's U, Kingston, ON. Trans. by Bernard Hœpffner as Préface. *Shoeless Joe*. By W.P. Kinsella. Trans. Bernard Hœpffner. Paris: Christian Bourgois Éditeur, 1993. 7-18. Abbr. as "On *Shoeless Joe*." *Quarry* 42.4 (1994): 68-73.
    Data gathered with the help of Paul Banfield, Jeremy Heil, and Don McLeod. TS is 11 pp. long. A sequence of five paragraphs that appeared both in the original TS and in the French translation is deleted following the fifth-last paragraph in the version published in *Quarry*. TS is 11 pp. long. Listed in 2., 8.

"Down the Natural Path: T. Coraghessan Boyle Envisions the Life and Times of John Harvey Kellogg, Prophet of Roughage and Abstinence." Rev. of *The Road to Wellville*, by T. Coraghessan Boyle. *Chicago Tribune* 9 May 1993, sec. Books: 1, 9.
    Data gathered with the help of Clark Blaise and Andrew C. McKague.

"A Revolutionary Priest in a Land of Despair." Rev. of *No Other Life*, by Brian Moore. *Newsday* 31 Aug. 1993: 54.
    Data gathered with the help of Clark Blaise and Andrew C. McKague.

Introduction. *Passage to Ararat*. By Michael J. Arlen. Saint Paul, MN: Hungry Mind, 1996. v-ix.
    Data gathered with the help of Clark Blaise.

"Rushdie as Novelist, Rushdie as Critic." *Selected Essays*. By Clark Blaise. Ed. John Metcalf and J.R. (Tim) Struthers. Emeryville, ON: Biblioasis, 2008.
    Selected and arranged and entitled by J.R. (Tim) Struthers, this piece includes and revises previously published material as follows: "A Novel of India's Coming of Age." Rev. of *Midnight's Children*, by Salman Rushdie. *The New York Times Book Review* 19 Apr. 1981: 1, 18-19 and "Rushdie as Critic: 'He

Engages Books with Expectation or Disillusionment. He Holds Nothing Back.'"
Rev. of *Imaginary Homelands: Essays and Criticism 1981-1991*, by Salman
Rushdie. *Sunday Newsday* 19 May 1991: 39, 44. Listed in 2., 7., 13.

3. On Some Short Story Writers

"Gordimer's Africa; Niland's Australia." Rev. of *The Late Bourgeois World*, by Nadine Gordimer, and *Pairs and Loners*, by D'Arcy Niland. *The Montreal Star* 30 July 1966, sec. Entertainments: 7.

Rev. of *The Streets of Summer*, by David Helwig. *Quarry* 19.3 (Spring 1970): 57-58.

"At Home in All Voices." Rev. of *The Love Parlour* and *The Broad Back of the Angel*, by Leon Rooke. *Canadian Literature* 81 (Summer 1979): 118-19. Rpt. (rev.) as "At Home in All Voices: Leon Rooke" in "Notes on the 'Canadian' Short Story." *Selected Essays*. By Clark Blaise. Ed. John Metcalf and J.R. (Tim) Struthers. Emeryville, ON: Biblioasis, 2008.

"On Easy Terms with Ghosts." Rev. of *The Oxford Book of French-Canadian Short Stories*, ed. Richard Teleky. *The New York Times Book Review* 9 Sept. 1984: 26.
    Data gathered with the help of Clark Blaise and Andrew C. McKague.

"Sheer Readability Neil Bissoondath's Greatest Talent." Rev. of *Digging Up the Mountains*, by Neil Bissoondath. *Quill & Quire* Mar. 1985: 71.
    Data gathered with the help of Andrew C. McKague.

"Stories of the Medieval in the Present Day." Rev. of *Beneath the Western Slopes*, by Patrick Roscoe, and *Medieval Hour in the Author's Mind*, by Ernest Hekkanen. *Quill & Quire* June 1987: 34.
    Data gathered with the help of Andrew C. McKague.

"Atwoodian Moments: The Passion, Wit and Stylishness of Margaret Atwood's Short Fiction." Rev. of *Wilderness Tips*, by Margaret Atwood. *Chicago Tribune* 24 Nov. 1991, sec. Books: 3.
    Data gathered with the help of Clark Blaise and Andrew C. McKague.

"Hairy Situations: Post-Chernobyl Werewolves and Other Modern Russian Nightmares." Rev. of *A Werewolf Problem in Central Russia and Other Stories*, by Victor Pelevin, trans. Andrew Bromfield. *San Francisco Chronicle* 21 Feb. 1999: RV-3.
    Data gathered with the help of Clark Blaise and Andrew C. McKague.

"Introduction: Reading John Metcalf." *Standing Stones: The Best Stories of John Metcalf*. By John Metcalf. Toronto: Thomas Allen, 2004. xiii-xvi. Rpt. (rev.) as "Reading John Metcalf" in "Notes on the 'Canadian' Short Story." *Selected Essays*. By Clark Blaise. Ed. John Metcalf and J.R. (Tim) Struthers. Emeryville, ON: Biblioasis, 2008.

"Notes on the 'Canadian' Short Story." *Selected Essays*. By Clark Blaise. Ed. John Metcalf and J.R. (Tim) Struthers. Emeryville, ON: Biblioasis, 2008.

Selected and arranged and entitled by J.R. (Tim) Struthers, this piece includes and revises previously published and unpublished material as follows: "At Home in All Voices." Rev. of *The Love Parlour* and *The Broad Back of the Angel*, by Leon Rooke. *Canadian Literature* 81 (Summer 1979): 118-19; "Introduction: Reading John Metcalf." *Standing Stones: The Best Stories of John Metcalf*. By John Metcalf. Toronto: Thomas Allen, 2004. xiii-xvi; the previously unpublished "A Stunning Glare: Alice Munro."

"A Stunning Glare: Alice Munro." In "Notes on the 'Canadian' Short Story." *Selected Essays*. By Clark Blaise. Ed. John Metcalf and J.R. (Tim) Struthers. Emeryville, ON: Biblioasis, 2008.

Title devised by J.R. (Tim) Struthers and approved by Clark Blaise via e-mail between them on 10 Mar. 2007.

4. On His Own Fiction

"Author's Introduction." *New Canadian Writing, 1968*. By David Lewis Stein, Clark Blaise, and Dave Godfrey. Toronto: Clarke, Irwin, 1968. 67-68.

"Why Authors Are Skeptical." *The Globe and Mail* 25 Apr. 1973: 7.
    Data in part gathered from *The Clark Blaise Papers* (1991), comp. Marlys Chevrefils. Published in "Letters to the Editor."

"[Canadian Convocation]." St. George's School, Montreal, QC. 30 May 1975. Address. "Canadian Convocation: Graduation Address – St. George's School." *Anthol* 4 (Winter 1975): 28-38. Print.
    Data in part gathered from *The Clark Blaise Papers* (1991), comp. Marlys Chevrefils, and with further help from Marlys Chevrefils. Title for original address devised by J.R. (Tim) Struthers and approved by Clark Blaise via e-mail between them on 25 Sept. 2008. Listed in 1., 4., 8.

"[The Books That Changed My Life]." From "The Book That Changed My Life: Or, at Any Rate, Altered It. Twenty Versions of That Exhilarating and Mind-Wrenching Experience That (Usually) Happens Just Once in a Lifetime," by Sandra Martin et al. *Saturday Night* May 1976: 34-35. Rpt. (abbr. and rev.) in "A North American Memoir: Revenge." *The North American Review* Dec. 1984: 57-58. Rpt. (abbr. and rev.) in "The Voice of Unhousement." *Resident Alien*. By Clark Blaise. Markham, ON: Penguin, 1986. 10-12.
    Title devised by J.R. (Tim) Struthers and approved by Clark Blaise via e-mail between them on 7 Sept. 2008. Listed in 4., 8.

"Autobiography." [Autobiography Symposium]. U of Iowa, Iowa City, IA. 13 Apr. 1978. Address. TS. The Clark Blaise Papers, Archives and Special Collections, U of Calgary Libraries and Cultural Resources, U of Calgary, Calgary, AB.
    Data in part gathered from *The Clark Blaise Papers* (1991), comp. Marlys Chevrefils, and with further help from Marlys Chevrefils. TS is 16 pp. long. Listed in 4., 5., 9., 10.

"The Cast and the Mold." *Stories Plus: Canadian Stories with Authors' Commentaries*. Ed. John Metcalf. Toronto: McGraw-Hill Ryerson, 1979. 27-29. Rpt. in *How Stories Mean*. Ed. John Metcalf and J.R. (Tim) Struthers. Critical Directions

3. Erin, ON: The Porcupine's Quill, 1993. 163-65. Rpt. (rev.) in "How Stories Mean." *Selected Essays*. By Clark Blaise. Ed. John Metcalf and J.R. (Tim) Struthers. Emeryville, ON: Biblioasis, 2008.

"The Truth Is: We Are All Laytons." *The Globe and Mail* 3 May 1980: 6.
    Data in part gathered from *Clark Blaise and His Works*, by Barry Cameron. Published in column entitled "The Mermaid Inn."

"[By a Curious Alchemy]." Humanities Week. Slayter Auditorium, Denison U, Granville, OH. 9 Nov. 1981. Address. TS. The Clark Blaise Papers, Archives and Special Collections, U of Calgary Libraries and Cultural Resources, U of Calgary, Calgary, AB.
    Data in part gathered from *The Clark Blaise Papers* (1991), comp. Marlys Chevrefils, and with further help from Clark Blaise and Marlys Chevrefils. Title chosen by Clark Blaise from suggestions offered by J.R. (Tim) Struthers via e-mail between them on 7 Sept. 2008. Read as an introduction to a revised version of Blaise's "An Unintentional Novel and an Unanticipated Autobiography" (cited separately in 7., 9.) during sesquicentennial celebrations at Denison U. TS is 3 pp. long. Listed in 4., 9., 13.

"Memories of Unhousement: A Memoir." *Salmagundi* 56 (Spring 1982): 3-25. Rpt. (abbr. and rev.) as "Memories of Unhousement." *Resident Alien*. By Clark Blaise. Markham, ON: Penguin, 1986. 165-84.
    Data gathered with the help of Clark Blaise. Listed in 4., 8.

"Portrait of the Artist as a Young Pup." *Canadian Literature* 100 (Spring 1984): 35-41. Rpt. (rev.) in *The Montreal Story Tellers: Memoirs, Photographs, Critical Essays*. Ed. J.R. (Tim) Struthers. Montreal: Véhicule, 1985. 65-72. Rpt. (abbr. and rev.) in "The Voice of Unhousement." *Resident Alien*. By Clark Blaise. Markham, ON: Penguin, 1986. 31-36. Rpt. (rev.) in *Selected Essays*. By Clark Blaise. Ed. John Metcalf and J.R. (Tim) Struthers. Emeryville, ON: Biblioasis, 2008.
    Listed in 4., 6., 8.

"Mentors." *Canadian Literature* 101 (Summer 1984): 35-41. Rpt. (abbr. and rev.) in "A North American Memoir: Revenge." *The North American Review* Dec. 1984: 59-60. Rpt. (rev.) in "The Voice of Unhousement." *Resident Alien*. By Clark Blaise. Markham, ON: Penguin, 1986. 15-24. Rpt. (rev.) in *Selected Essays*. By Clark Blaise. Ed. John Metcalf and J.R. (Tim) Struthers. Emeryville, ON: Biblioasis, 2008.
    Listed in 4., 6., 8.

"A North American Memoir: Revenge." *The North American Review* Dec. 1984: 56-60. Rpt. (abbr. and rev.) in "The Voice of Unhousement." *Resident Alien*. By Clark Blaise. Markham, ON: Penguin, 1986. 9-16, 24-26.

Data in part gathered from *The Clark Blaise Papers* (1991), comp. Marlys Chevrefils, and with further help from Andrew C. McKague. Listed in 4., 8.

"A Passage to Canada: How an American Writer Heeded the 'Daily Buttering' of the CBC To Return to the Land of His Parents." *Books in Canada* June-July 1985: 15-16. Rpt. (abbr. and rev.) in "The Voice of Unhousement." *Resident Alien*. By Clark Blaise. Markham, ON: Penguin, 1986. 26-30.

Data gathered with the help of Clark Blaise. Listed, in 4., 8.

"Clark Blaise." *Contemporary Authors: Autobiography Series*. Vol. 3. Ed. Adele Sarkissian. Detroit: Gale Research, 1986. 15-30. Rpt. (rev.) as "Autobiographical Essay: 1940-1984." *Selected Essays*. By Clark Blaise. Ed. John Metcalf and J.R. (Tim) Struthers. Emeryville, ON: Biblioasis, 2008.

Data gathered with the help of Clark Blaise and Andrew C. McKague. New title devised by J.R. (Tim) Struthers and approved by Clark Blaise via e-mail between them on 22 Sept. 2008. Listed in 4., 8., 9.

"Memories of Unhousement." *Resident Alien*. By Clark Blaise. Markham, ON: Penguin, 1986. 165-84.

This piece abbreviates and revises previously published material from "Memories of Unhousement: A Memoir," *Salmagundi* 56 (Spring 1982): 3-25. Listed in 4., 8.

"The Voice of Unhousement." *Resident Alien*. By Clark Blaise. Markham, ON: Penguin, 1986. 9-41.

This composite-essay or essay-in-fragments or, to invent a different term, 'essay-in-segments' abbreviates and revises previously published material as follows: pp. 9-16, from "A North American Memoir: Revenge," *The North American Review* Dec. 1984: 56-60; pp. 15-24, from "Mentors," *Canadian Literature* 101 (Summer 1984): 35-41; pp. 24-26, from "A North American Memoir: Revenge," *The North American Review* Dec. 1984: 56-60; pp. 26-30, from "A Passage to Canada: How an American Writer Heeded the 'Daily Buttering' of the CBC To Return to the Land of His Parents," *Books in Canada* June-July 1985: 15-16; pp. 30-36, from "Portrait of the Artist as a Young Pup," *The Montreal Story Tellers: Memoirs, Photographs, Critical Essays* (1985): 65-72; pp. 36-41, from "Tenants of Unhousement," *The Iowa Review* 13.2 (Spring 1982): 83-98. Listed in 4., 8.

"Chronology of Salience." *An Other I: The Fictions of Clark Blaise*. By Robert

Lecker. Toronto: ECW, 1988. 13-20.
    Listed in 4., 8., 9.

"Casting from the Shore." *The Second Macmillan Anthology*. Ed. John Metcalf and Leon Rooke. Toronto: Macmillan, 1989. 196-97.

Introduction. *Lunar Attractions*. By Clark Blaise. Sherbrooke Street 3. Erin, ON: Porcupine's Quill, 1990. 7-15.
    Listed in 4., 8., 9.

"To Begin, To Begin," "The Cast and the Mold," "On Ending Stories." *How Stories Mean*. Ed. John Metcalf and J.R. (Tim) Struthers. Critical Directions 3. Erin, ON: The Porcupine's Quill, 1993. 158-62, 163-65, 166-69. Rpt. (rev.) as "How Stories Mean." *Selected Essays*. By Clark Blaise. Ed. John Metcalf and J.R. (Tim) Struthers. Emeryville, ON: Biblioasis, 2008.
    Listed in 4., 5.

"The Zen of Writing." 1996. TS. Collection of the author, Clark Blaise, San Francisco, CA.
    Data gathered with the help of Clark Blaise. TS is 11 pp. long. Listed in 4., 8., 9.

"From Village to Millage: A Manchester Novel; Notes Toward a Franco-American Saga." Cultural Identity in French America: Legacy, Evolution, and the Challenges of Renewal / Identité culturelle en Amérique française: héritage, évolution, et défis au renouvellement. U of Maine and U d'Angers. Atlantic Oakes Hotel and Convention Center, Bar Harbor, ME. 23 May 1996. Address. TS. Collection of the author, Clark Blaise, San Francisco, CA. Trans. as "Création d'une conscience: notes pour une saga franco-américaine." Trans. Viateur Boutot. *Vision et visages de la Franco-Amérique*. Ed. Dean Louder, Jean Morisset, and Eric Waddell. Sillery, QC: Septentrion, 2001. 21-29, 323. Print.
    Data gathered with the help of Clark Blaise, Rhea J. Côté Robbins, Jim Bishop, Dean Louder, and Viateur Boutot. TS is 11 pp. long. Listed in 1., 4.

"[Autobiographical Annex: Clark Blaise]." In "BLAISE, Clark 1940- ." *Contemporary Authors: A Bio-Bibliographical Guide to Current Writers in Fiction, General Nonfiction, Poetry, Journalism, Drama, Motion Pictures, Television, and Other Fields*. Vol. 231. Project Ed. Julie Keppen. Farmington Hills, MI: Thomson Gale, 2005. 50-57. Rpt. (rev.) as "Autobiographical Annex: 1985-2006." *Selected Essays*. By Clark Blaise. Ed. John Metcalf and J.R. (Tim) Struthers. Emeryville, ON: Biblioasis, 2008.

Data gathered with the help of Clark Blaise and Andrew C. McKague. Title for original essay reproduces that on TS. Collection of the author, Clark Blaise, San Francisco, CA. New title devised by J.R. (Tim) Struthers and approved by Clark Blaise via e-mail between them on 22 Sept. 2008. Listed in 4., 8., 9., 12.

Afterword. *World Body*. By Clark Blaise. Introd. Michael Augustin. Erin, ON: Porcupine's Quill, 2006. 213. Vol. 4 of *The Selected Stories of Clark Blaise*. 4 vols. 2000-06.

5. On Fiction and Interpretation

"To Begin, To Begin." *The Narrative Voice: Short Stories and Reflections by Canadian Authors*. Ed. John Metcalf. Toronto: McGraw-Hill Ryerson, 1972. 22-26. Rpt. in *Fiction International* 4-5 (1975): 5-8. Rpt. in *How Stories Mean*. Ed. John Metcalf and J.R. (Tim) Struthers. Critical Directions 3. Erin, ON: The Porcupine's Quill, 1993. 158-62. Rpt. (rev.) in "How Stories Mean." *Selected Essays*. By Clark Blaise. Ed. John Metcalf and J.R. (Tim) Struthers. Emeryville, ON: Biblioasis, 2008.
     Data gathered with the help of Andrew C. McKague.

[Introduction]. *Here & Now: Best Canadian Stories*. Ed. Clark Blaise and John Metcalf. Ottawa: Oberon, 1977. 5-6.

"Autobiography." [Autobiography Symposium]. U of Iowa, Iowa City, IA. 13 Apr. 1978. Address. TS. The Clark Blaise Papers, Archives and Special Collections, U of Calgary Libraries and Cultural Resources, U of Calgary, Calgary, AB.
     Data in part gathered from *The Clark Blaise Papers* (1991), comp. Marlys Chevrefils, and with further help from Marlys Chevrefils. TS is 16 pp. long. Listed in 4., 5., 9., 10.

[Introduction]. *79: Best Canadian Stories*. Ed. Clark Blaise and John Metcalf. Ottawa: Oberon, 1979. 5-6.

[Introduction]. *80: Best Canadian Stories*. Ed. Clark Blaise and John Metcalf. Ottawa: Oberon, 1980. 5-6.

"[On Moral Fiction]." In "A Writers' Forum on Moral Fiction." By Max Apple, Russell Banks, et al. *Fiction International* 12 (1980): 7-8.
     Data gathered with the help of Clark Blaise and Andrew C. McKague. Title devised by J.R. (Tim) Struthers and approved by Clark Blaise via e-mail between them on 12 July 2008.

"The Human Synthesizer." *Rampike* 2.1-2 (1982): 45.
     Data in part gathered from *An Other I: The Fictions of Clark Blaise* (1988), by Robert Lecker.

"On Ending Stories." *The Canadian Forum* Sept. 1982: 7, 37. Rpt. in *Making It New: Contemporary Canadian Stories*. Ed. John Metcalf. Toronto: Methuen, 1982. 32-35. Rpt. in *How Stories Mean*. Ed. John Metcalf and J.R. (Tim) Struthers. Critical Directions 3. Erin, ON: The Porcupine's Quill, 1993. 166-69. Rpt. (rev.) in "How Stories Mean." *Selected Essays*. By Clark Blaise. Ed. John Metcalf and J.R. (Tim) Struthers. Emeryville, ON: Biblioasis, 2008.

"[Personalizing History and Politics]." In "A Conversation with Nadine Gordimer." By Robert Boyers, Clark Blaise, Terence Diggory, Jordan Elgrably. *Salmagundi* 62 (Winter 1984): 9-12, 13, 16-18.
    Data gathered with the help of Clark Blaise. Title devised by J.R. (Tim) Struthers and approved by Clark Blaise via e-mail between them on 25 July 2008.

"To Begin, To Begin," "The Cast and the Mold," "On Ending Stories." *How Stories Mean*. Ed. John Metcalf and J.R. (Tim) Struthers. Critical Directions 3. Erin, ON: The Porcupine's Quill, 1993. 158-62, 163-65, 166-69. Rpt. (rev.) as "How Stories Mean." *Selected Essays*. By Clark Blaise. Ed. John Metcalf and J.R. (Tim) Struthers. Emeryville, ON: Biblioasis, 2008.
    Listed in 4., 5.

"Writing a Myth." Introduction to panel discussion "Writing a Myth." The Intl. Writing Program. English-Philosophy Building, U of Iowa, Iowa City, IA. Fall 1996. Address. TS. Collection of the author, Clark Blaise, San Francisco, CA.
    Data gathered with the help of Clark Blaise. TS is 4 pp. long.

"The Craft of the Short Story." 28th Annual Southampton Coll. Writers Conf. Southampton Coll. of Long Island U, Southampton, NY. 23 July 2003. Address. *Proteus* [Southampton Coll. of Long Island U] (2003): 220-27. Print. Rpt. in *The Southampton Review* 1.1 (Summer-Autumn 2007): 22-28. Rpt. in *Canadian Notes & Queries* 72 (Fall-Winter 2007): 28-31. Rpt. (rev.) in *Selected Essays*. By Clark Blaise. Ed. John Metcalf and J.R. (Tim) Struthers. Emeryville, ON: Biblioasis, 2008.
    Data gathered with the help of Clark Blaise.

"The Justice-Dealing Machine." *Writers on Writing: The Art of the Short Story*. Ed. Maurice A. Lee. Contributions to the Study of World Lit. 128. Westport, CT: Praeger, 2005. 221-25. Rpt. (rev.) in *Selected Essays*. By Clark Blaise. Ed. John Metcalf and J.R. (Tim) Struthers. Emeryville, ON: Biblioasis, 2008.
    Data gathered with the help of Clark Blaise.

6. On Some Artists, Fellow Writers, Mentors

"[Sam Tata's India – and Mine]." 1976. TS. The Clark Blaise Papers, Archives and Special Collections, U of Calgary Libraries and Cultural Resources, U of Calgary, Calgary, AB.

  Data in part gathered from *The Clark Blaise Papers* (1991), comp. Marlys Chevrefils, and with further help from Clark Blaise, Marlys Chevrefils, and Sorouja Moll. Title given by Clark Blaise in an e-mail to J.R. (Tim) Struthers on 18 July 2008. This material consists of three linked pieces entitled "Photography and Writing," "An Asian Education," and "Sam Tata's India – and Mine" written for a planned but unrealized national exhibit and catalogue of ninety India photographs by Montrealer Sam Tata. TS is 13 pp. long. Listed in 6., 8.

Blaise, Clark, and Bharati Mukherjee. "[On Satyajit Ray's *The Chess-Players*]." 1978. TS. The Clark Blaise Papers, Archives and Special Collections, U of Calgary Libraries and Cultural Resources, U of Calgary, Calgary, AB.

  Data in part gathered from *The Clark Blaise Papers* (1991), comp. Marlys Chevrefils, and with further help from Clark Blaise and Marlys Chevrefils. Title devised by J.R. (Tim) Struthers and approved by Clark Blaise via e-mail between them on 26 July 2008. TS is 11 pp. long.

"Alan Weinstein: An Informal Memoir." *Alan Weinstein: 20 Years*. Guelph, ON: Macdonald Stewart Art Centre, 1983. 13-15.

  Data in part gathered from *The Clark Blaise Papers* (1991), comp. Marlys Chevrefils, and with further help from Sorouja Moll.

"Portrait of the Artist as a Young Pup." *Canadian Literature* 100 (Spring 1984): 35-41. Rpt. (rev.) in *The Montreal Story Tellers: Memoirs, Photographs, Critical Essays*. Ed. J.R. (Tim) Struthers. Montreal: Véhicule, 1985. 65-72. Rpt. (abbr. and rev.) in "The Voice of Unhousement." *Resident Alien*. By Clark Blaise. Markham, ON: Penguin, 1986. 31-36. Rpt. (rev.) in *Selected Essays*. By Clark Blaise. Ed. John Metcalf and J.R. (Tim) Struthers. Emeryville, ON: Biblioasis, 2008.

  Listed in 4., 6., 8.

"Mentors." *Canadian Literature* 101 (Summer 1984): 35-41. Rpt. (abbr. and rev.) in "A North American Memoir: Revenge." *The North American Review* Dec. 1984: 59-60. Rpt. (rev.) in "The Voice of Unhousement." *Resident Alien*. By

Clark Blaise. Markham, ON: Penguin, 1986. 15-24. Rpt. (rev.) in *Selected Essays*. By Clark Blaise. Ed. John Metcalf and J.R. (Tim) Struthers. Emeryville, ON: Biblioasis, 2008.

> Listed in 4., 6., 8.

"Engle's Literary Legacy for the World." *The Des Moines Register* 4 Apr. 1991, sec. A: 16.

> Data gathered with the help of Clark Blaise, Andrew C. McKague, and Joann Donaldson.

Foreword. *Appalachian Mettle*. By Paul Bennett. Superior, WI: Savage, 1997. 12.

> Data gathered with the help of Clark Blaise.

"No Names Please." *Americans*. Ed. Jane Davis. *The Reader* 19 (Autumn 2005): 106-09. Rpt. in *Canadian Notes & Queries* 70 (Fall-Winter 2006): 8-9.

> Data gathered with the help of Clark Blaise. Listed in 6., 8.

7. On Some Writers of Autobiography, Memoir, Personal Nonfiction

"Chinese Attitudes." Rev. of *Love and Hate in China*, by Hans Koningsberger. *The Montreal Star* 10 Sept. 1966, sec. Entertainments: 7.

"An Informal Account of a Writer's Life." Rev. of *It Has Its Charms*, by Charles W. Morton, and *Westward Lies Heaven*, by Petru Dumitriu. *The Montreal Star* 10 Dec. 1966, sec. Entertainments: 11.
    Listed in 2., 7.

"[An Unintentional Novel and an Unanticipated Autobiography]." Denison Honors Colloquium. ATO House, Denison U, Granville, OH. 17 Apr. 1979. Address. TS. The Clark Blaise Papers, Archives and Special Collections, U of Calgary Libraries and Cultural Resources, U of Calgary, Calgary, AB. Rev. and introd. by "[By a Curious Alchemy]." Humanities Week. Slayter Auditorium, Denison U, Granville, OH. 9 Nov. 1981. Address. TS. The Clark Blaise Papers, Archives and Special Collections, U of Calgary Libraries and Cultural Resources, U of Calgary, Calgary, AB.
    Data in part gathered from *The Clark Blaise Papers* (1991), comp. Marlys Chevrefils, and with further help from Clark Blaise and Marlys Chevrefils. Title for original version and revised version of address and title for new piece (cited separately in 4., 9., 13) used to introduce revised version were chosen by Clark Blaise from suggestions offered by J.R. (Tim) Struthers via e-mail between them on 25 July 2008 and 7 Sept. 2008. Original version was read on the occasion of Blaise's visit to Denison U to receive an honorary doctorate. TS is 19 pp. long. New piece and revised version were presented during sesquicentennial celebrations at Denison U. TS of new piece is 3 pp. long; TS of revised version is 20 pp. long. Listed in 7., 9.

"Family Memoir." Rev. of *Mamaji*, by Ved Mehta. *The New York Times Book Review* 21 Oct. 1979: 7, 51.
    Data gathered with the help of Andrew C. McKague.

"Four Senses & Imagination." Rev. of *Vedi* and *A Family Affair: India Under Three Prime Ministers*, by Ved Mehta. *The New York Times Book Review* 17 Oct. 1982: 12, 36.

Data gathered with the help of Andrew C. McKague.

"Incognito." Rev. of *Incognito*, by David Young, photographs by Jim Lang. *Canadian Literature* 101 (Summer 1984): 106-09.

"Thanks for the Memoirs: Five Writers on Distilling a Life's Essence." Rev. of *Inventing the Truth: The Art and Craft of Memoir*, ed. William Zinsser. *The Washington Post* 17 Nov. 1987: D8.
Data gathered with the help of Clark Blaise and Andrew C. McKague.

"Notes by Native Americans: Insulted, Injured and Angry." Rev. of *I Tell You Now: Autobiographical Essays by Native American Writers*, ed. Brian Swann and Arnold Krupat. *The Washington Post* 7 Feb. 1988, sec. Book World: 9.
Data gathered with the help of Clark Blaise and Andrew C. McKague.

"Calcutta Is the Measure of All Things." Rev. of *Show Your Tongue*, by Günter Grass, trans. John E. Woods. *The New York Times Book Review* 21 May 1989: 12.
Data gathered with the help of Andrew C. McKague.

"Southern Discomfort: V.S. Naipaul, Acerbic Observer of the Third World, Announces His Admiration for American Rednecks." Rev. of *A Turn in the South*, by V.S. Naipaul. *Saturday Night* June 1989: 61-63.
Data gathered with the help of Andrew C. McKague. Listed in 1., 7.

"Rushdie as Critic: 'He Engages Books with Expectation or Disillusionment. He Holds Nothing Back.'" Rev. of *Imaginary Homelands: Essays and Criticism 1981-1991*, by Salman Rushdie. *Sunday Newsday* 19 May 1991: 39, 44. Rpt. (rev.) in "Rushdie as Novelist, Rushdie as Critic." *Selected Essays*. By Clark Blaise. Ed. John Metcalf and J.R. (Tim) Struthers. Emeryville, ON: Biblioasis, 2008.
Data gathered with the help of Clark Blaise and Andrew C. McKague. Listed in 7., 13.

"Rushdie as Novelist, Rushdie as Critic." *Selected Essays*. By Clark Blaise. Ed. John Metcalf and J.R. (Tim) Struthers. Emeryville, ON: Biblioasis, 2008.
Selected and arranged and entitled by J.R. (Tim) Struthers, this piece includes and revises previously published material as follows: "A Novel of India's Coming of Age." Rev. of *Midnight's Children*, by Salman Rushdie. *The New York Times Book Review* 19 Apr. 1981: 1, 18-19 and "Rushdie as Critic: 'He Engages Books with Expectation or Disillusionment. He Holds Nothing Back.'" Rev. of *Imaginary Homelands: Essays and Criticism 1981-1991*, by Salman Rushdie. *Sunday Newsday* 19 May 1991: 39, 44. Listed in 2., 7., 13.

8. Autobiographical Writing

"From Notebook 1, Bombay." *Davinci* 4 (Autumn 1975): 26-28.
Data in part gathered from *The Clark Blaise Papers* (1991), comp. Marlys Chevrefils.

"[Canadian Convocation]." St. George's School, Montreal, QC. 30 May 1975. Address. "Canadian Convocation: Graduation Address – St. George's School." *Anthol* 4 (Winter 1975): 28-38. Print.
Data in part gathered from *The Clark Blaise Papers* (1991), comp. Marlys Chevrefils, and with further help from Marlys Chevrefils. Title for original address devised by J.R. (Tim) Struthers and approved by Clark Blaise via e-mail between them on 25 Sept. 2008. Listed in 1., 4., 8.

"[Sam Tata's India – and Mine]." 1976. TS. The Clark Blaise Papers, Archives and Special Collections, U of Calgary Libraries and Cultural Resources, U of Calgary, Calgary, AB.
Data in part gathered from *The Clark Blaise Papers* (1991), comp. Marlys Chevrefils, and with further help from Clark Blaise, Marlys Chevrefils, and Sorouja Moll. Title given by Clark Blaise in an e-mail to J.R. (Tim) Struthers on 18 July 2008. This material consists of three linked pieces entitled "Photography and Writing," "An Asian Education," and "Sam Tata's India – and Mine" written for a planned but unrealized national exhibit and catalogue of ninety India photographs by Montrealer Sam Tata. TS is 13 pp. long. Listed in 6., 8.

"[The Books That Changed My Life]." From "The Book That Changed My Life: Or, at Any Rate, Altered It. Twenty Versions of That Exhilarating and Mind-Wrenching Experience That (Usually) Happens Just Once in a Lifetime," by Sandra Martin et al. *Saturday Night* May 1976: 34-35. Rpt. (abbr. and rev.) in "A North American Memoir: Revenge." *The North American Review* Dec. 1984: 57-58. Rpt. (abbr. and rev.) in "The Voice of Unhousement." *Resident Alien*. By Clark Blaise. Markham, ON: Penguin, 1986. 10-12.
Title devised by J.R. (Tim) Struthers and approved by Clark Blaise via e-mail between them on 7 Sept. 2008. Listed in 4., 8.

"[Where Was I When Bobby Kennedy Died?]" *Where Were You?: Memorable Events of the Twentieth Century*. Ed. Sandra Martin and Roger Hall. Toronto:

Methuen, 1981. 229-30.

 Data in part gathered from *The Clark Blaise Papers* (1991), comp. Marlys Chevrefils. Title given reproduces that on TS in The Clark Blaise Papers, Archives and Special Collections, U of Calgary Libraries and Cultural Resources, U of Calgary, Calgary, AB. Title approved by Clark Blaise via e-mail to J.R. (Tim) Struthers on 21 Sept. 2008.

"Memories of Unhousement: A Memoir." *Salmagundi* 56 (Spring 1982): 3-25. Rpt. (abbr. and rev.) as "Memories of Unhousement." *Resident Alien*. By Clark Blaise. Markham, ON: Penguin, 1986. 165-84.

 Data gathered with the help of Clark Blaise. Listed in 4., 8.

"Tenants of Unhousement." *The Iowa Review* 13.2 (Spring 1982): 83-98. Rpt. (abbr. and rev.) in Introduction and "The Voice of Unhousement." *Resident Alien*. By Clark Blaise. Markham, ON: Penguin, 1986. 1, 36-41. Rpt. (rev.) in Chapter Fourteen and Chapter Fifteen of *I Had a Father: A Post-Modern Autobiography*. By Clark Blaise. Reading, MA: Addison-Wesley, 1993. Toronto: Harper-Collins, 1993.

 Data gathered with the help of Clark Blaise. Listed in 8., 9.

"Portrait of the Artist as a Young Pup." *Canadian Literature* 100 (Spring 1984): 35-41. Rpt. (rev.) in *The Montreal Story Tellers: Memoirs, Photographs, Critical Essays*. Ed. J.R. (Tim) Struthers. Montreal: Véhicule, 1985. 65-72. Rpt. (abbr. and rev.) in "The Voice of Unhousement." *Resident Alien*. By Clark Blaise. Markham, ON: Penguin, 1986. 31-36. Rpt. (rev.) in *Selected Essays*. By Clark Blaise. Ed. John Metcalf and J.R. (Tim) Struthers. Emeryville, ON: Biblioasis, 2008.

 Listed in 4., 6., 8.

"Mentors." *Canadian Literature* 101 (Summer 1984): 35-41. Rpt. (abbr. and rev.) in "A North American Memoir: Revenge." *The North American Review* Dec. 1984: 59-60. Rpt. (rev.) in "The Voice of Unhousement." *Resident Alien*. By Clark Blaise. Markham, ON: Penguin, 1986. 15-24. Rpt. (rev.) in *Selected Essays*. By Clark Blaise. Ed. John Metcalf and J.R. (Tim) Struthers. Emeryville, ON: Biblioasis, 2008.

 Listed in 4., 6., 8.

"A North American Memoir: Revenge." *The North American Review* Dec. 1984: 56-60. Rpt. (abbr. and rev.) in "The Voice of Unhousement." *Resident Alien*. By Clark Blaise. Markham, ON: Penguin, 1986. 9-16, 24-26.

 Data in part gathered from *The Clark Blaise Papers* (1991), comp. Marlys Chevrefils, and with further help from Andrew C. McKague. Listed in 4., 8.

"A Passage to Canada: How an American Writer Heeded the 'Daily Buttering' of the CBC To Return to the Land of His Parents." *Books in Canada* June-July 1985: 15-16. Rpt. (abbr. and rev.) in "The Voice of Unhousement." *Resident Alien*. By Clark Blaise. Markham, ON: Penguin, 1986. 26-30.

Data gathered with the help of Clark Blaise. Listed, in 4., 8.

"Clark Blaise." *Contemporary Authors: Autobiography Series*. Vol. 3. Ed. Adele Sarkissian. Detroit: Gale Research, 1986. 15-30. Rpt. (rev.) as "Autobiographical Essay: 1940-1984." *Selected Essays*. By Clark Blaise. Ed. John Metcalf and J.R. (Tim) Struthers. Emeryville, ON: Biblioasis, 2008.

Data gathered with the help of Clark Blaise and Andrew C. McKague. New title devised by J.R. (Tim) Struthers and approved by Clark Blaise via e-mail between them on 22 Sept. 2008. Listed in 4., 8., 9.

Introduction. *Resident Alien*. By Clark Blaise. Markham, ON: Penguin, 1986. 1-3.

This piece abbreviates and revises previously published material from "Tenants of Unhousement." *The Iowa Review* 13.2 (Spring 1982): 83-98. Listed in 8., 9.

"Memories of Unhousement." *Resident Alien*. By Clark Blaise. Markham, ON: Penguin, 1986. 165-84.

This piece abbreviates and revises previously published material from "Memories of Unhousement: A Memoir." *Salmagundi* 56 (Spring 1982): 3-25. Listed in 4., 8.

"The Voice of Unhousement." *Resident Alien*. By Clark Blaise. Markham, ON: Penguin, 1986. 9-41.

This composite-essay or essay-in-fragments or, to invent a different term, 'essay-in-segments' abbreviates and revises previously published material as follows: pp. 9-16, from "A North American Memoir: Revenge," *The North American Review* Dec. 1984: 56-60; pp. 15-24, from "Mentors," *Canadian Literature* 101 (Summer 1984): 35-41; pp. 24-26, from "A North American Memoir: Revenge," *The North American Review* Dec. 1984: 56-60; pp. 26-30, from "A Passage to Canada: How an American Writer Heeded the 'Daily Buttering' of the CBC To Return to the Land of His Parents," *Books in Canada* June-July 1985: 15-16; pp. 30-36, from "Portrait of the Artist as a Young Pup," *The Montreal Story Tellers: Memoirs, Photographs, Critical Essays* (1985): 65-72; pp. 36-41, from "Tenants of Unhousement," *The Iowa Review* 13.2 (Spring 1982): 83-98. Listed in 4., 8.

"A Middle-Aged Orphan." *The New York Times Magazine* 27 Apr. 1986: 64. Rpt. (rev.) in Chapter One of *I Had a Father: A Post-Modern Autobiography*. By Clark

Blaise. Reading, MA: Addison-Wesley, 1993. Toronto: HarperCollins, 1993. Data in part gathered from *An Other I: The Fictions of Clark Blaise* (1988), by Robert Lecker, and with further help from Andrew C. McKague.

"Cross-Cultural Marriages." *Chatelaine* Aug. 1986: 44. Data gathered with the help of Andrew C. McKague. Published in column entitled "Me Tarzan, You Jane."

"Chronology of Salience." *An Other I: The Fictions of Clark Blaise*. By Robert Lecker. Toronto: ECW, 1988. 13-20.
    Listed in 4., 8., 9.

"The Border as Fiction." *The Border as Fiction [and] Borderlines and Borderlands in English Canada: The Written Line*. By Clark Blaise and by Russell Brown. Borderlands Monograph Ser. 4. Orono, ME: Borderlands Project, The Canadian-American Center, U of Maine, 1990. 1-12. Rpt. (trans.) as "La frontière comme fiction." *Une frontière dans la tête: Culture, institutions et imaginaire canadiens*. By Lauren McKinsey and Victor Konrad, Roger Gibbins, et al. Pref. Albert Desbiens. Trans. Marie-José Daoust, Jean Papineau, and Laurent-Michel Vacher. Montreal: Liber, 1991. 133-50. Rpt. (abbr. and rev.) in Chapter Six of *I Had a Father: A Post-Modern Autobiography*. By Clark Blaise. Reading, MA: Addison-Wesley, 1993. Toronto: HarperCollins, 1993. Rpt. (rev.) in *Selected Essays*. By Clark Blaise. Ed. John Metcalf and J.R. (Tim) Struthers. Emeryville, ON: Biblioasis, 2008.
    Data gathered with the help of Clark Blaise, Rhea J. Côté Robbins, Jim Bishop, Russell Brown, Robert Lecker, and Victor Konrad. Listed in 1., 8.

Introduction. *Lunar Attractions*. By Clark Blaise. Sherbrooke Street 3. Erin, ON: Porcupine's Quill, 1990. 7-15.
    Listed in 4., 8., 9.

"Latin Americans of the North." First annual colloquium of la Chaire pour le développement de la recherche sur la culture d'expression française en Amérique du Nord (CEFAN), l'université Laval. Petit Séminaire de Québec, Faculté d'architecture, l'université Laval, Sainte-Foy, QC. 16 June 1990. Address. *Le Québec et les francophones de la Nouvelle-Angleterre*. Ed. Dean Louder. Sainte-Foy, QC: Presses de l'université Laval, 1991. 227-37. Print. Rpt. (rev.) in Chapter Seven to Chapter Thirteen of *I Had a Father: A Post-Modern Autobiography*. By Clark Blaise. Reading, MA: Addison-Wesley, 1993. Toronto: HarperCollins, 1993.
    Data gathered with the help of Clark Blaise, Jim Bishop, Dean Louder,

Jeanne Valois, Guy Dinel, and James Lambert. Listed in 1., 8., 9.

"The Thing: The Real Thing." *The Movie That Changed My Life.* Ed. David Rosenberg. New York: Viking/Penguin, 1991. 50-59.
    Data gathered with the help of Clark Blaise. Listed in 1., 8.

"[Memory, Europe, and the East-West Dialogue]." Lahti Intl. Writers' Reunion. Mukkula Manor Hotel, Mukkula, Fin. 18 June 1991. Address. TS and reel-to-reel tape (now digitized). Kirjallisuusarkisto, Suomalaisen Kirjallisuuden Seura [The Literary Archives, The Finnish Literature Society], Helsinki, Fin.
    Data gathered with the help of Clark Blaise, Mirja Halonen, and Ilkka Välimäki. Title given by Clark Blaise in the Epilogue to *I Had a Father: A Post-Modern Autobiography.* By Clark Blaise. Reading, MA: Addison-Wesley, 1993. Toronto: HarperCollins, 1993. Title confirmed by Clark Blaise via e-mail with J.R. (Tim) Struthers on 19 Sept. 2008. TS is 5 pp. long. Listed in 1., 8.

"Introduction to *Shoeless Joe.*" 1992. TS. Quarry Press Fonds, Queen's U Archives, Kathleen Ryan Hall, Queen's U, Kingston, ON. Trans. by Bernard Hœpffner as Préface. *Shoeless Joe.* By W.P. Kinsella. Trans. Bernard Hœpffner. Paris: Christian Bourgois Éditeur, 1993. 7-18. Abbr. as "On *Shoeless Joe.*" *Quarry* 42.4 (1994): 68-73.
    Data gathered with the help of Paul Banfield, Jeremy Heil, and Don McLeod. TS is 11 pp. long. A sequence of five paragraphs that appeared both in the original TS and in the French translation is deleted following the fifth-last paragraph in the version published in *Quarry.* TS is 11 pp. long. Listed in 2., 8.

"I Had a Father: A Post-Modern Autobiography." Magnum Readings. Magnum Book Store, Ottawa, ON. 27 Sept. 1992. Address. *I Had a Father: A Post-Modern Autobiography.* Magnum Readings 15. Ottawa, ON: Magnum Book Store, 1992. Print. Rpt. (rev.) in Introduction and Chapter One to Chapter Three of *I Had a Father: A Post-Modern Autobiography.* By Clark Blaise. Reading, MA: Addison-Wesley, 1993. Toronto: HarperCollins, 1993.
    Data gathered with the help of John Metcalf. The Magnum Readings material consists of thirty-six pages of subsequently revised TS "Here first published in an edition of thirty copies of which four are *hors de commerce* and twenty-six are numbered and signed." Listed in 1., 8.

"Culture Wars in Lake County." 1994. TS. Collection of the author, Clark Blaise, San Francisco, CA.
    Data gathered with the help of Clark Blaise. TS is 22 pp. long. Listed in 1., 8.

"Eating in Tokyo." 1994. TS. Collection of the author, Clark Blaise, San Francisco, CA.

Data gathered with the help of Clark Blaise. TS is 20 pp. long, including almost 11 pp. of text proper and more than 9 pp. of "notes for sidebars." Listed in 1., 8.

"Some Thoughts on Canadian and Australian Fiction." Meiji U Intl. Exchange Programs. Center for Intl. Programs, Meiji U, Tokyo. 9 May 1994. Address. *Here, There and Everywhere*. By Clark Blaise. Meiji U Intl. Exchange Programs Guest Lecture Ser. 1. Tokyo: Center for Intl. Programs, Meiji U, 1994. 32-52, 72. Print. Rpt. (rev.) in *Selected Essays*. By Clark Blaise. Ed. John Metcalf and J.R. (Tim) Struthers. Emeryville, ON: Biblioasis, 2008.

Data gathered with the help of Clark Blaise and Rick Visentin. Listed in 1., 8.

"Teaching Experience," "Teaching Areas," "Professional Work 1990- 93." *Here, There and Everywhere*. By Clark Blaise. Meiji U Intl. Exchange Programs Guest Lecture Ser. 1. Tokyo: Center for Intl. Programs, Meiji U, 1994. 76, 76, 77-78.

Data gathered with the help of Clark Blaise and Rick Visentin.

"Ruth." *Communion: Contemporary Writers Reveal the Bible in Their Lives*. Ed. David Rosenberg. New York: Anchor/Doubleday, 1996. 103-13.

Data gathered with the help of Clark Blaise. Listed in 1., 8.

"The Zen of Writing." 1996. TS. Collection of the author, Clark Blaise, San Francisco, CA.

Data gathered with the help of Clark Blaise. TS is 11 pp. long. Listed in 4., 8., 9.

"Quebec's Soul City." *The Wilson Quarterly* 20.1 (Winter 1996): 68-75.

Data gathered with the help of Clark Blaise and Andrew C. McKague. Listed in 1., 8.

"The International Novel." The Loft Literary Center, Minneapolis, MN. 7 Sept. 1996. Address. *Selected Essays*. By Clark Blaise. Ed. John Metcalf and J.R. (Tim) Struthers. Emeryville, ON: Biblioasis, 2008. Print.

Data gathered with the help of Clark Blaise, Dara Syrkin, and Jerod Santek. Listed in 1., 8.

"Looking at India: An Iowa Perspective." Narratives of Displacement in South Asian Experience, Movement and Memory Workshop, U of Iowa South Asian Studies Program. Pappajohn Business Building, U of Iowa, Iowa City, IA. 26

Sept. 1996. Address. Audiocassette. Collection of Paul R. Greenough, Iowa City, Iowa. TS. Collection of the author, Clark Blaise, San Francisco, CA.

Data gathered with the help of Clark Blaise, Susan K. Lohafer, Jo Dickens, Jonathan Wilcox, Peter Nazareth, Mary Nazareth, Nancy L. Baker, David F. McCartney, Philip A. Lutgendorf, Frederick M. Smith, and Paul R. Greenough. TS is 9 pp. long. Listed in 1., 8.

"Kerouac in Black and White." *Ishmael Reed's Konch Magazine* 9 (Fall 1996-Spring 1997): 12-15. Reissued on Web. <http://www.ishmaelreed.com/articles/blaise1.html>. Rpt. (rev.) in *Selected Essays*. By Clark Blaise. Ed. John Metcalf and J.R. (Tim) Struthers. Emeryville, ON: Biblioasis, 2008.

Data gathered with the help of Clark Blaise and Robin Philpot. This printed piece (later posted online) was followed, after the journal switched to publishing online in 1998, by Robin Philpot's online piece "Kerouac, Blaise, Quebec: In Black and White" (cf. <http://www.ishmaelreed.com/articles/Philpot.html>) in *Ishmael Reed's Konch Magazine* ([Fall 1998]). An earlier printed piece by Robin Philpot, "Quebec: Bucking the Monoculturalists' Current," had appeared – without Blaise knowing it, he states in an e-mail to J.R. (Tim) Struthers on 13 Sept. 2008 – in *Ishmael Reed's Konch Magazine* 8 (Fall 1995): 18-20. Blaise and Philpot subsequently published two more items in the same journal, as noted later in this section. Listed in 1., 8.

"First Class from India." 1997. TS. Collection of the author, Clark Blaise, San Francisco, CA.

Data gathered with the help of Clark Blaise. TS is 7 pp. long.

"[On the Multiculturalism Debate]." U.S./Canadian Writers' Perspectives on the Multiculturalism Debate: A Round Table Discussion and Reading at Harvard U. Moderated by Graham Huggan and Winfried Siemerling; with panelists Clark Blaise, Dionne Brand, Nicole Brossard, George Elliott Clarke, Bharati Mukherjee, Paul Yee. Harvard Hall, Harvard U, Cambridge, MA. 10 May 1997. Address. In "U.S./ Canadian Writers' Perspectives on the Multiculturalism Debate: A Round-Table Discussion at Harvard University." By Graham Huggan, Winfried Siemerling, et al. *Canadian Literature* 164 (2000): 87-93. Print.

Data gathered with the help of Winfried Siemerling. Title devised by J.R. (Tim) Struthers and approved by Clark Blaise via e-mail between them on 11 July 2008. Listed in 1., 8.

"Sci-Fi & I." Scholars Convocation. Grinnell Coll., Grinnell, IA. 19 Feb. 1998. Address. Grinnell Coll. Archives, Burling Lib., Grinnell Coll. Libs., Grinnell Coll., Grinnell, IA. Videotape. TS. Collection of the author, Clark Blaise, San

Francisco, CA.

Data gathered with the help of Clark Blaise, Paula Smith, and Cheryl Neubert. TS is 9 pp. long. Listed in 1., 8.

"Racism in Québec: A Response to Robin Philpot." *Ishmael Reed's Konch Magazine* ([Fall 1999]). Web. <http://www.ishmaelreed.com/articles/Blaise2.html>.

Data gathered with the help of Clark Blaise and Robin Philpot. This online response to Robin Philpot's online piece "Kerouac, Blaise, Quebec: In Black and White" (cf. <http://www.ishmaelreed.com/articles/Philpot.html>) published a year earlier in *Ishmael Reed's Konch Magazine* ([Fall 1998]) was posted with Robin Philpot's follow-up online response to it "Reply to Clark Blaise" (cf. <http://www.ishmaelreed.com/articles/philpot1.html>) in *Ishmael Reed's Konch Magazine* ([Fall 1999]). Listed in 1., 8.

"Exile and Memory." Cultural Section U.S. Consulate General Monterrey. Monterrey, Mex. 24 Sept. 2003. Address. *Selected Essays*. By Clark Blaise. Ed. John Metcalf and J.R. (Tim) Struthers. Emeryville, ON: Biblioasis, 2008. Print.

Data gathered with the help of Clark Blaise. Listed in 1., 8.

"Border-Crossing." Crossing Borders: The Immigrant Voice in American Lit. Key West Literary Seminar. San Carlos Institute, Key West, FL. 9 Jan. 2004. Address. Rev. as "The Smuggler's Son Grows Older." *Clark Blaise, Proprietor.* Ed. J.R. (Tim) Struthers. *Short Story* 15.2 (Fall 2007): 57-64. Print. Rpt. (rev.) in *Selected Essays*. By Clark Blaise. Ed. John Metcalf and J.R. (Tim) Struthers. Emeryville, ON: Biblioasis, 2008.

Data gathered with the help of Clark Blaise. Listed in 1., 8.

"Minding the Gap." Arts and Religious Studies Convocation. McGill U, Montreal, QC. 2 June 2004. Address. Rev. as "The Subtle Contingencies of History." *Canadian Notes & Queries* 67 (Spring-Summer 2005): 4-6. Print.

Data gathered with the help of Clark Blaise. Address delivered on the occasion of Clark Blaise's receiving an honorary doctorate from McGill U. Listed in 1., 8., 12.

"Water." Freshman Global Lecture Ser. Southampton Coll. of Long Island U, Southampton, NY. 13 Sept. 2004. Address. TS. Collection of the author, Clark Blaise, San Francisco, CA.

Data gathered with the help of Clark Blaise and Anne Algieri. TS. is 18 pp. long. Listed in 1., 8.

"[Autobiographical Annex: Clark Blaise]." In "BLAISE, Clark 1940- ." *Contemporary Authors: A Bio-Bibliographical Guide to Current Writers in Fiction, General Nonfiction, Poetry, Journalism, Drama, Motion Pictures, Television, and Other Fields.* Vol. 231. Project Ed. Julie Keppen. Farmington Hills, MI: Thomson Gale, 2005. 50-57. Rpt. (rev.) as "Autobiographical Annex: 1985-2006." *Selected Essays.* By Clark Blaise. Ed. John Metcalf and J.R. (Tim) Struthers. Emeryville, ON: Biblioasis, 2008.

    Data gathered with the help of Clark Blaise and Andrew C. McKague. Title for original essay reproduces that on TS. Collection of the author, Clark Blaise, San Francisco, CA. New title devised by J.R. (Tim) Struthers and approved by Clark Blaise via e-mail between them on 22 Sept 2008. Listed in 4., 8., 9., 12.

"No Names Please." *Americans.* Ed. Jane Davis. *The Reader* 19 (Autumn 2005): 106-09. Rpt. in *Canadian Notes & Queries* 70 (Fall-Winter 2006): 8-9.

    Data gathered with the help of Clark Blaise. Listed in 6., 8.

"A Delayed Disclosure." *Brick: A Literary Journal* 78 (Winter 2006): 108-15. Rpt. (rev.) in *Selected Essays.* By Clark Blaise. Ed. John Metcalf and J.R. (Tim) Struthers. Emeryville, ON: Biblioasis, 2008.

    The title cited here is what appears at the start of the actual piece in its first published form in *Brick: A Literary Journal.* Another title, "A Memoir of Childhood," is given in the list of contents there.

"The 'Wickedness' of Herman Melville." 2007. TS. Collection of the author, Clark Blaise, San Francisco, CA.

    Data gathered with the help of Clark Blaise. TS is 11 pp. long. Listed in 1., 8.

9. On His Own Autobiographical Writing

"Hot from India." *Books in Canada* May 1977: 41.

Data in part gathered from *The Clark Blaise Papers* (1991), comp. Marlys Chevrefils Published in "Letters to the Editor."

"Autobiography." [Autobiography Symposium]. U of Iowa, Iowa City, IA. 13 Apr. 1978. Address. TS. The Clark Blaise Papers, Archives and Special Collections, U of Calgary Libraries and Cultural Resources, U of Calgary, Calgary, AB.

Data in part gathered from *The Clark Blaise Papers* (1991), comp. Marlys Chevrefils, and with further help from Marlys Chevrefils. TS is 16 pp. long. Listed in 4., 5., 9., 10.

"[An Unintentional Novel and an Unanticipated Autobiography]." Denison Honors Colloquium. ATO House, Denison U, Granville, OH. 17 Apr. 1979. Address. TS. The Clark Blaise Papers, Archives and Special Collections, U of Calgary Libraries and Cultural Resources, U of Calgary, Calgary, AB. Rev. and introd. by "[By a Curious Alchemy]." Humanities Week. Slayter Auditorium, Denison U, Granville, OH. 9 Nov. 1981. Address. TS. The Clark Blaise Papers, Archives and Special Collections, U of Calgary Libraries and Cultural Resources, U of Calgary, Calgary, AB.

Data in part gathered from *The Clark Blaise Papers* (1991), comp. Marlys Chevrefils, and with further help from Clark Blaise and Marlys Chevrefils. Title for original version and revised version of address and title for new piece (cited separately in 4., 9., 13) used to introduce revised version were chosen by Clark Blaise from suggestions offered by J.R. (Tim) Struthers via e-mail between them on 25 July 2008 and 7 Sept. 2008. Original version was read on the occasion of Blaise's visit to Denison U to receive an honorary doctorate. TS is 19 pp. long. New piece and revised version were presented during sesquicentennial celebrations at Denison U. TS of new piece is 3 pp. long; TS of revised version is 20 pp. long. Listed in 7., 9.

"[By a Curious Alchemy]." Humanities Week. Slayter Auditorium, Denison U, Granville, OH. 9 Nov. 1981. Address. TS. The Clark Blaise Papers, Archives and Special Collections, U of Calgary Libraries and Cultural Resources, U of Calgary, Calgary, AB.

Data in part gathered from *The Clark Blaise Papers* (1991), comp. Marlys

Chevrefils, and with further help from Clark Blaise and Marlys Chevrefils. Title chosen by Clark Blaise from suggestions offered by J.R. (Tim) Struthers via e-mail between them on 7 Sept. 2008. Read as an introduction to a revised version of Blaise's "An Unintentional Novel and an Unanticipated Autobiography" (cited separately in 7., 9.) during sesquicentennial celebrations at Denison U. TS is 3 pp. long. Listed in 4., 9., 13.

"Tenants of Unhousement." *The Iowa Review* 13.2 (Spring 1982): 83-98. Rpt. (abbr. and rev.) in Introduction and "The Voice of Unhousement." *Resident Alien*. By Clark Blaise. Markham, ON: Penguin, 1986. 1, 36-41. Rpt. (rev.) in Chapter Fourteen and Chapter Fifteen of *I Had a Father: A Post-Modern Autobiography*. By Clark Blaise. Reading, MA: Addison-Wesley, 1993. Toronto: Harper-Collins, 1993.
    Data gathered with the help of Clark Blaise. Listed in 8., 9.

"Clark Blaise." *Contemporary Authors: Autobiography Series*. Vol. 3. Ed. Adele Sarkissian. Detroit: Gale Research, 1986. 15-30. Rpt. (rev.) as "Autobiographical Essay: 1940-1984." *Selected Essays*. By Clark Blaise. Ed. John Metcalf and J.R. (Tim) Struthers. Emeryville, ON: Biblioasis, 2008.
    Data gathered with the help of Clark Blaise and Andrew C. McKague. New title devised by J.R. (Tim) Struthers and approved by Clark Blaise via e-mail between them on 22 Sept 2008. Listed in 4., 8., 9.

Introduction. *Resident Alien*. By Clark Blaise. Markham, ON: Penguin, 1986. 1-3.
    This piece abbreviates and revises previously published material from "Tenants of Unhousement," *The Iowa Review* 13.2 (Spring 1982): 83-98. Listed in 8., 9.

Blaise, Clark, and Bharati Mukherjee. "How It All Turned Out . . . ." *Days and Nights in Calcutta*. By Clark Blaise and Bharati Mukherjee. Markham, ON: Penguin, 1986. 301, 303-14.
    Listed in 1., 9.

"A Canadian Alien?" *The New York Times Book Review* 9 Nov. 1986: 65.
    Data gathered with the help of Andrew C. McKague. Published in "Letters."

"Chronology of Salience." *An Other I: The Fictions of Clark Blaise*. By Robert Lecker. Toronto: ECW, 1988. 13-20.
    Listed in 4., 8., 9.

Introduction. *Lunar Attractions.* By Clark Blaise. Sherbrooke Street 3. Erin, ON: Porcupine's Quill, 1990. 7-15.

    Listed in 4., 8., 9.

"Latin Americans of the North." First annual colloquium of la Chaire pour le développement de la recherche sur la culture d'expression française en Amérique du Nord (CEFAN), l'université Laval. Petit Séminaire de Québec, Faculté d'architecture, l'université Laval, Sainte-Foy, QC. 16 June 1990. Address. *Le Québec et les francophones de la Nouvelle-Angleterre.* Ed. Dean Louder. Sainte-Foy, QC: Presses de l'université Laval, 1991. 227-37. Print. Rpt. (rev.) in Chapter Seven to Chapter Thirteen of *I Had a Father: A Post-Modern Autobiography.* By Clark Blaise. Reading, MA: Addison-Wesley, 1993. Toronto: Harper-Collins, 1993.

    Data gathered with the help of Clark Blaise, Jim Bishop, Dean Louder, Jeanne Valois, Guy Dinel, and James Lambert. Listed in 1., 8., 9.

"Your Nearest Exit May Be Behind You: Autobiography and the Post-Modernist Moment." Life Likenesses: The Seductions of Biography. Longfellow Hall, Harvard U, Cambridge, MA. 15 Oct. 1993. Address. *The Seductions of Biography.* Ed. Mary Rhiel and David Suchoff. New York: Routledge, 1996. 201-09. Print.

    Data gathered with the help of Clark Blaise. Listed in 9., 10.

"The Last Post(s): Some Thoughts on Post-Deconstruction and Post-Modernism and Contemporary Autobiography." Meiji U Intl. Exchange Programs. Center for Intl. Programs, Meiji U, Tokyo. 18 May 1994. Address. *Here, There and Everywhere.* By Clark Blaise. Meiji U Intl. Exchange Programs Guest Lecture Ser. 1. Tokyo: Center for Intl. Programs, Meiji U, 1994. 53-70. Print.

    Data gathered with the help of Clark Blaise and Rick Visentin. Listed in 9., 10.

Blaise, Clark. "Prologue." *Days and Nights in Calcutta.* By Clark Blaise and Bharati Mukherjee. Saint Paul, MN: Hungry Mind, 1995. ix, xi-xiii.

"The Zen of Writing." 1996. TS. Collection of the author, Clark Blaise, San Francisco, CA.

    Data gathered with the help of Clark Blaise. TS is 11 pp. long. Listed in 4., 8., 9.

"[Autobiographical Annex: Clark Blaise]." In "BLAISE, Clark 1940- ." *Contem-*

porary Authors: A Bio-Bibliographical Guide to Current Writers in Fiction, General Nonfiction, Poetry, Journalism, Drama, Motion Pictures, Television, and Other Fields. Vol. 231. Project Ed. Julie Keppen. Farmington Hills, MI: Thomson Gale, 2005. 50-57. Rpt. (rev.) as "Autobiographical Annex: 1985-2006." *Selected Essays.* By Clark Blaise. Ed. John Metcalf and J.R. (Tim) Struthers. Emeryville, ON: Biblioasis, 2008.

Data gathered with the help of Clark Blaise and Andrew C. McKague. Title for original essay reproduces that on TS. Collection of the author, Clark Blaise, San Francisco, CA. New title devised by J.R. (Tim) Struthers and approved by Clark Blaise via e-mail between them on 22 Sept 2008. Listed in 4., 8., 9., 12.

10. On Autobiography and Interpretation

"Autobiography." [Autobiography Symposium]. U of Iowa, Iowa City, IA. 13 Apr. 1978. Address. TS. The Clark Blaise Papers, Archives and Special Collections, U of Calgary Libraries and Cultural Resources, U of Calgary, Calgary, AB.

Data in part gathered from *The Clark Blaise Papers* (1991), comp. Marlys Chevrefils, and with further help from Marlys Chevrefils. TS is 16 pp. long. Listed in 4., 5., 9., 10.

"Your Nearest Exit May Be Behind You: Autobiography and the Post-Modernist Moment." Life Likenesses: The Seductions of Biography. Longfellow Hall, Harvard U, Cambridge, MA. 15 Oct. 1993. Address. *The Seductions of Biography*. Ed. Mary Rhiel and David Suchoff. New York: Routledge, 1996. 201-09. Print.

Data gathered with the help of Clark Blaise. Listed in 9., 10.

"The Last Post(s): Some Thoughts on Post-Deconstruction and Post-Modernism and Contemporary Autobiography." Meiji U Intl. Exchange Programs. Center for Intl. Programs, Meiji U, Tokyo. 18 May 1994. Address. *Here, There and Everywhere*. By Clark Blaise. Meiji U Intl. Exchange Programs Guest Lecture Ser. 1. Tokyo: Center for Intl. Programs, Meiji U, 1994. 53-70. Print.

Data gathered with the help of Clark Blaise and Rick Visentin. Listed in 9., 10.

11. Nonfiction

"A Canada-India Literary Link in Need of Help." *The Globe and Mail* 20 May 1977: 7.

Data in part gathered from *The Clark Blaise Papers* (1991), comp. Marlys Chevrefils.

"Race Incidents Make India Wary of Canada." *The Globe and Mail* 13 July 1977: 7.

Data in part gathered from *The Clark Blaise Papers* (1991), comp. Marlys Chevrefils.

"The Important Things Begin Where the Game Leaves Off." *TV Guide* (Canada) 26 July 1980: 16-17, 19-20.

Data in part gathered from *Clark Blaise and His Works* (1985), by Barry Cameron, and from *The Clark Blaise Papers* (1991), comp. Marlys Chevrefils. The title cited here is what appears at the start of the actual piece. On the front cover, the title stated is "Baseball – A Fan's Notes." Another title, "Baseball: A Game of Inches," is given in the list of contents.

"How Can This Team Lose?" *Sport* Oct. 1982: 40-41, 43-44, 48.

Data in part gathered from *The Clark Blaise Papers* (1991), comp. Marlys Chevrefils.

"Canada – Is It Going, Going . . . Gone?: Unity, Always Tenuous, Has Been Undermined by the U.S. Free Trade Pact." *Newsday* 27 Aug. 1990: 41. Rpt. as "Free Trade and the Demise of Canada." *The Buffalo News* 31 Aug. 1990: C3.

Data gathered with the help of Andrew C. McKague.

"The Canadian Who Tamed Time," "Fleming's CV," "What Is Time?" *The Globe and Mail* 31 Mar. 2001: F9.

Data gathered with the help of Andrew C. McKague. Abbr. and rev. from "5 The Decade of Time, 1875-85," "Foreword: The Gauge Age," "1 The Discovery of Time" of *Time Lord: Sir Sandford Fleming and the Creation of Standard Time*. By Clark Blaise. London: Weidenfeld & Nicolson, 2000. New York: Pantheon, 2001. Rpt. as *Time Lord: The Remarkable Canadian Who Missed His Train and Changed the World*. Toronto: Alfred A. Knopf Canada, 2001.

"The Measurement of Time." *The Fine Art of Watches: A Special Report.* [*International Herald Tribune*] [*The New York Times*] [Paris] 31 Mar. 2005: vii.
    Data gathered with the help of Clark Blaise and Andrew C. McKague.

12. On His Own Nonfiction

Blaise, Clark, and Bharati Mukherjee. Introduction. *The Sorrow and the Terror: The Haunting Legacy of the Air India Tragedy.* By Clark Blaise and Bharati Mukherjee. Markham, ON: Penguin, 1988. ix-xxii.

    This 1988 paperback edition offers a much-expanded version of the Introduction in the original 1987 hardcover edition, including fuller comments on the authors' research methods. Listed in 1., 12.

"Passion and the Nonfiction Subject." Middlebury Coll. Bread Loaf Writers' Conf. Middlebury, VT. 16 Aug. 1999. Address. Media Archives, Special Collections, Main Library, Middlebury Coll., Middlebury, VT. Audiocassette.

    Data gathered with the help of Clark Blaise, Noreen Cargill, and Danielle Rougeau. Listed in 12., 13.

"Minding the Gap." Arts and Religious Studies Convocation. McGill U, Montreal, QC. 2 June 2004. Address. Rev. as "The Subtle Contingencies of History." *Canadian Notes & Queries* 67 (Spring-Summer 2005): 4-6. Print.

    Data gathered with the help of Clark Blaise. Address delivered on the occasion of Clark Blaise's receiving an honorary doctorate from McGill U. Listed in 1., 8., 12.

"[Resolving the Nightmare of Time]." Time Contemplates and Celebrates the Windy City. Chicago Humanities Festival. Julius Lewis Auditorium, Alliance Française de Chicago, Chicago, IL. 13 Nov. 2004. Address. TS. Collection of the author, Clark Blaise, San Francisco, CA.

    Data gathered with the help of Clark Blaise and Amanda Burr. Title given by Clark Blaise in an e-mail to J.R. (Tim) Struthers on 4 Mar. 2007. TS is 18 pp. long. Listed in 1., 12.

"[Autobiographical Annex: Clark Blaise]." In "BLAISE, Clark 1940- ." *Contemporary Authors: A Bio-Bibliographical Guide to Current Writers in Fiction, General Nonfiction, Poetry, Journalism, Drama, Motion Pictures, Television, and Other Fields.* Vol. 231. Project Ed. Julie Keppen. Farmington Hills, MI: Thomson Gale, 2005. 50-57. Rpt. (rev.) as "Autobiographical Annex: 1985-2006." *Selected Essays.* By Clark Blaise. Ed. John Metcalf and J.R. (Tim) Struthers. Emeryville, ON: Biblioasis, 2008.

Data gathered with the help of Clark Blaise and Andrew C. McKague. Title for original essay reproduces that on TS. Collection of the author, Clark Blaise, San Francisco, CA. New title devised by J.R. (Tim) Struthers and approved by Clark Blaise via e-mail between them on 22 Sept. 2008. Listed in 4., 8., 9., 12.

"The Possibility of Cultural Transformation in a Time of Cultural Extremism]." Open Inquiry in the Face of Cultural Extremism. NAFSA: Assoc. of Intl. Educators. Queen Elizabeth Hotel, Montreal, QC. 22 May 2006. Address. TS. Collection of the author, Clark Blaise, San Francisco, CA.

Data gathered with the help of Clark Blaise and Andrew C. McKague. Title devised by J.R. (Tim) Struthers and approved by Clark Blaise via e-mail between them on 13 July 2008. TS is 15 pp. long. Listed in 1., 12.

13. On Nonfiction and Interpretation

"White Method, Black Subject." Rev. of *Urban Blues*, by Charles Keil. *The Montreal Star* 3 Sept. 1966, sec. Entertainments: 6.

Data in part gathered from *The Clark Blaise Papers* (1991), comp. Marlys Chevrefils.

"[By a Curious Alchemy]." Humanities Week. Slayter Auditorium, Denison U, Granville, OH. 9 Nov. 1981. Address. TS. The Clark Blaise Papers, Archives and Special Collections, U of Calgary Libraries and Cultural Resources, U of Calgary, Calgary, AB.

Data in part gathered from *The Clark Blaise Papers* (1991), comp. Marlys Chevrefils, and with further help from Clark Blaise and Marlys Chevrefils. Title chosen by Clark Blaise from suggestions offered by J.R. (Tim) Struthers via e-mail between them on 7 Sept. 2008. Read as an introduction to a revised version of Blaise's "An Unintentional Novel and an Unanticipated Autobiography" (cited separately in 7., 9.) during sesquicentennial celebrations at Denison U. TS is 3 pp. long. Listed in 4., 9., 13.

"Not Unlike a Unicorn." Rev. of *Saroyan: A Biography*, by Lawrence Lee and Barry Gifford, and *Ararat: A Special Issue on William Saroyan*, ed. Leo Hamalian. *American Book Review* May-June 1986: 22-23.

Data in part gathered from *The Clark Blaise Papers* (1991), comp. Marlys Chevrefils, and with further help from Andrew C. McKague.

"Joseph Conrad's Many Lives." Rev. of *Joseph Conrad: A Biography*, by Jeffrey Meyers. *The Washington Post* 21 Apr. 1991, sec. Book World: 5, 13.

Data gathered with the help of Clark Blaise and Andrew C. McKague.

"Rushdie as Critic: 'He Engages Books with Expectation or Disillusionment. He Holds Nothing Back.'" Rev. of *Imaginary Homelands: Essays and Criticism 1981-1991*, by Salman Rushdie. *Sunday Newsday* 19 May 1991: 39, 44. Rpt. (rev.) in "Rushdie as Novelist, Rushdie as Critic." *Selected Essays*. By Clark Blaise. Ed. John Metcalf and J.R. (Tim) Struthers. Emeryville, ON: Biblioasis, 2008.

Data gathered with the help of Clark Blaise and Andrew C. McKague. Listed in 7., 13.

"India's Queen Lear." Rev. of *Mother India: A Political Biography of Indira Gandhi*, by Pranay Gupte. *Los Angeles Times* 26 Apr. 1992, sec. Book Review: 1, 7.

Data gathered with the help of Clark Blaise and Andrew C. McKague.

"Time, Technology and the Value of Slowing Down for the Future." Rev. of *The Clock of the Long Now: Time and Responsibility*, by Stewart Brand. *San Francisco Chronicle* 11 July 1999: RV-4.

Data gathered with the help of Clark Blaise and Andrew C. McKague.

"Passion and the Nonfiction Subject." Middlebury Coll. Bread Loaf Writers' Conf. Middlebury, VT. 16 Aug. 1999. Address. Media Archives, Special Collections, Main Library, Middlebury Coll., Middlebury, VT. Audiocassette.

Data gathered with the help of Clark Blaise, Noreen Cargill, and Danielle Rougeau. Listed in 12., 13.

"[The Aperture Approach]." Writing and Publishing Nonfiction Books. Moderated by Jason Roberts; with panelists Joyce Maynard, Mary Roach, David Ewing Duncan, Clark Blaise. 826 Valencia, San Francisco, CA. 20 Nov. 2005. Address. TS. Collection of the author, Clark Blaise, San Francisco, CA.

Data gathered with the help of Clark Blaise. Title devised by J.R. (Tim) Struthers and approved by Clark Blaise via e-mail between them on 13 July 2008. TS is 2 pp. long.

"Lost and Found." Rev. of *Ghost Empire: How the French Almost Conquered North America*, by Philip Marchand. *Canadian Notes & Queries* 72 (Fall-Winter 2007): 85-87.

"Rushdie as Novelist, Rushdie as Critic." *Selected Essays*. By Clark Blaise. Ed. John Metcalf and J.R. (Tim) Struthers. Emeryville, ON: Biblioasis, 2008.

Selected and arranged and entitled by J.R. (Tim) Struthers, this piece includes and revises previously published material as follows: "A Novel of India's Coming of Age." Rev. of *Midnight's Children*, by Salman Rushdie. *The New York Times Book Review* 19 Apr. 1981: 1, 18-19 and "Rushdie as Critic: 'He Engages Books with Expectation or Disillusionment. He Holds Nothing Back.'" Rev. of *Imaginary Homelands: Essays and Criticism 1981-1991*, by Salman Rushdie. *Sunday Newsday* 19 May 1991: 39, 44. Listed in 2., 7., 13.

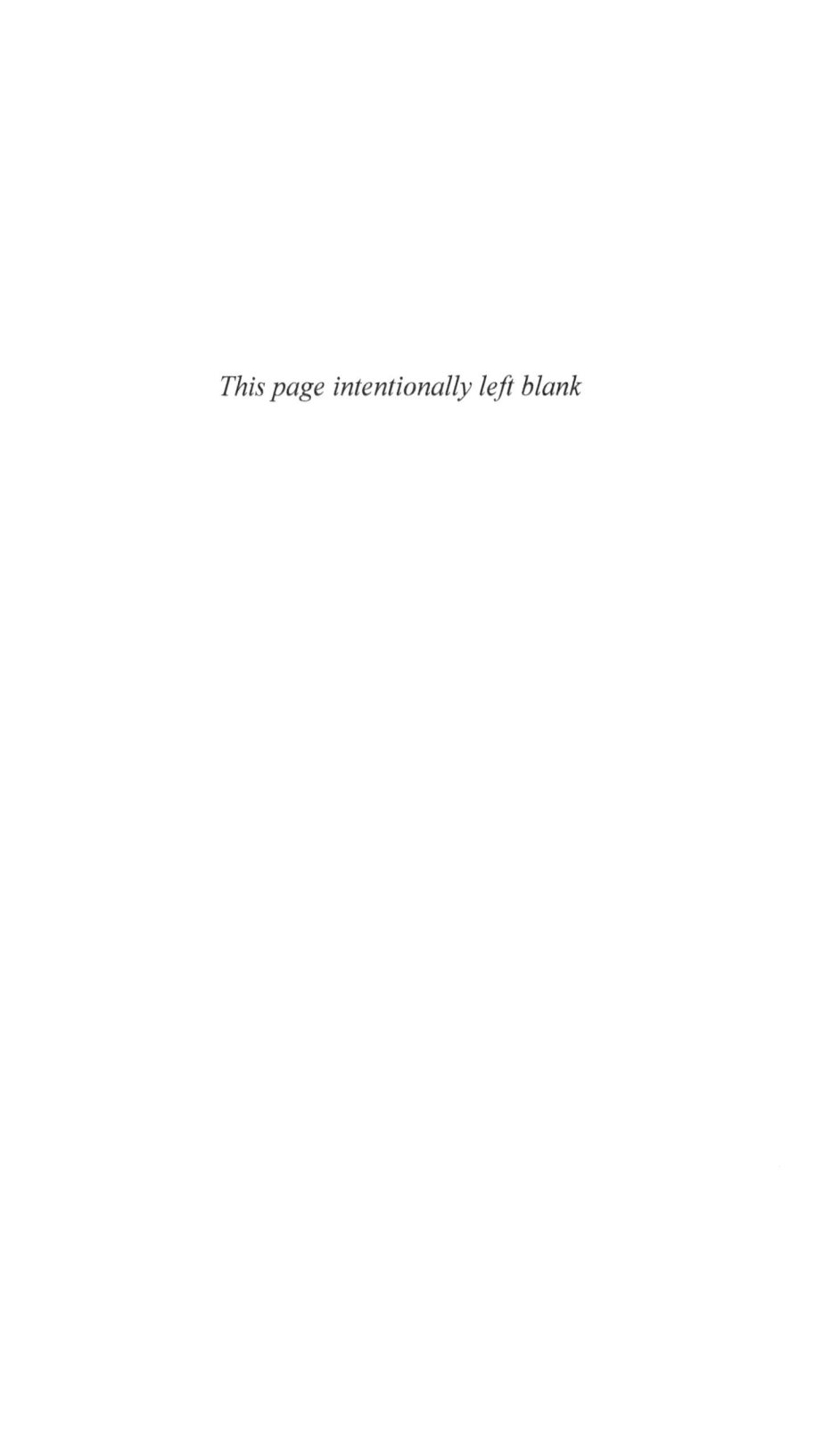

This page intentionally left blank

This page intentionally left blank

About the Author

Clark Blaise is the author of 18 books of fiction and nonfiction, including nine volumes of short stories. Two autobiographical works, *Resident Alien* and *I Had a Father*, concern his French-Canadian identity; two other nonfiction titles (co-authored with his wife, Bharati Mukherjee), *Days and Nights in Calcutta* and *The Sorrow and the Terror*, involve his experience of India. He was born in the state of North Dakota in 1940 to Canadian parents, and raised in a variety of settings in the United States and Canada. Between 1966 and 1978 he and his family lived in Montreal, followed by two years in Toronto; in 1980 he returned to the United States as a Canadian immigrant. He has been a professor in a dozen universities, among them the University of Iowa where he has taught in the Writers' Workshop on different occasions and served as Director of the International Writing Program for many years, and the University of California-Berkeley where he now teaches writing. In 2003 he won the Pearson Prize in Canada (for *Time Lord*, his study of the Canadian engineer who invented standard time) and received an Academy Award from the American Academy of Arts and Letters for his lifetime achievement in literature.

www.ingramcontent.com/pod-product-compliance
Lightning Source LLC
Chambersburg PA
CBHW031052020726
47495CB00007B/1835